Turning Points

IN WORLD HISTORY

World War I

Donald J. Murphy, *Book Editor*

Daniel Leone, *President*
Bonnie Szumski, *Publisher*
Scott Barbour, *Managing Editor*

Greenhaven Press, Inc., San Diego, California

Every effort has been made to trace the owners of copyrighted material. The articles in this volume may have been edited for content, length, and/or reading level. The titles have been changed to enhance the editorial purpose.

Library of Congress Cataloging-in-Publication Data

World War I / Donald J. Murphy, book editor.
   p.   cm. — (Turning points in world history)
   Includes bibliographical references and index.
   ISBN 0-7377-0932-4 (pbk. : alk. paper)
   ISBN 0-7377-0933-2 (lib. : alk. paper)
   1. World War, 1914–1918. I. Title: World War One. II. Title: World War I. III. Murphy, Donald J., 1936– . IV. Turning points in world history (Greenhaven Press)
D521 .W635 2002
940.3—dc21   2001033513

Cover photo: © Corbis
Library of Congress: 27, 147

Printed in the U.S.A.

Contents

Foreword   9

Introduction   11

Chapter 1: The Origins of World War I

**1. An Explosive Mix: Nationalism and   33
Military Alliances** *by H. Stuart Hughes*
The peace of Europe was undermined before 1914 by
two converging developments: first, the agitation by sup-
pressed national minorities in Eastern Europe and the
Balkans and, second, the dangerous actions of Austria-
Hungary and Germany on the eve of war.

**2. The Causes of War: Sharing the Blame   41
by Michael J. Lyons
Responsibility for starting World War I was widely
shared among the great powers of Europe. Serbia and
Austria-Hungary probably deserve somewhat more
blame than Russia, Germany, France, or Great Britain,
but all contributed to the outbreak of war.

**3. The Trigger of War: The Assassination of   47
Franz Ferdinand** *by Robert K. Massie*
The incident that sparked the outbreak of war was the
assassination of the heir to the Austro-Hungarian
throne, Archduke Franz Ferdinand, by Bosnian Serb terrorists in Sarajevo in June 1914. The assassination gave
Austria-Hungary a pretext to attack Serbia with German
support.

**4. Britain's Intervention: A Great Mistake?   56
by Niall Ferguson
The coming of World War I is often viewed as an inevitable event, with Germany most at fault in unleashing
general war, but Germany aimed more for economic
than military dominance of Europe. Great Britain was
not very threatened by German economic expansion and
could have avoided its costly military intervention.

Chapter 2: The War Expands and Intensifies, 1914–1916

1. **A War of Attrition** *by Christopher Andrew*   64
   The European powers that went to war in August 1914
   believed that offensive action would produce a quick victory. Instead, defenses capitalized on technologies like
   the machine gun to inflict a massive loss of life. By late
   1916, the warring coalitions were mobilizing their populations for complete victory, not a compromise.

2. **The Eastern Front: Success and Failure**   73
   by James L. Stokesbury
   The battle lines on the eastern front of the Great War
   were more fluid than on the deadlocked western front.
   Germany inflicted punishing defeats on Russia's forces,
   but Russian forces continued fighting. Russia's autocratic,
   inept regime, however, was on the brink of total collapse.

3. **Slaughter: The Battle of Verdun** *by John F. Wukovits*   82
   In 1916, Germany launched a massive attack on the
   French position at Verdun with the goal of grinding up
   the French forces defending the strategic site. Instead,
   Germany chewed up its own armies as badly as the
   French, without capturing Verdun, revealing the terrible
   price of a war of attrition.

4. **The Battle of the Somme** *by S.L.A. Marshall*   92
   The British attack along the Somme River in northern
   France in July 1916 also revealed the bloody futility of
   offensive warfare on the western front. Despite losing an
   incredible sixty thousand soldiers on the first day of battle, General Douglas Haig continued the futile offensive
   for five more months.

5. **Tragedy at Gallipoli** *by William R. Griffiths*   99
   The British-led Dardanelles, or Gallipoli, campaign of
   1915 tried to regain the initiative by defeating Turkey at
   the strategic point between the Mediterranean and Black
   Seas. Poor planning and execution undermined the Allied effort, forcing withdrawal and defeat.

6. **The War in the Trenches: Guns and Gas** *by John Ellis*   110
   The miseries of trench warfare engulfed ordinary soldiers of both the Allies and the Central Powers by late
   1914. Massive artillery bombardments and the use of
   poison gas created a hellish experience for the troops.

Chapter 3: Russian Revolution, American Intervention, and German Defeat, 1917–1918

1. Russia Leaves the War: Revolution *by Martin Gilbert*   119
Revolution in Russia in March 1917 toppled the czarist
government, but the liberal democratic regime that replaced it would itself be overthrown by the Bolsheviks
(Communists) in November. Russia's armies disintegrated as a result of German attacks and Russia's internal
collapse. The Bolsheviks, true to their propaganda and
responding to popular demand, made a quick peace with
Germany, shocking the Allies.

2. President Wilson's Decision for War   126
by Richard Hofstadter
The United States was drawn into the war because of its
one-sided economic and financial commitment to the
Allies at the expense of Germany. President Woodrow
Wilson searched for a peaceful alternative to U.S. intervention, but his own policies undermined this hope.
Wilson abandoned his strategy of "peace without victory" for one of peace through victory.

3. The Failure of Germany's Submarine Gamble   132
by Trevor Wilson
Germany's unrestricted submarine warfare campaign
after February 1917 endangered the Allies' prospects.
After inflicting heavy losses on Allied and neutral shipping on the Atlantic, however, the U-boat challenge was
beaten back by the new Allied convoy system.

4. Peace with Victory: Wilson's Fourteen Points   144
by John Milton Cooper Jr.
In the wake of social unrest among the war-weary belligerents, the Bolshevik revolution in Russia, and calls
for a just rather than an imperialistic peace, Woodrow
Wilson proposed his famous Fourteen Points for postwar peace in January 1918. Germany would seize on
these moderate terms to sue for an armistice in November 1918.

5. The Central Powers Collapse *by Keith Robbins*   150
In the spring of 1918, Germany unleashed a last, great
offensive on the western front, hoping to defeat Britain
and France before American troops could cross the Atlantic. The German bid for victory fell short, and an

Allied and American counteroffensive finally forced Germany's defeat in November 1918.

Chapter 4: The Home Fronts

1. Mobilizing the Home Front for Total War   162
by Gordon A. Craig
World War I developed into a total war not only on the battlefields and seas but also on the "home fronts" of the belligerents. The war encouraged centralized governmental controls, regimented economies, and governmental intrusion into civil liberties.

2. Civilians at War: Blockades Test the Home Fronts   171
by Arthur Marwick
The home fronts of the warring nations were tested by economic warfare waged by both sides. Germany's submarine blockade of Great Britain countered the British naval blockade of the parts of Europe controlled by Germany. For the home front populations, the experience of war included food shortages, rationing, strikes, and outright hunger.

3. Germany's Home Front Ordeal *by Laurence Moyer*   179
By the winter of 1916–1917, the German home front showed signs of stress and privation. A potato harvest failure led to the substitution of the unappetizing turnip as a staple of the national diet. The declining quality of bread and the shortage of coal for heating added to civilian discontent, which eventually led to collapse and revolution by 1918.

4. Women, War, and Work *by Gail Braybon*   184
World War I increased job opportunities for women in sectors such as munitions, transportation, agriculture, and white-collar services. Yet the war did not, as myth would have it, transform women's social and economic status. Traditional views of women's economic and social roles were reasserted at war's end, and female job gains, on the whole, did not outlast the war.

5. Anti-German Hysteria in the United States   196
by Meirion Harries and Susie Harries
The United States entered World War I in 1917 despite much American apathy and some opposition to interven-

tion. The propaganda activities of the Wilson administration's Committee on Public Information gave a hysterical anti-German tone to the war effort that generated
crude attacks on German Americans and German influ-
ences in American culture.

Chapter 5: Peace and the Legacy of World War I

1. **A Troubled Peace** *by David Thomson*   202
The Paris Peace Conference of 1919 faced the enormous
task of making peace amid the ruins of war and revolutionary upheavals. Despite lofty expectations at the start,
Allied peacemakers had to settle for unsatisfactory compromises on Germany and Eastern Europe.

2. **How World War I Led to World War II** *by P.M.H. Bell* 209
Many historians argue that World War I and its aftermath led inevitably to the outbreak of World War II
(1939–1945). The entire era is viewed as a new Thirty
Years' War, even more destructive than the seventeenth-
century religious wars of the same name. Europe was so
deeply damaged and destabilized between 1914 and 1923
that a second disastrous war was unavoidable.

3. **The Perils of Peacemaking in a War-Torn World**   222
by Robert H. Ferrell
The failures of the Paris Peace Conference were partly
due to the personal limitations of the "Big Three" heads
of state who made the key decision there: Wilson, Lloyd
George, and Clemenceau. But even more significant
were impersonal factors like the economic drawbacks of
the reparations settlement imposed on Germany and
the hatreds and disillusionment that gripped postwar
Europe.

4. **World War I and the Rise of Totalitarian**   228
Dictatorships *by Jack J. Roth*
World War I marked a turning point in world history.
Liberal democracy was badly damaged, a development
apparent by the 1920s and '30s. Extremist movements
took power in Russia, Italy, and Germany in the form of
communism, fascism, and Nazism. These totalitarian
states built on the "total war" policies of some of the
belligerent states in World War I.

5. The Scars of Total War *by Jay Winter and Blaine Baggett* 235
The physical and psychological consequences of war cast
a shadow in the postwar era over the battlefield veterans,
their families, and society at large. Blind, crippled, and
mentally anguished veterans became a somber reminder
of the Great War.

Appendix of Documents   243

Chronology   274

For Further Research   276

Index   280

Foreword

Certain past events stand out as pivotal, as having effects and outcomes that change the course of history. These events are often referred to as turning points. Historian Louis L. Snyder provides this useful definition:

> A turning point in history is an event, happening, or stage which thrusts the course of historical development into a different direction. By definition a turning point is a great event, but it is even more—a great event with the explosive impact of altering the trend of man's life on the planet.

History's turning points have taken many forms. Some were single, brief, and shattering events with immediate and obvious impact. The invasion of Britain by William the Conqueror in 1066, for example, swiftly transformed that land's political and social institutions and paved the way for the rise of the modern English nation. By contrast, other single events were deemed of minor significance when they occurred, only later recognized as turning points. The assassination of a little-known European nobleman, Archduke Franz Ferdinand, on June 28, 1914, in the Bosnian town of Sarajevo was such an event; only after it touched off a chain reaction of political-military crises that escalated into the global conflict known as World War I did the murder's true significance become evident.

Other crucial turning points occurred not in terms of a few hours, days, months, or even years, but instead as evolutionary developments spanning decades or even centuries. One of the most pivotal turning points in human history, for instance—the development of agriculture, which replaced nomadic hunter-gatherer societies with more permanent settlements—occurred over the course of many generations. Still other great turning points were neither events nor developments, but rather revolutionary new inventions and innovations that significantly altered social customs and ideas, military tactics, home life, the spread of knowledge, and the human condition in general. The developments of writing, gunpowder, the printing press, antibiotics, the electric light, atomic energy, television, and the computer, the last two of which have recently ushered in the world-altering information age, represent only some of these innovative turning points.

Each anthology in the Greenhaven Turning Points in World History series presents a group of essays chosen for their accessibility. The anthology's structure also enhances this accessibility. First, an introductory essay provides a general overview of the principal events and figures involved, placing the topic in its historical context. The essays that follow explore various aspects in more detail, some targeting political trends and consequences, others social, literary, cultural, and/or technological ramifications, and still others pivotal leaders and other influential figures. To aid the reader in choosing the material of immediate interest or need, each essay is introduced by a concise summary of the contributing writer's main themes and insights.

In addition, each volume contains extensive research tools, including a collection of excerpts from primary source documents pertaining to the historical events and figures under discussion. In the anthology on the French Revolution, for example, readers can examine the works of Rousseau, Voltaire, and other writers and thinkers whose championing of human rights helped fuel the French people's growing desire for liberty; the French *Declaration of the Rights of Man and Citizen*, presented to King Louis XVI by the French National Assembly on October 2, 1789; and eyewitness accounts of the attack on the royal palace and the horrors of the Reign of Terror. To guide students interested in pursuing further research on the subject, each volume features an extensive bibliography, which for easy access has been divided into separate sections by topic. Finally, a comprehensive index allows readers to scan and locate content efficiently. Each of the anthologies in the Greenhaven Turning Points in World History series provides students with a complete, detailed, and enlightening examination of a crucial historical watershed.

Introduction

World War I, known as the "Great War," decisively shaped the entire twentieth century. It was the first phase in a century of total war. Militarily, World War I introduced new large-scale weapons, including combat aircraft, tanks, submarines, flame throwers, and chemical agents. The war also increased the firepower of heavy artillery and machine guns, two of the most deadly weapons of the conflict. Politically, World War I was an essential precondition to the rise of the totalitarian movements that shaped the twentieth century. Communism in Russia, fascism in Italy, and Nazism in Germany all had their start in the outcome of World War I. Even the Holocaust had a World War I counterpart— Turkey's killing of millions of Armenians in 1914–1915.

The war of 1914–1918 also caused the collapse and disappearance of no less than four great empires. The regimes of the Romanovs of Russia, the Habsburgs of Austria-Hungary, the Hohenzollerns of Germany, and the Ottomans of Turkey all disappeared. In the wake of the collapse of these old regimes, a dozen new "successor" states emerged in Central and Eastern Europe.

Economically, World War I disrupted national budgets, financial markets, and international trade. Most economic historians see the war as a fundamental factor in the onset of the Great Depression in 1929. Socially and culturally, the First World War also profoundly affected the Western world, the Middle East, Africa, and Asia as well. Before 1914, confidence in progress, science, and reason marked the educated elite class in the West. The experience of four years of brutal warfare shattered these ideals. As French writer Paul Valery observed at war's end, Europe had been deeply wounded in mind and spirit. For famed psychologist Sigmund Freud, the war showed that the human race was a species with ineradicable destructive instincts. Clearly, World War I stands out as a seismic shift in world history.

The Coming of War: 1914

The causes of World War I were controversial from the start. Even during the opening months of the conflict, the combatants were issuing carefully doctored "official" justifications of their own actions and condemnations of those of their foes. In more recent decades, however, historians have pinpointed a multiplicity of factors that combined to produce the war.

Germany, united under the leadership of Otto von Bismarck, emerged after its victory over France in 1870 as the strongest military power on the European continent. The new Germany solidified its international position in 1882 when it created the Triple Alliance with Austria-Hungary and Italy. With the ascension of Wilhelm II to the German throne in 1888, however, the elderly Bismarck's policy of diplomatic maneuvering to avoid the encirclement of Germany by isolating France was abandoned. The rash young kaiser and his advisers antagonized both Russia and France. This led to a Russian-French alliance in 1894. The alliance between republican France and the reactionary czarist Russian monarchy stunned Europe. And from that point, European international relations became increasingly strained, marked by a succession of diplomatic crises that on several occasions after 1905 brought Europe close to war. In 1904, Great Britain ended a centuries-long conflict with its cross-Channel rival, France, and joined in a loose pact of understanding, or entente. Then, in 1907, Great Britain and Russia, two countries that had dueled for power and influence for decades in Asia and the Middle East, joined in a similar entente. Europe was divided into a complicated and increasingly unstable balance of power, pitting the Triple Alliance against the Triple Entente.

Accelerating the tensions between the two alliance systems was an escalating armaments race on land and sea. Between 1870 and 1914, the major European powers (with the exception of Britain) adopted compulsory military conscription, providing a huge military reserve in case of war. Military spending rose sharply, especially in the decade before

1914. Beginning in the 1890s, Germany challenged the British domination of the seas by launching a battleship fleet. Britain had no intention of giving up its historic superiority, however, and built even more battleships, called Dreadnoughts, to outnumber the German fleet.

In addition to the rival alliances and rising militarization, the European political and social order was rife with internal tensions. A formidable antiwar socialist movement existed in all the major nations. Socialists pledged (somewhat ambivalently) to wage a general strike if war threatened and their own governments mobilized. Unfortunately for peacemakers, nationalism proved stronger than internationalism even among socialists and the working classes. Over the course of the period from 1870 to 1914, a modern "mass society" came into existence in Europe. The masses won the right to vote in all the major states of the continent. Compulsory free public education systems raised literacy levels and broke down local and regional barriers to national unity. Schoolchildren were indoctrinated in nationalist values and patriotic versions of national history. Assisting the schools in nationalizing the populace were the new mass-circulation newspapers and magazines, with their sensationalism and superpatriotism. Nationalism stands as the single most dominating factor in the origins of the Great War. And at no time was nationalism more potent and inflammatory than in the summer of 1914 when Europe stumbled into war.

The connection between nationalism and the outbreak of general war in 1914 is best seen in the explosive Balkans. In the decade before 1914, the Balkan region of southeastern Europe was a combustible cross-point of frustrated and violent national aspirations. Austria-Hungary was a deeply divided empire encompassing dominant German-speaking Austrians and autonomous Hungarians as well as suppressed nationalities such as the Czechs, Slovaks, Croats, and, most troublesome for the Vienna government, Serbs. In 1908, Austria-Hungary annexed the province of Bosnia, which contained a large Serbian population. Russia, asserting itself in the role of protector of the Slavic and Eastern Orthodox

Serbs, vigorously denounced Austria-Hungary's action, but it failed to prevent the annexation.

In 1912–1913, the region was rocked by two wars between different combinations of small Balkan states plus Turkey. The overall effect of these wars enhanced Serbia's power as a leader of the anti-Habsburg discontent in the region. By 1914, Austria-Hungary felt that its existence as a multicultural empire was in peril unless it suppressed a Serbia that it alleged was promoting subversion among the empire's Balkan Slavic subjects. Russia, meanwhile, was determined not to back down again from a confrontation over a region that it, too, aspired to influence. In June 1914, the confrontation between Austria-Hungary and Russia in the Balkans finally ignited the European powder keg when a young Bosnian Serb, Gavrilo Princip, assassinated Austro-Hungarian archduke and heir apparent Franz Ferdinand at Sarajevo on June 28, 1914.

Despite the dangerous international frictions and large armies in 1914 Europe, the Sarajevo assassination and the crisis that followed took the governments and people by surprise. Europe had experienced a century of peace with only brief and limited conflicts between 1854 and 1878. But Austria-Hungary's ultimatum to Serbia on July 23, endorsed by Germany, triggered a growing crisis that swept all the major powers, except Italy, into general war within two weeks. On July 28, Austria-Hungary declared war after the Serbs refused the humiliating terms of the ultimatum from Vienna. Russia, meanwhile, put pressure on Austria-Hungary by mobilizing its armies. Germany viewed the Russian action as provocative because the mobilization also included Russian forces on Germany's eastern borders. On August 1, Germany declared war on Russia. Since Germany's long-standing war plan called for attacking France by way of Belgium to win a quick victory before dealing with Russia in the east, it proceeded to declare war on France and invade Belgium. Belgium chose to resist German intervention. Finally, on August 4, Great Britain honored its ambiguous commitment to aid France, citing the German violation of Belgian neutrality as its reason for declaring war on Germany. The third Balkan war of the decade had escalated to a general European war.

Why did no effective initiatives for peace exist to avoid the disastrous drift toward general war? The potency of nationalism again provides the best clue to the failure of peacemaking in 1914. Different nations bore different levels of responsibility for the outbreak of war. Serbia encouraged extremists like Princip. Austria-Hungary's ultimatum to Serbia virtually demanded that Serbia abandon its sovereignty. Russia's clumsy mobilization, thanks to the weak, vacillating Czar Nicholas II, contributed to the sad outcome since it alarmed Germany. France's contribution to the final crisis seems relatively insignificant.

Germany arguably carries the heaviest blame for war. It allowed its junior partner Austria-Hungary too much discretion to risk a wider war by taking action against Serbia. In addition, as historian Samuel R. Williamson Jr. observes, "the German war plans in 1914 were simple, dangerous, and exceptionally mechanical."[1] That is, the Germans were committed to a preventive offensive war in which they planned to crush France quickly and then wheel east to defeat Russia. They miscalculated the British response, thinking Britain would stand aside or react too slowly. But Britain ultimately could not allow Germany to attain dominance in Western Europe, which would also put German warships on the English Channel.

Stalemate and a Widening War

The European nations went to war in the summer of 1914 with remarkable enthusiasm. Cheering crowds in the great cities of Europe were convinced of their own country's righteousness. But by late 1914, the German plan to crush France's armies by a powerful flanking attack through Belgium was stopped near Paris at the First Battle of the Marne. The Russian invasion of Germany's province of East Prussia was halted by a major German victory at Tannenberg, and the Austro-Hungarian attack into Serbia was thrown back. Soon, the armies of Germany, France, and Britain were not advancing on the western front. Instead, they were digging elaborate defensive trenches stretching from the English

Channel on the French-Belgian border all the way to the Swiss frontier hundreds of miles to the southeast. The great stalemate on the western front had begun; it would not be broken for almost four years. In the east, major German advances would drive Russian forces eastward, but no decisive victory would be attained. The opposing belligerents slowly realized that no short-war victory, in the east or west, was possible. A long, costly struggle lay ahead.

As the Allies and the Central Powers grappled with the deadlock in early 1915, they took steps that widened the war and helped convert it into a total war. By this point, Germany had already won Turkey to its side at the strategic meeting point of Europe and the Middle East. As the Allies realized that no breakthrough in the west was likely, they mounted an indirect attack on the Central Powers by attempting to capture the Turkish Straits in a 1915 naval and land campaign that ended in failure. Bulgaria, meanwhile, would join the Central Powers in late 1915, participating in a successful invasion of Serbia that year along with German and Austro-Hungarian forces. Italy, after a brief neutrality at the start of the war, joined the Allied side after the Allies promised postwar territorial gains at the expense of Austria-Hungary. Bitter, bloody battles on the Alpine borders between these two powers continued until the end of the war. The British extended military operations into the Middle East (against the Ottoman Turks) and into Africa against Germany's few colonies there. Greece entered the war with the Allies in 1916, as did Romania. The Romanians timed their intervention poorly and were overrun by German forces in late 1916. Meanwhile, naval warfare flared at sea.

Toward Total War

In 1915, as Jay Winter and Blaine Baggett argue in *The Great War and the Shaping of the 20th Century*, traditional methods of battle gave way to total war. At the Second Battle of Ypres on the western front, Germany introduced the use of chlorine gas, which caused blindness, choking, and panic among its victims. It briefly terrorized French army units, but because the gas relied on the direction the wind was blowing, it sometimes incapacitated the users. Soon, both the Allies and the Germans were employing increasingly deadly chemical agents and packing them in artillery shells. Gas masks became required as a defensive measure. Only fear of the chaos that unlimited use of the weapon might produce inhibited governments from employing it more.

Another event marking the onset of total war was the sinking of the British passenger liner *Lusitania* by German submarine U-20 in May 1915. Submarine warfare was Germany's deadly response to a tightening British naval blockade that denied Germans foodstuffs and other "noncontraband" goods. The death of more than twelve hundred civilians, including more than one hundred Americans, on the *Lusitania* outraged Allied and American public opinion and created a crisis in German-American relations. That same year also saw German dirigibles launch primitive bombing raids on Britain's cities, also killing civilians. Finally, along their northeastern battle line with Russia, the Turks resorted to the first large-scale example of twentieth-century genocide against an Armenian population whose loyalty they distrusted. Civilians were increasingly the victims of a widening war.

Also paving a path for an increasingly bloody and total war was the way in which the coalitions launched military offensives for political and diplomatic reasons. As several recent historians maintain, the combatant nations were concerned not only with recruiting possible new allies but also with retaining existing allies. Therefore, taking the offensive would impress the potential ally and reassure and take military pressure off existing allies. The British attack on the Somme in July 1916, with sixty thousand casualties on the first day of battle alone, was largely intended to relieve German pressure against the French at the great battle at Verdun. It was also meant to assist the Russian armies that had been battered by Germany the previous year.

The Horrors of Battle

While politicians and generals ordered great offensives, the suffering and dying on the battlefronts was the fate of the ordinary soldiers on both sides. There is no more lasting impression of World War I than the horrific conditions that soldiers in the trenches experienced. As German artist and soldier Otto Dix exclaimed,

> Lice, rats, barbed wire, fleas, shells, bombs, underground caves, corpses, blood, liquor, mice, cats, artillery, filth, bullets, mortars, fire, steel, that is what war is. It is the work of the devil.[2]

Dix's bitter account was matched by British and French soldiers. The mechanization of warfare by World War I gave an immense advantage to the defense, once the first offensives of the war had failed. The machine gun, in particular, proved a deadly defensive weapon. The general staffs, especially those of France and Britain, failed to revise pre-1914 offensive doctrines in light of the realities of trench defenses, based on barbed wire, machine guns, and artillery. Though offensive-oriented military doctrines accepted by the British and French generals were obsolete by 1914, the generals continued with suicidal frontal attacks through 1917. As historian Norman Stone suggests, the generals' contempt for the intelligence and well-being of the peasant and working-class soldier made them indifferent to the heavy sacrifice of lives on the battlefield.

The soldiers underwent unspeakable hardships in these campaigns. Although they did receive regular periods of rear-line duty and rest leave, they faced constant challenges and dangers. Mud, rain, cold, and snow added to the troops' miseries. Soldiers undertook long marches with packs weighing up to eighty-five pounds, often at night through winding trenches. Added to this was the fatigue of trench construction and repair, sentry duty, and other difficult tasks. Finally, in battle, soldiers faced the terrifying symphony of rifle, machine-gun, mortar, and heavy artillery fire. Poison gas was especially horrendous in its effects, attacking lungs, faces, and eyes, although countermeasures like the gas mask reduced casualties somewhat later in the war. Throughout World War I, the fear of death in the chaos of battle was a constant. On many battlefields, soldiers fought on while wounded and dead comrades lay by their sides, the wounded crying for help, the dead grotesque reminders of what might lie ahead for them at any moment.

Total War on the Home Front

As total war deepened in 1916, it led to expanding government economic controls on the home fronts. The epic battles of that year were a British-French attack at the Somme and the German bid to bleed the French army into submission by an attack at Verdun. Almost 2 million soldiers were sacrificed in these prolonged ordeals, but the military stalemate was unchanged. This carnage without victory resulted in intensified pressure on the home fronts to mobilize entire populations and all available resources to continue the war effort. Because of the heavy losses at the battlefront, the belligerents had to carefully allocate their diminished man power. Britain abandoned its prewar liberal principles and introduced military conscription after its volunteer forces were slaughtered at the Somme. Britain, France, and Germany imposed controls on the allocation of labor, shifting man power from civilian to munitions manufacturing and other war-essential work. Labor unions were persuaded or pressured into no-strike pledges. One of the most significant developments in the wartime mobilization of labor was the massive entry of women into war-related occupations, including munitions. The vital contribution of women on the industrial front was summed up by French general Joseph Joffre: "If women working in the factories stopped for twenty minutes," he said, "France would lose the war."[3] Workers on the home fronts also suffered from food shortages and had to endure government rationing of everyday necessities such as bread, sugar, dairy goods, and meat. Germans, for example, saw their bread become darker and less digestible. To conserve flour, the German government even allowed wood shavings and sand to be added to bread.

Another aspect of mobilizing the civilian population for total war was government propaganda to sustain the war effort. Governments had to persuade their people that the war was justified and that sacrifice was necessary. They also had to maintain this public backing till the end of the war. As a result, a "politics of hate" infected the home fronts of the warring European nations. The enemy was portrayed as immoral and responsible for the war. British propaganda cast Germans as the evil "Huns." Germany, in turn, portrayed the British as a selfish commercial people.

What was new in World War I was not just the intensity of the propaganda but its scope and its use of the cinema. Charlie Chaplin, a British actor-comedian and international movie star, made several popular and patriotic war films. Chaplin and other film stars also keynoted enthusiastic rallies in the United States promoting the sale of war bonds among the general public. Despite a coal shortage by 1918, Germany made sure that its movie theaters would not close because of a lack of heating. Propaganda on the home fronts was more evidence of the total mobilization of minds and materials that emerged during the Great War.

1916: Clashing War Aims

Historian S.L. Mayer, reflecting on the failure of nearly all the offensives through the end of 1916, summarized the situation of both sides: "Technology, which was assumed to be able to achieve anything, had failed as the armies themselves had failed. . . . Yet, since neither side would accept a peace without victory, victory had to be achieved."[4] Another historian, David Stevenson, observes that by late 1916 the war involved a "triple deadlock" involving diplomacy, the battlefronts, and the home fronts. Diplomatically, the belligerents' war aims were starkly different and incompatible with those of their foes. Among the major belligerents, Germany envisioned an empire of direct or indirect control extending "from Belgium to Baghdad." Russia demanded control of Constantinople at the Turkish Straits; the other Allies readily agreed to this to keep Russia fighting. Italy was promised Austrian territory in the Alps and along the Adriatic coast in secret treaties with the Allies in 1915. France's war aims included the elimination of "Prussian militarism" within Germany (breaking its military power), the return of Alsace-Lorraine, and even the loss of the vital German Rhineland.

Britain's war goals also included overturning "Prussian militarism," in addition to the German evacuation from Belgium and northern France, the surrender of the German fleet, its African colonies, and British control over vital parts of the Middle East, mostly under Ottoman Turkish rule before 1914.

On the home fronts, a consensus in support of total victory still held in each belligerent state through the end of 1916. Solidarity was weakest in Russia and was eroding significantly in Austria-Hungary and Germany. Unity at home waned to a lesser degree in France, Italy, and Britain. Although less enthusiastically than at the start of the war, home front populations still continued to believe that their own nations had acted honorably and in self-defense since 1914.

1917: A Turning Point

In 1917, three events broke the grinding stalemate that had prevailed since late 1914. Germany, under its new military leadership team of Generals Paul von Hindenburg and Erich Ludendorff, decided to gamble on an unrestricted submarine offensive to force Britain to make peace. The obvious danger was that this policy would assure that the United States entered the war. But German military strategists believed that Germany was being so severely damaged by the Allied naval blockade that a bold escalation against Britain was necessary even if the United States entered the conflict on the side of the Allies. In response to Germany's all-out U-boat offensive that began on January 31, 1917, against neutral and Allied shipping around the British Isles, the United States broke diplomatic relations with Berlin in early February 1917. Two months later, after mounting attacks on American vessels, the United States declared war on Germany—the second turning point. Finally, czarist Russia, staggering under the burden of military losses, inflation, shortages, and peasant and worker discontent, collapsed in March 1917.

These events showed that previous solid coalitions were starting to unravel. Russia would establish a provisional republican government; the moderate liberals and socialist leaders there continued the war. Continuing the war, however, would contribute to the provisional government's overthrow in November 1917 by the hitherto insignificant Bolshevik Party (Communists). Meanwhile, Germany's key partner, Austria-Hungary, showed increased signs of wavering in the face of internal unrest that was intensified by agitation for autonomy from suppressed nationality groups like the Czechs and the Slovaks. The death of Emperor Franz Joseph in December 1916 after a reign of sixty-eight years brought to the throne a peace-oriented successor, Emperor Karl. As a result, Austria-Hungary began to actively promote diplomatic contacts to leave the war, but its unwillingness or inability to untie itself from Germany frustrated this effort.

Calls for peace had mounted by the close of 1916, as all the nations faced huge casualties, rising labor discontent, and general war-weariness on the home fronts. These rumblings never quite managed to destroy the support for war in any of the main fighting nations, except Russia in 1917. But the discontent forced governments to at least appear to explore the possibilities of peace.

While the war raged, the Allies were desperate for American troops to be raised, trained, and dispatched to France as soon as possible. This need became even more apparent since Russia, in mid-1917, seemed incapable of further military efforts on the eastern front. If American troops did not arrive in Europe soon, Germany might shift forces to the western front and launch a crushing attack on a French army that had experienced widespread mutinies in its ranks and on a British army that was also very hard-pressed.

The year 1917 was a low point for the Allies, even though the Central Powers were themselves plagued by food shortages and social unrest. In November 1917, Lenin and the Bolshevik Party overthrew the weakened Russian republican government, culminating in the disintegration of Russia's armies and a vast internal breakdown. The Bolsheviks quickly focused on the popular agenda of peace, bread, and land. In December, Italian armies collapsed in the wake of the German and Austro-Hungarian attack at Caporetto, although a new defense line was propped up to prevent a further breakthrough. Peace proposals were now advanced from diverse sources: European socialists and trade unionists, the German Reichstag (Parliament), Pope Benedict XV, and British conservative leader Lord Lansdowne. The longing for peace in the face of seemingly endless war was clear.

The debate over peace terms intensified in early 1918. The new Bolshevik regime called for immediate peace and soon agreed to an armistice with Germany. On the Allied home fronts, discontent grew in the wake of internal unrest and because of Bolshevik revelations of secret treaties that suggested that the Allies were as imperialistic as the Germans. On January 8, 1918, President Woodrow Wilson outlined American terms for a peace settlement in his Fourteen Points address. Wilson's Fourteen Points were an effort to counter the Bolshevik call for immediate peace, to stir up peace sentiment inside the Central Powers, and to reassure the discontented Allied liberals and socialists. It was also an instrument of psychological warfare. The speech defined an American bid to shape the postwar peace on the basis of the liberal capitalist ideals that also shaped Wilson's Latin American and Asian policies. Besides endorsing freedom of the seas, reduced barriers to international trade, and the establishment of a League of Nations, Wilson stressed the principle of national self-determination and, in effect, a German retreat in both the east and west. The speech did help undermine support within Austria-Hungary and had an impact on German morale, too.

Even though the Allies gave tentative support to most of the Fourteen Points, Wilson's peace proposals did not alter the U.S. commitment to the goal of military victory over Germany. When Berlin in March 1918 imposed an extremely harsh peace on Russia, Wilson pledged "force to the utmost, force without stint or limit"[5] against Germany. Britain and France redoubled their commitment to victory at the same time. In the end, despite the numerous pleas for peace from late 1916 to early 1918, peace did not come.

Indeed, Germany's harsh actions in dictating peace to Russia, and also Romania in early 1918, assured a continued Allied pursuit of military victory, not a negotiated, compromise peace. British prime minister David Lloyd George and French premier Georges Clemenceau, were as unyielding as Wilson in their commitment to a complete Allied military victory.

1918: Defeat of the Central Powers

Even before the harsh Treaty of Brest-Litovsk Germany imposed on Bolshevik Russia in March 1918, it began shifting dozens of divisions from the now-quiet eastern front to the west. In what are sometimes called the Ludendorff offensives, named after its leading military planner, the Germans once again gambled on victory, this time through a massive blow at French and British forces in northern France. Germany hoped that these Allied powers would sue for peace under the weight of the new German assault before the vast, fresh man power of the Allies' new "associate," the United States, was ready for full-scale battle in France. Germany's great spring offensive scored some stunning initial successes as a result of new tactical innovations and the superior coordination of artillery and infantry. The drive threatened to split the British and French armies and capture Paris. But the Allies quickly strengthened their coordination and by July began a counteroffensive, which was enhanced by the increasing participation of fresh American divisions under General John Pershing. The Allied advance gained increased momentum by August and September, and the German military leaders came to the realization that defeat was inevitable. What proved decisive was not the increased presence of American divisions, though that was a factor; it was the German knowledge that huge additional American forces were on their way to the battlefront. As historian John Keegan suggests,

> After four years of a war in which they had destroyed the Tsar's army, trounced the Italians and Rumanians, demoralized the French and, at the very least, denied the British

clear-cut victory, [the Germans] were now confronted with an army whose soldiers sprang, in uncountable numbers, as if from soil sown with dragons' teeth.[6]

The German army retreated but did not completely collapse. But whereas the Allies could plan for a war into 1919 because of abundant man power and weaponry, Germany faced increased desertions and declining morale since its last-gasp offensive had failed. German man power could not match that of the Allies, especially with the addition of hundreds of thousands of American troops. In September 1918, the German military encouraged a new German government to sue for peace on the basis of President Wilson's Fourteen Points and related peace proposals. By November 1918, revolution within Germany signaled defeat on the German home front as well.

In the postwar era, German leaders would allege that the German army was not beaten in battle but was the victim of a "stab in the back" by subversive liberal and leftist elements at home. This was a myth: Germany's military elite made the decision to seek an end to the war, knowing full well that it could not win the war after August 1918. At the same time, in the fall of 1918, Germany's lesser allies—Austria-Hungary, Bulgaria, and Turkey—collapsed and sued for peace with the Allies as well. On November 11, 1918, the guns on the western front fell silent. The most catastrophic war in human history till that time had ended. But the four years of agony and destruction cast a giant shadow over efforts to build a lasting peace.

A Flawed Peace

The Allies would dictate the terms of the final peace settlement at the Paris Peace Conference of 1919. Most decisions were made by the "Big Three," U.S. president Woodrow Wilson, British prime minister David Lloyd George, and French premier Georges Clemenceau. An apt description of the chaos and confusion reigning at the massive conference was that of British diplomat and eyewitness Harold Nicolson. He called the meeting "a riot in a parrothouse."[7] To begin with, the planning and organization of the assembly were badly flawed. Committees studied technical aspects of the peace settlement without adequate consultation with other committees. The conferees were also subject to a bombardment of publicity, for hundreds of newspapermen, film cameras, and spokesmen for numerous causes were in attendance. Advocates of oppressed colonial peoples such as Vietnam's Ho Chi Minh and T.E. Lawrence on behalf of the Arabs tried unsuccessfully to influence the decision makers. The peace settlement would be a hastily and badly crafted effort.

Yet under the circumstances, the various treaties signed near Paris in 1919 and the early 1920s were perhaps as good as the extremely poor circumstances permitted. In 1919, at the end of four years of death, hunger, stoked-up hatreds, social upheaval, and economic disruption, Europe was not likely to fashion a just, lasting peace. As Jay Winter and Blaine Baggett argue, the "politics of hatred" produced by the war poisoned the peacemaking process. In 1919, Europe faced massive obstacles to any stable peace: Bolshevik Russia survived in a state of civil war and battled foreign (Allied) intervention; Central and Eastern Europe were wracked by economic breakdown and spreading hunger; revolutionary movements of the left in Germany and Hungary and rightist movements in Germany and Italy bid for power; four empires and thrones in Central and Eastern Europe disappeared while weak new national states emerged; finally, an influenza epidemic that would kill more people than the World War itself devastated Europe and the world between 1918 and 1920.

The victors' settlement with Germany was the core of the final peace treaty. The treaty became official when it was dictated by the Allies to a German delegation at the Palace of Versailles on June 28, 1919, the fifth anniversary of the assassination at Sarajevo. Despite the Allied promise to base the peace settlement on Wilson's liberal Fourteen Points, Germany was forced to accept responsibility for the war in Article 231, the "war guilt" clause. Besides withdrawing from Alsace-Lorraine, Belgium, and Poland, it had to reduce its army to one hundred thousand and surrender its navy to

On June 28, 1919, government officials gathered in the Hall of Mirrors to witness the signing of the Treaty of Versailles. The peace treaty officially ended World War I.

Britain. Germany also lost all its colonies in Africa and Asia. Finally, Germany was ordered to pay heavy reparations to the Allies, particularly France, Belgium, and Britain, for not only war damage but additional costs such as war pensions. Reparations provoked dissent even within the Allied camp. Economist John Maynard Keynes, an adviser to the British peace delegation, assailed the vindictive spirit and punitive economic terms of the treaty as likely to hinder rather than help European economic recovery.

The "war guilt" clause, in particular, became a rallying point for opposition by both extreme right wing and moderate German nationalists. Behind these drastic provisions was France's determination to weaken Germany so that it would never pose a danger to France again. Clemenceau was concerned about little else than security against Germany, which he believed could not be trusted to Woodrow Wilson's vague liberal visions or even to Great Britain's future support. Indeed, with the end of the war, British leaders became increasingly worried that France, not Germany, might do more to disrupt the peace by a shortsighted vindictive policy toward a now republican but resentful and economically prostrate Germany.

The United States contributed significantly to the failure of the Versailles settlement. France wanted a British and American military pledge to come to its aid if it was threatened in the future by Germany. Unfortunately, the U.S. Senate rejected any such commitment. Given that rejection, France then redoubled its determination to squeeze Germany economically through the reparations payments in order to permanently weaken its foe and achieve military security. The United States also failed to cancel or reduce Allied war debts it was owed, loans the Allies could not repay given their troubled postwar economic condition. Even Wilson's greatest achievement at Paris, the League of Nations (a key provision of the treaty), was repudiated by the Senate when it also rejected the treaty in 1920.

The peace conference also focused on Central and Eastern Europe. Here, however, it mainly ratified the emergence of new independent states from the wreckage of the Hohenzollern, czarist, and Habsburg empires. These new states included Poland, Czechoslovakia, and Yugoslavia. Unfortunately, the creation of these small, unstable states on the borders of a Communist Russia and a resentful Germany only weakened the long-run balance of power in the region.

Elsewhere, Italy's territorial demands caused trouble at the peace conference, since its demands for territorial spoils at the expense of both Austria and Yugoslavia violated the principle of self-determination. In the Middle East, further violations of the principle of national self-determination would occur as Britain and France allocated former Ottoman lands inhabited by Arab peoples (including Palestine) to themselves under the cover of League of Nations "mandates."

Modern historians still disagree about the overall significance of the Treaty of Versailles and the results of the Paris Peace Conference. The weaknesses of the peace settlement go far to explain the coming of World War II two decades later. Yet the hatreds of the Great War itself undermined the chances for a lasting peace even before the conference met. As soon as the treaty was signed, the Allies themselves, especially the British, began trying to make its terms more lenient to the defeated. In time, this became known as appeasement, a sign of moderation and reason toward the vanquished. Unfortunately, Nazism in Germany during the 1920s and '30s made the Versailles treaty a scapegoat, as it worked to undermine the new republican government there. Once in power, the Nazis soon repudiated all treaty restraints and rearmed, but Britain and France continued and intensified appeasement. As historian Alan Sharp concludes, the Versailles settlement might have worked if it was either a more generous peace from the start or its terms had been vigorously enforced. In the end, it was the worst of both worlds: too vindictive in its terms and then not enforced effectively and consistently.

The Legacy of the Great War

The First World War is arguably the pivotal event of the twentieth century. It marked the eclipse of European global predominance that dated back to the sixteenth century. Out of the war, the United States emerged the world's leading economic power. Communism took hold in Russia, and small "successor" states were created in Eastern and Central Europe, most of which still exist today. The rise of fascism and Nazism in Europe is incomprehensible without reference to the impact of World War I. Their use of naked force against both internal foes and foreign nations reflected the culture of violence stemming from the war. The world economic depression that began in 1929 owed heavily to the profound economic dislocations of the war. Finally, the coming of World War II has been viewed as a nearly inevitable result of the deep wounds opened by the Great War. Soon after the Versailles treaty, French general Ferdinand Foch forecast prophetically that the treaty was only "an armistice for twenty years."[8] The Great War and failed peace settlement made probable a second, more terrible war. In their study of its lasting significance, Jay Winter and Blaine Baggett capture the paradox of the war: Technological and scientific progress was coupled with brute force, a regression in human history. As Winter and Baggett note, "The trajectory of human progress was fractured: technological change leaped forward yet political life moved backward into a new age of cruelty, made worse by the new and more efficient machinery of degradation and death."[9]

The human costs of the Great War are apparent in the 8 to 10 million servicemen who died in the war. Germany lost nearly 2 million men. Russia, France, and Austria-Hungary all lost well over a million soldiers, and Britain and Italy somewhat less than a million. The U.S. casualties included forty-eight thousand battlefield deaths, less than those of Canada or Australia, but American losses were considerable given the short time the American forces were in action. Smaller countries such as Serbia, Romania, and Belgium also paid a steep price in both civilian and military lives.

In the postwar period, the crippled and maimed veterans were a constant reminder of the horror of the war. The "men with broken faces," as some were called in France, lacked acceptance and understanding in postwar society. In addition to the physically damaged, hundreds of thousands of veterans suffered from psychological problems caused by the indescribable experience in the trenches. Some of these veterans experienced "shell shock," a malady similar to what today is called post-traumatic stress disorder.

The Great War profoundly influenced the arts and literature of the 1920s and '30s. It accelerated the acceptance of a modern perspective characterized by uncertainty and a questioning of all ideas and values. A long list of writers and artists served in the war and explored its meanings in their work. Erich Maria Remarque, a German who served on the western front, wrote about the sufferings of frontline soldiers in an international best-seller in 1929 called *All Quiet on the Western Front*. American Ernest Hemingway, who served as an ambulance medic on the Italian front, defined a modern as opposed to a romantic response to the war experience in his novel *A Farewell to Arms*. A character in the novel declares that "abstract words such as glory, honor, courage, or hallow were obscene" and that the "sacrifices were like the stockyards at Chicago."[10] During and after the war, such outstanding British soldier-poets as Wilfred Owen, Siegfried Sassoon, and Robert Graves crafted poems that conveyed the predicament of men seeking to survive the mechanized terror of modern warfare.

One of the most creative productions representing the First World War was the sculpture of German artist Kathe Kollwitz. To memorialize her son's death on the western front, Kollwitz returned after the war to the Belgian cemetery where he was buried to sculpt statues of two grieving parents—herself and her husband. Her work expressed a deep sense of guilt on her part for not having worked to prevent the tragedy of 1914 in the first place. The legacy of the war would create the preconditions for a larger, more terrible war from 1939 to 1945. In that war, Kathe Kollwitz lost a grandson on the battlefield as well.

To this day, the Great War remains a transforming event in the making of the contemporary world.

Notes

1. Samuel R. Williamson Jr., "The Origins of the War," in Hew Strachan, ed., *World War I: A History*. Oxford, England: Oxford University Press, 1998, p. 23.

2. Quoted in Jay Winter and Blaine Baggett, *The Great War and the Shaping of the 20th Century*. New York: Penguin Studio, 1996, pp. 99–101.

3. Quoted in Gerald J. De Groot, "The First World War as Total War," in Martin Pugh, ed., *A Companion to European History, 1871–1945*. Oxford, England: Oxford University Press, 1997, p. 271.

4. S.L. Mayer, "Introduction," in A.J.P. Taylor, ed., *History of World War I*. London: Octopus Books, 1974, p. 84.

5. Quoted in David Stevenson, *The First World War and International Politics*. Oxford, England: Oxford University Press, 1988, p. 202.

6. John Keegan, *The First World War*. New York: Knopf, 1999, pp. 411–12.

7. Harold Nicolson, *Peacemaking 1919*. London: Methuen, 1964, p. 152.

8. Quoted in P.M.H. Bell, *The Origins of the Second World War in Europe*. 2nd ed. London: Longman, 1997, p. 16.

9. Winter and Baggett, *The Great War and the Shaping of the 20th Century*, p. 361.

10. Quoted in *Bartlett's Familiar Quotations*. 15th ed. Boston: Little Brown, 1980, p. 844.

Chapter 1

The Origins of World War I

Turning|Points
IN WORLD HISTORY

An Explosive Mix: Nationalism and Military Alliances

H. Stuart Hughes

H. Stuart Hughes (1916–1999) had a distinguished career as a teacher and scholar at Harvard and the University of California, San Diego. Hughes's major interest was European intellectual history in the twentieth century. In this excerpt from his elegant survey *Contemporary Europe*, H. Stuart Hughes explains how nationalism and the rival alliance systems led Europe toward war in 1914. The Balkan region of southeast Europe was an especially combustible mix of rival great powers and suppressed nationalities. Serbian nationalists in the annexed Austro-Hungarian province of Bosnia wanted to pull Bosnia out from the Austro-Hungarian empire. Hughes also explains Russia's decision to support Serbia. Russia's decision led to a general European war. Hughes concludes that Austria-Hungary and Germany were primarily responsible for the war and holds France relatively blameless.

The First World War was produced by the confluence of two explosive pressures: the aspirations of the national minorities in Central and Eastern Europe and the dynamic of the rival alliance systems among the Great Powers. Either one of these had in itself an enormous war potential; together they brought about a steady drift toward armed hostilities that in retrospect seems irresistible.

The Nationalities Problem

The question of national minorities was almost exclusively a Central and Eastern European concern. . . .

Excerpted from *Contemporary Europe: A History*, 4th ed., by H. Stuart Hughes. Copyright © 1976, 1972, 1966, 1961 by Prentice-Hall, Inc. Used with permission.

Austria-Hungary had the most serious minority problems, and the Dual Monarchy was often referred to less as a nation than as a mere conglomeration of nationalities. In Germany, the overwhelming majority of the inhabitants spoke German and felt themselves to be Germans (its Polish population constituted the outstanding exception). Even in the Russian Empire, the Great Russian nationality formed the central core of the state and easily dominated the others. For Russia, the chief problem lay in the western borderlands, where the Finns, the small Baltic peoples, and, most important, the Poles, all had standing complaints of one sort or another against rule from St. Petersburg.

In the partitions that destroyed the independence of Poland in the late eighteenth century, Russia received the largest share. The rest had gone to Prussia and Austria. Hence from the very start, the Polish problem had involved all three eastern powers. All three had an interest in the maintenance of the *status quo*, while Austria followed a calculated policy of giving its own Poles the position of a favored minority within the state.

Austrian policy dealt otherwise with two other branches of European Slavdom. The Czechs and the South Slavs looked to Russia for deliverance, and they had it in their power to rend the whole Austrian state asunder. The Czechs of Bohemia and Moravia had long ago lost their separate national existence: like the Poles, they lived on hopes and historical memories. The South Slavs, though culturally less advanced than the Czechs, were closer to independence. Part in and part out of the Austro-Hungarian Empire, they were in a position that naturally aroused maximum awareness of every national injustice.

In 1903 the Serbian monarchy had reverted to the ambitious and Russian-oriented Karageorgevich dynasty. An aggressive anti-Austrian policy was the result. The Serbian leaders longed to have their country assume for the South Slavs the role that nineteenth-century Prussia had played for the Germans and Piedmont for the Italians—the core around which unity would be achieved. To fellow Serbs just across the border, and to the Croats and Slovenes farther west, Serbia promised the liberation of all the South Slavs within the confines of the Austro-Hungarian Empire. This pledge had taken on greater urgency since 1908 when—to the intense indignation of the Serbs—Austria annexed the South Slav provinces of Bosnia and Herzegovina, which had been technically still under Turkish suzerainty [political control].

The Bosnian crisis of 1908 was one of the periodic international crises which in the years after the turn of the century brought the powers closer and closer to war and which were usually Balkan in origin. The great exceptions, of course, were the two crises over Morocco in 1905 and 1911, which eventually resulted in French acquisition of that promising domain. The year following the French triumph, however, international attention returned to the Balkans, and it remained riveted on Balkan problems until the outbreak of the World War itself.

In 1912 and 1913, the small nations of this area went to war, first to deprive Turkey of nearly all its remaining European territory and subsequently to quarrel over the spoils. The Turks had been the oppressors of the Balkan peoples for more than five hundred years; the Balkan drive for national liberation, which began in the early nineteenth century, was completed in the First Balkan War of 1912–1913. But independence settled nothing. No Balkan nation was satisfied with its boundaries of 1913. Each had fellow nationals living within its neighbors' borders. Bulgaria had been humiliated in the Second Balkan War (June–July 1913), when the others had banded together against her. Greece coveted long stretches of Bulgaria's and Turkey's Aegean seacoast. Rumania sought the liberation of Transylvania from Hungarian rule. And Serbia—the most ambitious of the lot—stood in a particularly difficult position, with a Bulgarian minority inside its borders while it looked north and west in an attitude of unreserved hostility toward the Austro-Hungarian oppressors of its "blood brothers." It was obvious to any astute observer of the Balkan scene that the settlement of 1913 was no more than an uneasy truce. . . .

The Rival Alliances

The system of European alliances worked reasonably smoothly in the period from 1870 to 1890. Britain continued in its traditional detachment; the French nursed their grievance over the loss of Alsace-Lorraine; and Austria-Hungary and Italy moved into a defensive alliance with Germany. The new German Empire held the center of the stage. Its chancellor, Prince Bismarck, kept insisting that Germany was now a satisfied power. By reassuring Russia and isolating France, he held apart the only two powers that

Survival of the Militarily Fittest

In this excerpt from her classic study of the first month of World War I, historian Barbara Tuchman suggests how Germany may have contributed to the outbreak of war. Tuchman makes reference to General Friedrich von Bernhardi's book Germany and the Next War *(1911), which illustrated how nationalism, social Darwinism, and militarism had become a dangerous combination by this time, particularly in Germany.*

As a twenty-one-year-old cavalry officer in 1870, [Friedrich von] Bernhardi had been the first German to ride through the Arc de Triomphe when the Germans entered Paris. Since then flags and glory interested him less than the theory, philosophy, and science of war as applied to "Germany's Historic Mission." . . . He had served as chief of the Military History section of the General Staff, was one of the intellectual elite of that hard-thinking, hard-working body, and author of a classic on cavalry before he assembled . . . the book [*Germany and the Next War*] that was to make his name a synonym for Mars [the Roman god of war].

War, he stated, "is a biological necessity"; it is the carrying out among humankind of "the natural law, upon which all the laws of Nature rest, the law of the struggle for existence." Nations, he said, must progress or decay; "there can be no standing still," and Germany must choose "world power or downfall." Among the nations Germany "is in social-political respects at could possibly threaten the *status quo* in Central Europe.

With Bismarck's dismissal by the young Emperor William II in 1890, international relations moved into a graver phase. Within four years, Russia and France had signed a military agreement. By 1900, the German alliance with Italy had virtually become a dead letter. The British, alarmed by their isolation among the Great Powers that the Boer War [1899–1902, in South Africa] had revealed, reached a "cordial understanding" with France in 1904. In 1907, the new alliance system was completed when Britain and Russia

---

the head of all progress in culture" but is "compressed into narrow, unnatural limits." She cannot attain her "great moral ends" without increased political power, an enlarged sphere of influence, and new territory. This increase in power, "befitting our importance," and "which we are entitled to claim," is a "political necessity" and "the first and foremost duty of the State." In his own italics Bernhardi announced, "What we now wish to attain must be *fought for*," and from here he galloped home to the finish line: "Conquest thus becomes a law of necessity."

Having proved the "necessity" (the favorite word of German military thinkers), Bernhardi proceeded to method. Once the duty to make war is recognized, the secondary duty, to make it successfully, follows. To be successful a state must begin war at the "most favorable moment" of its own choosing; it has "the acknowledged right . . . to secure the proud privilege of such initiative." Offensive war thus becomes another "necessity" and a second conclusion inescapable: "It is incumbent on us . . . to act on the offensive and strike the first blow." Bernhardi did not share the Kaiser's concern about the "odium" that attached to an aggressor. Nor was he reluctant to tell where the blow would fall. It was "unthinkable," he wrote, that Germany and France could ever negotiate their problems. "France must be so completely crushed that she can never cross our path again"; she "must be annihilated once and for all as a great power."

Barbara Tuchman, *The Guns of August*. New York: Macmillan, 1962, pp. 10–11.

achieved a similar settlement of past differences.

In theory, then, the Powers stood three against three: a Triple Alliance—Germany, Austria-Hungary, and Italy—faced a looser Triple Entente—Britain, France, and Russia. In reality, the situation was rather less neat. Germany and Austria could no longer count on Italy. Within the rival coalition, only France and Russia were bound by a true alliance. Moreover, during the period 1890–1907, the balance had turned heavily against Germany. Although the Germans were probably the strongest single nation in the world—as their war record was to prove—they felt "encircled" by the united hostility of the second, third, and fourth European powers.

The Drift Toward War

In 1914, the merits of this contention were far from obvious. Each nation was absorbed in its own internal difficulties. For the second decade of the century had brought a break in economic prosperity and in the prevailing mood of optimism. Everywhere, the political militants were on the move. In Germany, the Reichstag elections of 1912 had made the Social Democrats the strongest party in the state. In Britain, the attempt of the Liberal government to grant home rule to Ireland had occasioned a mutiny among the army officers and a stalemate in civil-military relations. In Italy, the Socialists had taken a sharp turn to the left and in June 1914, engaged in a week of local rioting. France alone remained calm. Indeed, with radical influence weakened, with the passage of the three-year service law, and the election of the nationalist Raymond Poincaré as president, France seemed stronger, more confident, and more united than it had been at any time since the defeat of 1870.

The assassination at Sarajevo on June 28 rudely shook the statesmen of Europe out of domestic absorptions. In view of the tense relations between Serbia and Austria-Hungary in 1914, no one in Europe should have been surprised that the fuse which set off the great explosion was lighted here. Far from being—as journalists phrased it—an "obscure corner" of Europe, the capital of Bosnia was as likely a place as any for the great war to begin. The heir to the Austro-Hungarian throne, the Archduke Francis Ferdinand, might have known that he took his life in his hands when he ventured to pay a state visit there. No act was better calculated to stir Serbian resentment, and it was natural that the assassin should be a young Bosnian heated to fever by Serbian propaganda.

From this point on, individual national responsibilities for the great conflict unrolled with an iron logic. Serbia had only an indirect complicity in the assassination. Although its prime minister knew in a general way what was afoot, the slayers of the archduke were in no sense the agents of the Serbian government that the Austrians claimed. Moreover, when the Austrians followed up the assassination with a severe ultimatum, the Serbs agreed to nearly all their terms. They drew the line only at the unprecedented demand that Austro-Hungarian officials participate, *within Serbian territory*, in the investigation of the crime. It was the Austrians, rather, who bore the prime responsibility for the ensuing conflict in that they purposely made their requirements unacceptable in order to settle once for all—by war if necessary—with their upstart neighbors to the south. Next to them came the Germans, who in effect gave the Austrians a "blank check" by promising unlimited support to the nation which they correctly regarded as their only reliable ally, and by pressing it to act quickly against Serbia so as to split apart the Triple Entente.

The original Austro-German policy was predicated on the assumption that the war could be "localized." What made it a Europe-wide conflict was the Russian decision to support the Serbs. This brought the whole alliance system into play; for if Russia went to the aid of Serbia against Austria-Hungary, she also had to be prepared to face the German Empire. Still worse, the Russian military machine was slow and cumbersome, and if the country was to mobilize at all, technical considerations obliged it to do so fully and against *both* its potential enemies. Thus when the Russians were ostensibly doing nothing more than offering to protect their Serbian "brothers" against Austria-Hungary, it looked in Berlin as though they were also threatening Germany itself. In the frenzied weeks between the assassination and the outbreak of the conflict, it was the Russians who began the process of "escalation" by mobilizing prematurely; but it was the Germans who bore the responsibility for precipitating matters by declaring war on both France and the tsarist Empire.

In this succession of events, French responsibility was minimal. It has been argued that the French did not act with sufficient energy to restrain their Russian allies. But in reality they were kept in the dark about what the Russians were doing; the latter deceived them about the extent of the mobilization until it was a *fait accompli* [an accomplished fact]. The French government accepted the fact of war with resolution and confidence; but it did nothing to bring it about. Indeed it took up arms not so much in fidelity to its Russian ally as in defense of a European equilibrium which appeared threatened by German hegemony [dominance].

Even the British did not wholly escape responsibility, for they kept the Germans guessing up to the very last as to whether they would intervene—thus encouraging the war party within the Reich—and they justified their final decision not on its true ground (their secret military commitments to France) but on the ground of the German invasion of Belgium, which made a better impression on the British public.

Thus the melancholy sequence unfolded: Austria-Hungary threatened Serbia, Russia supported Serbia, Germany supported Austria, France supported Russia, Britain supported France. Italy alone remained aloof. On August 4, 1914, the armies started to move. The First World War had begun.

The Causes of War: Sharing the Blame

Michael J. Lyons

In the following viewpoint, historian Michael J. Lyons discusses the degrees of responsibility of each of the major European powers for the outbreak of the war, distributing the blame widely. Lyons teaches history at North Dakota State University in Fargo. He has published well-received short studies of both World War I and World War II.

From the start of hostilities, each of the opposing sides blamed the other for causing the war. Historians soon joined in and have continued to this very day to argue about who or what caused the catastrophe. Although it is unlikely that complete agreement will ever be forthcoming, certain observations appear warranted.

The Central Powers: Serbia, Austria-Hungary, and Germany

The conspirators who carried out the assassination of Archduke Francis Ferdinand, with the active participation of . . . [the Serbian] Black Hand organization, clearly ignited "the spark that set the world afire." And although the Serbian government did not authorize their action, . . . other officials in Belgrade were certainly aware of the plot and did little to alert Vienna to the magnitude of the danger. Their anti-Austrian policies and Greater Serb ambitions had also contributed mightily to the deterioration of relations with the Dual Monarchy. They assumed, moreover, that if it came to a showdown with Austria-Hungary, Serbia's "big brother" Russia would back them up.

Excerpted from *World War I: A Short History*, by Michael J. Lyons. Copyright © 1994 by Prentice-Hall, Inc. Used with permission.

As for Austria-Hungary, it is hardly surprising that its leaders, outraged by the assassination of Francis Ferdinand, were convinced that Serbia was responsible and must be punished for this terrible crime. There is no doubt that, almost from the start of the crisis, most of them were resolved to go to war with Serbia. Whether Vienna would have actually translated this intent into reality without assurance of German support is less clear. But when Germany extended its "blank check," the Dual Monarchy pursued this policy with rigid single-mindedness, even at the risk of war with Russia, assuming that its "big brother" would provide the necessary support. Foreign Minister Leopold von Berchtold and the other Austro-Hungarian leaders seemed virtually to close their eyes to the possibility of Russian intervention, however. One historian has observed that Austro-Hungarian leaders conducted policy during the July crisis as though Russia did not exist. To them, all that mattered was the elimination of the Serbian menace. [Austro-Hungarian chief of staff general Franz] Conrad, of course, had long urged such action, and Berchtold appears to have been convinced by the success of his tough policy during the Albanian border dispute in 1913 that a hard-line approach would once again persuade the Russians to back down.

The leaders in Vienna took their desperate gamble to save the Hapsburg Empire from impending disintegration. If the Dual Monarchy was as weak as they feared, however, it is ironic that they believed it capable of waging war to the victorious conclusion they deemed necessary for its salvation. In reality, it does not appear that many of them felt very confident. Conrad, the archwarmonger, confided to his mistress that the coming war would be "a hopeless struggle." Nevertheless, he was willing to accept this outcome "because such an ancient monarchy and so grand an army cannot perish ingloriously."

German leaders certainly encouraged Austria-Hungary to take firm action against Serbia, believing that this was essential if the Dual Monarchy were to retain its position as a Great Power. They assumed, however, that if it came to war, it would be possible to "localize" the conflict, especially if

Vienna acted promptly while European opinion was still sympathetic to Austria-Hungary and hostile toward Serbia in the aftermath of the assassination. Indeed they were overly confident of Russian neutrality in the event of an Austro-Serbian war. Furthermore they were willing to risk Russian intervention to keep their ally in the ranks of the Great Powers. It is also certain that both [Prime Minister] Bethmann and [Chief of Staff] Moltke believed that Germany was in a better position to face war in 1914 than would be the case a few years later.

Some historians have contended that Bethmann and other German leaders made the decision to provoke a war as early as 1912 out of fear that the traditional political and social structure of Germany was in danger from the growing strength of the Social Democrats and the threat of government paralysis. According to this argument, Bethmann and his associates hoped to rally the German people, including the working class, behind the government in a great wartime crusade that would save the traditional system. Although German leaders clearly worried over the threat from the left and the danger to the stability of the government, this interpretation is not convincing. It appears that Germany based its response to the July crisis primarily on an appraisal of foreign policy considerations at the time. Berlin was convinced that Austria-Hungary must deal firmly with Serbia if it was to remain a Great Power. But Bethmann did attempt to restrain Austria-Hungary when it became increasingly obvious that war with Serbia would spark a general European conflict. He also resisted Moltke's persistent demands for mobilization until the last possible moment and may have unwittingly endangered Germany's hopes for victory in the process.

The Allied Powers: Russia, France, and Britain

Russia had long acted in an irresponsible manner by encouraging Serbia in its hostile policies toward Austria-Hungary. The machinations of Hartwig, the minister to Belgrade, were especially dangerous. Russia, of course, was also the first Great Power to order general mobilization. Critics of this action have pointed with scorn to the absence of an alternative plan for partial mobilization against Austria-Hungary only. Clearly the failure to provide for such a possibility represents a lamentable absence of flexibility. But even partial mobilization entailed serious danger. Moltke and other German generals were convinced that Germany could not wait for Russia to complete partial mobilization. Some of the military districts involved in such an operation bordered Germany as well as the Dual Monarchy. Moreover, the Schlieffen Plan [the German plan to quickly overwhelm France before confronting Russia, named for prewar chief of staff Alfred von Schlieffen] called for precise timing. Even a slight delay in putting it into effect might prove fatal. Finally, could the Germans stand idly by while the Russians brought their military strength to bear on Austria-Hungary?

Even if Russia believed that war was inevitable, as Sergei Sazonov, the Russian foreign minister, apparently did, it would have benefitted by delaying any kind of mobilization until Conrad had committed his forces against Serbia. The Russians had already initiated a period preparatory to war. This gave them several days advantage over their opponents, and by concentrating against the Serbs, Austria-Hungary would weaken its forces in Galicia opposite the Russians. In fact, the Austrians would not actually be able to start hostilities until August 12. It was conceivable, although doubtful, that the other powers might be able to work out the basis for a diplomatic settlement by then. But the leaders in St. Petersburg felt that they must take action to defend their little Serbian ally. By ordering mobilization, they enabled the chain reaction, initiated by Austria's declaration of war on Serbia, to continue its fateful course.

France also contributed to the increasingly explosive atmosphere during the July crisis. Critics have focused especially on the roles played by President [Raymond] Poincaré and [Georges] Paleologue, the French ambassador to St. Petersburg. Poincaré unquestionably contributed to strengthening the Triple Entente well before 1914, which made it more rigid and susceptible to a chain reaction. He and [French premier René] Viviani also encouraged Russia to stand firm while they were in St. Petersburg in July. It appears that the Russians welcomed their words as a "blank check." They no doubt strengthened Russia's resolve to back Serbia to the limit. And although Poincaré was at sea during the most critical days of the crisis, he failed to suggest any solution after his return to Paris. Paleologue assured the Russians of strong French support in the absence of Poincaré and Viviani despite having no authorization from Paris.

There are also those who believe that Britain might have persuaded the Germans to follow a more restrained policy had Foreign Secretary Grey announced early in the crisis that Berlin could not expect the British to stand aside in case of a German attack on France. But such criticism ignores the fact that Grey was reluctant to make such a statement without the support of Parliament, which at that time still knew nothing of the Anglo-French secret military and naval planning of the previous few years. In fact, Grey himself appears to have had difficulty recognizing the extent of British commitment to France and he clung to the belief that Britain retained a free hand until late in the crisis. To be sure, Grey is liable to criticism for the deviousness of his policy, not only in regard to his own people but also to other countries. France undoubtedly counted on British support until late in the crisis and based its encouragement of Russian firmness at least in part on this confidence. When it appeared that the British might not enter the war, French leaders not surprisingly felt betrayed. Grey, it seems, had become a prisoner of his own deviousness. He could not extricate himself from this dilemma until the other powers were already at war, and violation of Belgium's neutrality was a certainty. Grey also failed to offer any definite proposals for a way out of Europe's dilemma when he suggested a conference to mediate the Austro-Serbian dispute following the rupture of relations between the two countries.

It is questionable whether any of the Great Powers actually desired a general war when the July crisis began. But Austria-Hungary, justifiably angry with Serbia and assured of German backing, definitely sought a localized conflict, while Germany, Russia, and France appear to have been

willing to accept a general war, if conditions seemed sufficiently promising. But the extent of the general conflict that
began early in August 1914 was to be far greater than any of
them had anticipated. It was to lead to four years of ghastly
slaughter and would profoundly change the fabric of European society as well as the predominant position which the
Continent had enjoyed in the world for so long.

The Trigger of War: The Assassination of Franz Ferdinand

Robert K. Massie

Pulitzer Prize–winning biographer and historian Robert K. Massie has gained renown for his works *Nicholas and Alexandra* (1967) and *Peter the Great* (1980). Here he describes the fateful immediate cause of World War I—the assassination of Austria-Hungary's Archduke Franz Ferdinand by nineteen-year-old Bosnian Serb Gavrilo Princip at Sarajevo on June 28, 1914.

[British statesman] Winston Churchill . . . on March 17, 1914 . . . spoke somberly of the situation in Europe:

> The causes which might lead to a general war have not been removed and often remind us of their presence. There has not been the slightest abatement of naval and military preparation. On the contrary, we are witnessing this year increases of expenditure by Continental powers on armaments beyond all previous expenditure. The world is arming as it was never armed before. Every suggestion for arrest or limitation has so far been ineffectual.

Weapons were accumulating in the armories of states harboring bitter antagonisms. France had waited forty-four years for *revanche* [revenge] and the rejoining of Alsace and Lorraine. Russia, defeated in the Far East in 1905, humiliated in the Balkans in 1908, could not afford to suffer further abasement; if another challenge were offered by Austria and Germany, it would be accepted. Austria-Hungary, facing disintegration from within, believed it could save itself by striking down the external source of its difficulties, the Kingdom of Serbia. The Hapsburg monarchy had Germany's pledge of support. Germans were ready for war. Britain's gradual adherence to the Triple Entente made more real the [German] nightmare of Encirclement. Britain, for the moment distracted by Ireland, had fears in Europe—primarily of the German Fleet—but few antagonisms. Indeed, her traditional antagonisms with France and Russia had been resolved. Whether, or for what reasons, Britain would fight remained unclear.

In Churchill's words, "the vials of wrath were full."

"I shall not live to see the world war," Bismarck said to [German shipping magnate Albert] Ballin in 1891, "but you will. And it will start in the East."

A Tottering Empire

By the summer of 1914, the Austro-Hungarian Empire had shrunk from the days of Hapsburg magnificence, but it still was larger than any Continental power except Russia. The lands ruled by the Emperor Franz Josef were a patchwork of provinces, races, and nationalities spread across Central Europe and the upper Balkans. Three-fifths of the Empire's 40 million people were Slavs—Poles, Czechs, Slovaks, Serbs, Bosnians, Montenegrins—but the Empire was ruled by its two non-Slavic races, the Germanic Austrians and the Magyar Hungarians. The structure of government, a dual monarchy, reflected this arrangement: the Emperor of Austria was also the King of Hungary; Austrians and Magyars controlled the bureaucracy; there was place for the Slavs neither at court nor in the government.

Austria-Hungary's nemesis, a nation of free Slavs, the young, independent Kingdom of Serbia, was set close by the sprawling, multinational empire. Serbia's existence acted as a magnet on the restless populations of Austria's South Slav provinces: Bosnia, Herzegovina, and Montenegro. Inside Serbia and in the South Slav provinces, nationalists longed to break up the Hapsburg Empire and weld the dissident provinces into a single Greater South Slav Kingdom. Belgrade, capital of Serbia, was a center of inflammatory Slav propaganda distributed inside the Empire.

Ultimately, either the Emperor Franz Josef or his heir, the Archduke Franz Ferdinand, would decide how Austria would meet the Serbian challenge. If he lived long enough, it would be the Emperor, but in 1914 Franz Josef was eighty-four. His reign of sixty-six years, the longest in modern Europe, had been marked by a sequence of political defeats and personal calamities. The bald little gentleman with muttonchop whiskers had come to the throne in 1848 as a slim, wavy-haired youth of eighteen. He was still a young man when the northern Italian provinces, Lombardy and Venice, were stripped away. Defeat by Prussia in 1866 led to expulsion of Hapsburg influence in Germany. In 1867, Franz Josef's brother, blond, dreamy Maximilian, briefly installed as Emperor of Mexico, was executed by a firing squad on a Mexican hillside. Franz Josef's only son, rakish Crown Prince Rudolf, killed himself and his mistress in a suicide pact at Mayerling. Franz Josef's wife, Empress Elisabeth, once the most beautiful princess in Europe, withdrew after six years of marriage and wandered Europe for four decades until she was struck down by an anarchist's knife. Franz Josef's response to blows was to tighten his emotions and steel himself for further shocks. Facing political challenge, he vowed to maintain the authority of the Crown and the integrity of the Empire. He had no intention of appeasing the South Slavs by modifying the structure of government and giving them a voice.

This conciliatory course was proposed by Franz Josef's nephew and heir. The Archduke Franz Ferdinand, a ponderous, glowering man with brush-cut hair, had offended his uncle by marrying a Bohemian of insufficient rank, Countess Sophie Chotek. The old Emperor insisted that the Archduke renounce the throne for any children he might have from the marriage; Countess Sophie, wife of the future Emperor, although created a Duchess, was forced in public processions to walk behind the forty-four Hapsburg Archduchesses. Franz Ferdinand himself was restricted to ceremonial functions; he was allowed to inspect army barracks, attend maneuvers, and occasionally to visit provincial capitals. Time was on his side, but he worried that when, eventually, he came to the throne, the disintegration of the

Empire would be irreparably advanced. His solution to the problem of nationalist agitation in the South Slav provinces was to reconcile those populations by a radical reconstruction of the structure of the Imperial government: transformation of the Dual Monarchy into a Triad, in which the South Slavs shared power with the Austrians and Magyars. For these views, the Archduke was warmly disliked, especially by the Magyars, who did not relish the thought of diluting their own powerful grip on the Imperial administration.

Meanwhile, another solution for Austria's troubles was growing in popularity: eliminate the source of Slav agitation by crushing Serbia. To the conservative ruling class of the Empire, a preventive war seemed preferable to the kind of decomposition afflicting the Ottoman Empire and more bearable than the protracted negotiations and painful compromises that would be necessary to transform the dual structure into a triad. "Austria," reported the French Ambassador in Vienna on December 13, 1913, "finds herself in an impasse without knowing how she is to escape. . . . People here are becoming accustomed to the idea of a general war as the only possible remedy." The principal advocate of preventive war, General Count Franz Conrad von Hötzendorf, Chief of the General Staff of the Austrian Army, spoke of Serbia as "a dangerous little viper"; he longed to crush the "viper" in its nest. Twice, Austria had mobilized against Serbia, during the Bosnian annexation crisis of 1908–1909 and during the Balkan Wars of 1912–1913. Each time, Conrad had been held back; in 1908, because "at the last moment His Majesty was against it"; in 1912–1913, he complained that he had been "left in the lurch" by Germany.

By 1914, as Conrad knew, the Hapsburg monarchy was too weak to undertake initiatives, military or diplomatic, without assurance of German support. But Conrad also knew that German support must be forthcoming.

Germany Backs Austria-Hungary

The continued existence of Austria-Hungary was vital to the German Empire. Austria was the Reich's only reliable ally. If Austria disintegrated, Germany would face Russia, France, and possibly England alone. In the Wilhelmstrasse, therefore, the preservation of Austria as a Great Power became a cardinal point of German policy. Some German diplomatists worried about this virtually unqualified support for the Hapsburg monarchy. In May 1914, Baron von Tschirschky, the German Ambassador in Vienna, uttered a cry of near despair: "I constantly wonder whether it really pays to bind ourselves so tightly to this phantasm of a state which is cracking in every direction." Tschirschky's cry was ignored. "Our own vital interests demand the preservation of Austria," declared Chancellor von Bethmann-Hollweg.

The Austrian government understood and was prepared to exploit this German predicament. For months, the Kaiser and General von Moltke, Chief of the German General Staff, had given Austria explicit, hearty encouragement to take action against Serbia, even if it meant a German confrontation with Serbia's ally, Russia. On October 26, 1913, the Kaiser had a conversation in Vienna with Count Berchtold, the Austrian Foreign Minister. William began with high-flown talk of the "world historic process," declaring that a war was inevitable in which the Germanic peoples would have to stave off "a mighty impulse of Slavdom." "The Slavs were born to serve and not to rule, and this must be brought home to them," he continued. Specifically, in the case of Serbia, "If His Majesty Francis Joseph demands something, the Serbian Government must yield, and if she does not, then Belgrade will be bombarded and occupied until the will of His Majesty is fulfilled. You may rest assured that I stand behind you and am ready to draw the sword." As he spoke, William moved his hand to the hilt of his sword. The interview concluded with another pledge. "His Majesty ostentatiously used the occasion to assure me that we could absolutely and completely count on him," said Berchtold. "This was the red thread which ran through the utterances of the illustrious Sovereign and when I laid stress on this on taking my departure and thanked him as I left, His Majesty did me the honor to say that whatever came from the Vienna Foreign Office was a command for him."

Moltke had no doubt that war was imminent. He was ready. Like Conrad, he sensed that time was against the Triple Alliance, that the balance of power in Europe was shifting, that Serbia and Russia must be dealt with before the Russian Army was reequipped and the "Slav battering ram" could be driven home. On May 12, 1914, Conrad visited Karlsbad, where Moltke was taking a cure. "General von Moltke expressed the opinion that every delay meant a lessening of our chances," Conrad recorded. The Austrian chief agreed, adding pointedly that "the attitude of Germany in past years has caused us to let many favorable opportunities go by." He asked how long the coming "joint war against Russia and France would last; that is, how long before Germany would be able to turn against Russia with strong forces." Moltke replied, "We hope in six weeks after the beginning of operations to have finished with France, or at least so far as to enable us to direct our principal forces against the East."

Two weeks after the generals met, the Kaiser visited the Archduke Franz Ferdinand at his castle, Konopischt, in Bohemia. The Archduke's garden was famous for its roses and, officially, the German Emperor had come to admire the flowers in bloom. Over two days, William and Franz Ferdinand discussed the dangers posed to the Dual Monarchy and the Triple Alliance by Serbia. They agreed that something must be done. Russia was a factor, but it was the Archduke's opinion that internal difficulties in the Tsar's empire were too great to permit Russia to consider war.

Assassination in Sarajevo

Franz Ferdinand had another appointment at the end of June. He was scheduled to attend army maneuvers in the Bosnian mountains and, as a gesture to the South Slav population, he decided to pay a ceremonial visit to the Bosnian capital, Sarajevo. As a show of goodwill, he asked that the troops normally lining the streets for security during an Imperial visit be dispensed with. Except for a scattering of local policemen, the crowds were to have free access to the Heir to the Throne. On the morning of June 28, Franz Ferdinand, dressed in the pale blue tunic and red-striped black trousers of a cavalry general, with green plumes waving from his cap, sat in the open back seat of the second car, next to his wife, Sophie. Around him on the streets, he saw smiling faces and waving arms. Flags and decorative bright-colored rugs hung from the balconies; his own portrait stared back at him from the windows of shops and houses.

As the procession neared City Hall, the Archduke's chauffeur spotted an object as it was hurled from the crowd. He pressed the accelerator, and a bomb which would have landed in Sophie's lap exploded under the wheels of the car behind. Two officers were wounded and the young bomb-thrower was apprehended by the police. Franz Ferdinand arrived at City Hall shaken and furious. "One comes here for a visit," he shouted, "and is welcomed by bombs." There was an urgent conference. A member of the Archduke's suite asked whether a military guard could be arranged. "Do you think Sarajevo is filled with assassins?" replied the provincial governor.

It was decided to go back through the city by a different route from the one announced. On the way, the driver of the first car, forgetting the alteration, turned into one of the prearranged streets. The Archduke's chauffeur, following behind, was momentarily misled. He started to turn. An official shouted, "That's the wrong way!" At that moment, a slim nineteen-year-old boy stepped forward, aimed a pistol into the car, and fired twice. Sophie sank forward onto her husband's chest. Franz Ferdinand remained sitting upright and for a moment no one noticed that he had been hit. Then the governor, sitting in front, heard him murmur, "Sophie! Sophie! Don't die! Stay alive for our children!" His body sagged and blood from the severed jugular vein in his neck spurted across his uniform. He died almost immediately. Sophie, the Duchess of Hohenberg, died soon after. Fifteen minutes later, both bodies were laid in a room next to the ballroom where waiters were chilling champagne for his reception.

The assassin, Gavrilo Princip, was a native Bosnian, who, on trial, declared that he had acted to "kill an enemy of the

South Slavs" and also because the Archduke was "an energetic man who as ruler would have carried through ideas and reforms which stood in our way." Princip was part of a team of youthful assassins, all of whom were Bosnians and thus Austro-Hungarian subjects, belonging to a revolutionary movement whose object was to detach Bosnia and other Slav provinces from the Hapsburg monarchy and incorporate them into a Kingdom of Greater Serbia. They had been provided with six pistols and six bombs taken from the Serbian State Arsenal and smuggled with Serbian help across the frontier. The Serbian government was not involved, but the plot had been hatched in Belgrade. The organizers were members of a secret society of extreme Serbian nationalists known as the Black Hand.

The assassination horrified Europe. Sympathy lay overwhelmingly with the House of Hapsburg. Scarcely anyone questioned Austria-Hungary's right to impose some form of retribution. Sir Edward Grey, looking back, remembered, "No crime has ever aroused deeper or more general horror throughout Europe. . . . Sympathy for Austria was universal. Both governments and public opinion were ready to support her in any measures, however severe, which she might think it necessary to take for the punishment of the murderer and his accomplices." Despite their shock, most Europeans refused to believe that the assassination would lead to war. War, revolution, and assassination were the normal ingredients of Balkan politics. "Nothing to cause anxiety," announced [the newspaper] *Le Figaro* in Paris. "Terrible shock for the dear old Emperor," King George V noted in his diary.

In Vienna, Franz Josef accepted his nephew's demise with resignation, murmuring, "For me, it is a great worry less." Conrad von Hötzendorf, discreetly ecstatic, hailed the arrival of the long-awaited pretext for preventive war. Now there would be no mere punishment of "the murderer and his accomplices" but the crushing of the "viper," the demolition of the troublesome Serbian state. [Austro-Hungarian foreign minister] Count Berchtold, who hitherto had opposed preventive war, changed his mind and demanded that "the Monarchy with unflinching hand . . . tear asunder the threads which its foes are endeavoring to weave into a net above its head." Russia, patron of the Serbs, might object, but Russia could be confronted and forced to back away as she had been in 1909 by Austria's German ally. The key lay in Berlin; an Austrian decision for war must be contingent on Germany's guarantee against Russian intervention. The Emperor was cautious. Conrad came away from an interview with Franz Josef and recorded that the Emperor "does not feel certain of Germany and therefore hesitates to decide."

Britain's Intervention: A Great Mistake?

Niall Ferguson

Most historians of World War I agree that the war was probably inevitable. Many scholars also assign heavier responsibility for the war to Germany than to Russia, France, or Britain. Young British historian Niall Ferguson has brilliantly challenged this conventional wisdom in his controversial book, *The Pity of War*. Ferguson offers a novel rethinking of the war, including its causes. He argues that Britain is to blame for converting the July 1914 crisis into a *world* war. German war aims before August 1914 were limited, and mostly entailed a quest for economic dominance on the Continent, not sweeping Napoleonic military conquests. A notable feature of Ferguson's study is his use of "counterfactual," or "what if?," questions about the past. His provocative approach has rekindled new interest in the catastrophic Great War.

That Britain could have limited its involvement in a [European] continental war is a possibility which has been all but ignored by historians. Even those who deplore the *way* the war was fought generally neglect this. . . . Yet it should now be clear that the possibility was a very real one. [Prime Minister Herbert] Asquith and [Foreign Secretary Edward] Grey themselves later acknowledged this in their memoirs. Both men emphasized that Britain had not been obliged to intervene by any kind of contractual obligation to France. In Asquith's words, 'We kept ourselves free to decide, when the occasion arose, whether we should or should not go to war.'

Excerpted from *The Pity of War*, by Niall Ferguson. Copyright © 1999 by Niall Ferguson. Reprinted by permission of Basic Books, a member of Perseus Books, L.L.C.

Nor did Grey make any secret of the political opposition within his own [Liberal] party which had prevented him making a commitment to France in July. Despite his talk elsewhere of irresistible historical forces, he admitted that there had been a choice.

Of course, Grey naturally insisted that the Cabinet's choice had been the right one. But what were his arguments *against* neutrality? In his memoirs, he set these out:

> If we were to come in at all, let us be thankful that we did it at once—it was better so, better for our good name, better for a favourable result, than if we had tried to keep out and then found ourselves . . . compelled to go in. . . . [Had we not come in] we should have been isolated; we should have had no friend in the world; no one would have hoped or feared anything from us, or thought our friendship worth having. We should have been discredited . . . held to have played an inglorious part. We should have been hated.

For Grey, then, the war was at root 'a matter of honour': the legal commitment [based on earlier treaties] to Belgium and, even more, the moral commitment to France. . . . Grey's fundamental argument was that Britain could not risk a Germany victory, because such a victory would have made Germany 'supreme over all the Continent of Europe and Asia Minor'.

Germany's Limited Prewar Ambitions

But was that really the German objective? Was the Kaiser really Napoleon? The answer to that question depends, of course, on what one thinks Germany's 'war aims' actually were in 1914. According to [German historian] Fritz Fischer and his pupils they were every bit as radical as the [pre-1914] British Germanophobes feared. The war was an attempt 'to realize Germany's political ambitions, which may be summed up as German hegemony over Europe' through annexations of French, Belgian and possibly Russian territory, the founding of a Central European customs union and the creation of new Polish and Baltic states directly or indirectly under German control. In addition, Germany was to acquire new territory in Africa, so that her colonial possessions could be consolidated as a continuous Central African area. There was also to be a concerted effort to break up the British and Russian empires through fomenting revolutions.

Yet there is a fundamental flaw in Fischer's reasoning which too many historians have let pass. It is the assumption that Germany's aims as stated after the war had begun were the same as German aims beforehand. Thus [German chancellor Theodor von] Bethmann's 'September Programme'—'provisional notes for the direction of our policy' for a separate peace with France, drafted on the assumption of a swift German victory in the West—is sometimes portrayed as if it were the first open statement of aims which had existed before the outbreak of war. If this were true, then the argument that war was avoidable would collapse; for it is clear that no British government could have accepted the territorial and political terms which the September Programme proposed for France and Belgium, as these would indeed have realized the 'Napoleonic nightmare' by giving Germany control of the Belgian coast. But the inescapable fact is that no evidence has ever been found by Fischer and his pupils that these objectives existed *before* Britain's entry into the war. It is in theory possible that they were never committed to paper, or that the relevant documents were destroyed or lost, and that those involved subsequently lied rather than concede legitimacy to the 'war guilt' clause of the Versailles treaty. But it seems unlikely. All that Fischer can produce are the pre-war pipe-dreams of a few Pan-Germans [extreme nationalists] and businessmen, none of which had any official status, as well as the occasional bellicose utterances of the Kaiser [Wilhelm II, German emperor], an individual whose influence over policy was neither consistent nor as great as he himself believed. It is of course true that the Kaiser occasionally fantasized about 'a sort of Napoleonic supremacy', and that, when it belatedly dawned on him on 30 July that Britain would intervene, he gave vent to the wildest of global designs:

> Our consuls in Turkey and India, agents etc., must fire the whole Mohammedan world to fierce rebellion against this

hated, lying, conscienceless nation of shop-keepers; for if we are to be bled to death, England shall at least lose India.

[German chief of staff Helmuth von] Moltke too envisaged 'attempts . . . to instigate an uprising in India, if England takes a stand as our opponent. The same thing should be attempted in Egypt, also in the Dominion of South Africa.' But such flights of fancy . . . should not be seen as serious German war aims. Before the war the Kaiser was just as prone to remind British diplomats: 'We fought side by side a hundred years ago. I want our two nations to stand together again in front of the Belgian monument at Waterloo.' This was hardly Napoleonic talk. It is also of interest that as early as 30 July the Kaiser expected war with Britain to 'bleed Germany dry'. . . .

The Scope of German War Aims

The critical point is that had Britain not intervened immediately, Germany's war aims would have been significantly different from those in the September Programme. Bethmann's statement . . . of 29 July 1914 shows that he was prepared to guarantee the territorial integrity of both France and Belgium (as well as Holland) in return for British neutrality. Moltke's notorious 'Suggestions of a military-political nature' of 2 August said the same: the assurance that Germany 'would act with moderation in case of a victory over France . . . should be given . . . unconditionally and in the most binding form', along with guarantees of the integrity of Belgium. Had Britain in fact stayed out, it would have been foolish to have reneged on such a bargain. So Germany's aims would almost certainly not have included the territorial changes envisaged in the September Programme; . . . and they certainly would not have included the proposals for German control of the Belgian coast, which no British government could have tolerated. The most that would have remained, then, would have been the following proposals:

1. *France* . . . A war indemnity to be paid in instalments; it must be high enough to prevent France from spending

any considerable sums on armaments in the next 15–20 years. Furthermore: a commercial treaty which makes France economically dependent on Germany [and] secures the French market for our exports. . . . This treaty must secure for us financial and industrial freedom of movement in France in such fashion that German enterprises can no longer receive different treatment from French.

2. . . . We must create *a central European economic association* through common customs treaties, to include France, Belgium, Holland, Denmark, Austria-Hungary, Poland, and perhaps Italy, Sweden and Norway. This association will not have any common constitutional supreme authority and all its members will be formally equal, but in practice will be under German leadership and must stabilise Germany's economic dominance over *Mitteleuropa* [central Europe].

3. *The question of colonial acquisitions,* where the first aim is the creation of a continuous Central African colonial empire, will be considered later, as will that of the aims realised *vis-à-vis* Russia. . . .

4. *Holland.* It will have to be considered by what means and methods Holland can be brought into closer relationship with the German Empire. In view of the Dutch character, this closer relationship must leave them free of any feeling of compulsion, must alter nothing in the Dutch way of life, and must also subject them to no new military obligations. Holland, then, must be left independent in externals, but be made internally dependent on us. Possibly one might consider an offensive and defensive alliance, to cover the colonies; in any case a close customs association. . . .

To these points—in effect, the September Programme without annexations from France and Belgium—should be added the detailed plans subsequently drawn up to 'thrust [Russia] back as far as possible from Germany's eastern frontier and [break] her domination over the non-Russian vassal peoples'. These envisaged the creation of a new Polish state . . .

and the cession of the Baltic provinces (which would either be independent, incorporated in the new Poland or annexed by Germany itself). Even this edited version of the September Programme probably exaggerates the pre-war aims of the German leadership. [Bernhard von] Bülow, of course, was no longer Chancellor; but his comments to the Crown Prince in 1908 were not so different from Bethmann's view that war would strengthen the political left and weaken the Reich internally. . . .

The Kaiser's European Economic Union

Would the limited war aims outlined above have posed a direct threat to British interests? Did they imply a Napoleonic strategy? Hardly. All the economic clauses of the September Programme implied was the creation—some eighty years early, it might be said—of a German-dominated European customs union. Indeed, many of the official statements on the subject have a striking contemporary resonance: for example, [German historian] Hans Delbrück's, 'It is only a Europe which forms a single customs unit that can meet with sufficient power the over-mighty productive resources of the transatlantic world' [USA]; or Gustav Müller's enthusiastic call for a 'United States of Europe' (a phrase used before the war by the Kaiser). . . .

Even some of the German 'scaremongers' [alarmists] of the pre-war period had argued in these strangely familiar terms. . . . [One 'scaremonger'] had declared prophetically: 'The *union* of the European peoples alone can win back for them the undisputed political power and the dominion of the seas that they have lost. Today the centre of political gravity is in Washington, St Petersburg, and Tokyo.' . . . [Another] concludes: 'Only a peacefully united Europe can maintain itself against the growing strength of other races and against the economic domination of America. Unite! Unite! Unite!'

To be sure, Bethmann and his confidant Kurt Riezler had no doubt that this 'Middle European Empire of the German Nation' was merely 'the European disguise of our will to power.' Bethmann's aim, as Riezler put it in March 1917 was:

to lead the German Reich which by the methods of the Prussian territorial state . . . cannot become a world power . . . to
an imperialism of the European form, to organize the Continent from the centre outward (Austria, Poland, Belgium)
around our tacit leadership.

That is not the way German politicians talk today. But even
put like that, Germany's European project was not one with
which Britain, with her maritime empire intact, could not
have lived.

Of course, it was not to be: the bid for British neutrality
was, as we know, rejected. Yet German historians have been
too quick to dismiss Bethmann's proposal as wild miscalculation; or even to argue that the Germans themselves did not
expect to secure British neutrality. The evidence does not
bear this out. On the contrary, it shows that Bethmann's calculations were far from unreasonable. He can be forgiven for
not anticipating that, at the very last minute, the arguments
of Grey and [cabinet official Winston] Churchill would pre-
vail over the numerically stronger noninterventionists; and
that the majority of Members of Parliament would accept
what would prove to be the Foreign Secretary's most misleading assertion: 'If we are engaged in war, we shall suffer
but little more than we shall suffer even if we stand aside.'

Chapter 2

The War Expands and Intensifies, 1914–1916

A War of Attrition

Christopher Andrew

All the warring European nations entered the conflict in the summer of 1914 expecting victory after a short war. Then, in the Battle of the Marne in September 1914, the German invasion thrust was halted by French and British forces just short of Paris. This began four years of bloody, stalemated trench warfare on the "western front"—the main battleground of opposing armies extending from the English Channel at the Franco-Belgian border southeast-ward to the frontier of Switzerland. British historian Christopher Andrew explains how initial expectations of a swift victory quickly gave way to deadlock and carnage, particularly on the western front.

Almost no-one, in August 1914, had any idea of what war would be like. There had been moments in the decade be-fore the war when at least some generals had had a premo-nition of what lay in store for them. [German General Hel-muth von] Moltke had spoken in 1905 of 'a war that, even should we be victorious, will push our people to the limits of exhaustion'. [Joseph] Joffre, the French commander-in-chief, had spoken in 1912 of a war which might be 'of indef-inite duration'. These fears seemed to be forgotten in Au-gust 1914. No country possessed plans for a war of more than a few months. Most generals on both sides thought such plans unnecessary. 'You will be home', the Kaiser told the German army, 'before the leaves have fallen from the trees'. Only [Lord Horatio] Kitchener, recalled to become secretary of state for war on the day that Britain entered the conflict, foresaw a war which would involve millions of men and take years to decide.

Excerpted from *The First World War: Causes and Consequences,* Caxton's History of the World series, vol. 19, by Christopher Andrew (London: New Caxton Library Services, 1969). Copyright © 1969 The Hamlyn Publishing Group, Ltd.

And yet, on the Western Front [the main battlefront of the war, stretching from the English Channel and Belgium to the Swiss border] at least, the war was almost won and lost within the space of one campaign. In both 1870 and 1940 the French were routed by the Germans in six weeks. The same thing very nearly happened in 1914. Though Joffre knew of the Schlieffen Plan, he did not take it seriously. While the Germans were struggling through Belgium, the French would pour across the frontier into the heart of Germany. The whole French army in August 1914 shared Joffre's sublime confidence in attack. While the British and Germans tried to make themselves inconspicuous in khaki and field-grey, the French sought to make themselves as conspicuous as possible. Confident that their *élan* would shatter the enemy's nerve, their infantry went to battle in blue overcoats and red pantaloons. 'The French army', said its Field Regulations, 'knows no law but the offensive.' French *élan*, however, was no match for German firepower. The French assault on the German frontier ended in a series of disasters, collectively known as the Battles of the Frontiers. Unable to comprehend what had gone wrong, Joffre blamed the defeats on 'a lack of offensive spirit'.

The Germans, meanwhile, had swept through Belgium and were advancing into northern France. By the beginning of September they had reached the Marne, Paris was in a panic, and the French government had left for Bordeaux. The very speed of its advance, however, had led the German army to over-reach itself. Corps commanders were often out of touch both with headquarters and with one another. Moltke hardly knew where his armies were for days on end. Instead of enveloping Paris, as Moltke had planned, the German army wheeled to the south-east, leaving its flank exposed to a brilliantly successful counterattack on the Marne by the Paris garrison.

Some historians have since concluded that the Schlieffen Plan was doomed from the beginning. The French, however, believed that they had been saved only by a miracle: 'the miracle of the Marne'. Perhaps the crucial factor in the German failure was that Moltke had been forced, at a critical stage of the French campaign, to transfer two army corps to the Eastern Front to meet an unexpected Russian attack in East Prussia. The miracle of the Marne was won as much in East Prussia as on the Marne itself.

Killing Fields: Western and Eastern Fronts

The 'miracle of the Marne' was followed by a race to the sea, with each side trying, unsuccessfully, to turn the other's flank before the sea was reached. Though Germany had failed to win a quick victory, it still retained the initiative in the war. When the race to the sea was over, Germany remained in control of one-tenth of France's territory, 80 per cent of its coal, and almost the whole of its iron ore. For the next three and a half years Germany was usually content to remain on the defensive behind an impregnable line of trenches, against which the Allied armies battered in vain. At no time before the spring of 1918 did the front lines established during the race to the sea in 1914 vary in depth by as much as ten miles. 'The Western Front', wrote Robert Graves, 'was known among its embittered inhabitants as the Sausage Machine because it was fed with live men, churned out corpses, and remained firmly screwed in place.'

The reason for this stalemate was technological. The invention of barbed wire and the machine gun had given a temporary, but overwhelming, advantage to the defence. Only a further technological advance could turn the advantage once more in favour of attack. Some historians have argued that by the end of 1916 the invention of the tank already provided just such a technological advance, and that only the blindness of the French and British high commands prevented them from achieving a breakthrough. Until the closing months of the war, however, tanks were too deficient, both in quality and quantity, to end the stalemate on the Western Front. Even at their greatest victory, the battle of Amiens, in August 1918, 270 of a total of 415 tanks were destroyed in one day's fighting. Deadlock in the west continued for so long, not because generals were more incompetent than in the past but, quite simply, because they lacked the means to break it.

'The German lines in France', wrote Kitchener at the beginning of 1915, 'may be looked on as a fortress that cannot be carried by assault.' With the exception of Kitchener, however, most Allied generals were confident of an early breakthrough. The greatest criticism that can be levelled at the Allied commanders on the Western Front is not that they failed to make this breakthrough, but that they refused for so long, against all the evidence, to recognise the enormous strength of the enemy's position.

Joffre's plan to win the war in 1915 was for a gigantic pincer movement against the German lines, with Anglo-French forces attacking in Artois, and the French alone further south in Champagne. Offensives on these fronts continued intermittently throughout the year, none achieving an advance of more than three miles. At the end of the year Joffre comforted himself with the thought that, even if the Germans had yet to be defeated, they were being worn down by a war of attrition. Pinning his faith in inflated estimates of German losses, he refused, like most other Allied generals (and many later historians), to accept the simple truth that a war of attrition on the Western Front was bound to bear most heavily on the attacker. In fact, French and English losses in 1915 were almost double those of Germany: probably 1,600,000 killed and wounded as against 850,000 of the enemy.

Enormous though these losses were, they were surpassed by even greater losses in the east. In 1915 [Erich von] Falkenhayn, the new German commander-in-chief, had chosen to remain on the defensive in the west, whilst launching his main offensive in the east. In five months, between May and September 1915, Russia lost a million men in prisoners alone, at least a million more (perhaps far more) in killed and wounded, and more territory than the whole area of France. Judging by size alone, Falkenhayn had won what has been called 'the greatest battle in history'. But it was not, and could not be, a decisive victory. Though the Russians had been forced to retreat three hundred miles, they were left with a shorter line to defend, and still possessed vast reserves of manpower from which to replace their losses. In the east, as in the west, 1915 ended in deadlock.

Verdun: The Longest Battle

The plan of campaign devised by the Allies for 1916 simply proposed to repeat the mistakes of 1915 on a larger scale. Joffre convinced himself and many others that, on the Western Front at least, the Allies had been on the verge of a breakthrough in 1915, robbed of a victory only by a lack of heavy guns and ammunition. Next year, with plenty of munitions and the first British conscript armies, things would be different. As soon as sufficient shells were available, [British general Douglas] Haig told *The Times* correspondent, 'we could walk through the German lines at several places'. To make sure of victory in 1916 it was agreed to launch all-out offensives simultaneously on both the Western and the Eastern Fronts. Italy, which had entered the war on the side of the Allies in 1915, would join in with an attack on Austria from the south.

Falkenhayn's plan for victory was much more subtle. He proposed to win the war not by defeating the enemy in battle but by bleeding him to death—a new and ingenious addition to the theory of warfare. The power on whom Falkenhayn proposed to perform this experiment was France:

> Within our reach behind the French sector of the Western Front there are objectives for the retention of which the French General Staff would be compelled to throw in every man they have. If they do so, the forces of France will bleed to death—as there can be no question of voluntary withdrawal—whether we reach our goal or not.

Falkenhayn selected as his target the great French fortress of Verdun, already half encircled by German lines, and one of the few places on the Western Front where the defenders seemed to be at a disadvantage. German communications to the Verdun salient were excellent, and their heavy guns had closed all French routes to the fortress, except for one light railway and one road, which became known during the battle as the *voie sacrée*. Throughout the battle of Verdun supply remained as great a problem as the fighting itself. For months on end 3,000 lorries passed every day along the *voie sacrée* carrying 20,000 men and 4,000 tons of supplies.

The battle of Verdun became, as Falkenhayn had intended, the supreme symbol of attrition even in a war of attrition. It lasted ten months, from February to November 1916, longer than any battle had ever lasted before. In no other battle in the history of warfare have so many died on so small an area of ground. As the battle progressed, however, it became increasingly clear that Falkenhayn had made one fatal miscalculation. 'Germany is perfectly free', he had written, 'to accelerate or draw out the offensive, to intensify it or to break it off from time to time as suits its purpose.' After the first week of the battle Falkenhayn's freedom of action had disappeared. Just as French prestige was involved in the defence of Verdun, so German prestige increasingly demanded its capture. The battle of Verdun ended by bleeding the German army almost as disastrously as it bled the French.

In the summer of 1916, however, Germany came very close to victory. Had Germany been able to press home its attack after the capture of Fort Vaux on 7 June, it could, in the opinion of the historian of the battle, Alistair Horne, 'almost certainly have broken through to Verdun'. In June 1916, as in the other great crisis of the war in September 1914, the French were saved by a Russian offensive in the east. Partly in response to desperate appeals from France to relieve the pressure on Verdun, Brusilov, the ablest of the Russian generals, attacked the Austrians on the south-east front with forty divisions. Many German officers had long believed that, by its alliance with Austria, 'Germany was fettered to a corpse'. They were confirmed in this opinion by the spectacular success of the Brusilov offensive. What began as a diversionary attack rapidly turned into a rout of the Austrian army along a three hundred mile front. By the time German troops arrived to try and stem the Austrian retreat in September, Brusilov had taken almost half a million prisoners.

Despite its ultimate failure, the Brusilov offensive had far-reaching consequences on both the Eastern and Western

Fronts. In the east it brought nearer the disintegration of the Austrian Empire. In the west it changed the course of the battle for Verdun. At a crucial moment, Falkenhayn was forced to divert to the Eastern Front divisions intended to push home the assault on Verdun. At a time when French reserves were almost exhausted, General [Henri Philippe] Pétain, who had been summoned to the defence of Verdun, was given a vital ten days' breathing space in which to strengthen his defences and bring up fresh troops. When the Germans were able to resume their offensive, on 22 June, their chance of victory had gone.

The Somme Offensive

Verdun was a turning point in the history of the Western Front. From now on, the main burden of the fighting passed from France to Britain. The French had been so weakened at Verdun that they were no longer capable of assuming the major role in the planned summer offensive on the Somme. When the battle began on 1 July the French contingent had been reduced by Verdun from forty to fourteen divisions alongside Haig's twenty-five. Yet what successes were achieved on the first day of the offensive were due mainly to the French. The latter moved swiftly in small groups supported by machine guns, using methods learnt from the Germans at Verdun, and overran most of the German front line. The British, weighed down by sixty-six pound packs, advanced at walking pace in even lines, presenting the German machine guns with their best target of the war. As one line of British troops was cut down, so others came on, regularly spaced at intervals of a hundred yards. On 1 July the British lost almost 60,000 men killed and wounded in a single day: more than on any other day in the history of the British army, greater, too, than the losses suffered by any other army on any day of the First World War.

Neither Haig nor any of his staff officers had any idea of the extent of the catastrophe that had befallen them. Haig wrote in his diary on the following day: 'The enemy has undoubtedly been severely shaken. Our correct course, therefore, is to press him hard with the least possible delay.' The battle of the Somme was to last five months. Only when the winter rains had reduced the battleground to a wilderness of mud was Haig, at last, forced to call a halt. When the battle ended, though the front line had here and there advanced about five miles, some of the objectives set for the first day's offensive had still not been achieved. Like Joffre after the battle of Champagne a year before, Haig comforted himself with the delusion, strengthened by inflated estimates of enemy casualties, that the Somme had been successful as a battle of attrition. 'The results of the Somme', he wrote, 'fully justify confidence in our ability to master the enemy's power of resistance'.

A Fight to the Finish

'The wars that are won', it has been said, 'never are the wars that were begun.' Wars, once begun, invariably generate war aims for which the combatants would never at the outset have gone to battle. Thus it was after 1914. Russia would not have started a war to capture Constantinople and the Straits [between the Mediterranean and Black Seas] nor Germany for the creation of a Belgian satellite, nor France for the recovery of Alsace-Lorraine. Yet once they had gone to war for other reasons, all these ambitions, and others like them, were swiftly adopted as war aims. And war aims multiplied still further as each side struggled to win over neutrals or retain existing allies by territorial bribes.

Italy's entry into the war, in 1915, was preceded by a protracted auction in which each side competed for its favours and Italy played off one against the other. Much the same process preceded the entry of Bulgaria on the side of the Central Powers in 1915 and Rumania on the side of the Allies a year later, though—like Italy—neither significantly influenced the outcome of the war. Despite the stalemate in the war at the end of 1916, despite the growing exhaustion on each side, the extent of the war aims of each alliance condemned attempts to arrange a compromise peace to inevitable failure. Neither side was prepared to accept anything approaching a return to the status quo of July 1914, though both were understandably reluctant to reveal the full extent of their ambitions.

There was one further reason why a compromise peace was impossible. The French writer, de Tocqueville, had long ago predicted that though democracies might be reluctant to involve themselves in war, once embarked on war they would not readily make peace. In an age of mass education, the people of Europe were no longer content to accept the pretexts which for centuries had served as an excuse for war. They needed to believe, instead, that they were involved in a moral crusade to protect civilisation itself. Only such a cause could justify the millions of lives whose sacrifice the war demanded. To bolster its belief in the rightness of its cause, each side convinced itself of the wickedness of its opponent. British people swiftly came to credit Germans with a variety of mythical atrocities: priests hung as clappers in cathedral bells, crucified prisoners of war, and children with their hands cut off. With so evil an enemy a compromise peace must be unthinkable. As [Britain's] Lloyd George put it shortly before he succeeded [Herbert] Asquith as prime minister in December 1916: 'The fight must be to a finish— to a knock-out.'

The Eastern Front: Success and Failure

James L. Stokesbury

Canadian historian James L. Stokesbury (1934–1995) has written histories of both world wars and the Korean War. In this selection, he focuses on the relatively fluid battle lines of the eastern front compared with those in the west. The war between the Central Powers and Russia in the east was, however, indecisive through the end of 1916. Stokesbury notes that while Germany experienced frustration because Russian defeats did not lead to a general Russian collapse, the Russian war effort, in fact, had been fatally undermined by its autocratic and grossly inefficient leadership.

Just as the Allies had their disagreements over where and how to win the war, so did the Germans. They lacked the wide range of strategic options that general command of the seas gave their enemies, yet there were still enough possibilities to generate heated argument. Their main efforts might be directed west against France and Britain, east against Russia, or rather less profitably southeast in the Balkans, or south against Italy. The latter two merely rounded out the map, for the major opportunities and dangers lay east and west. [German general Erich] von Falkenhayn believed, and events were to show him the more nearly correct, that the war could and should be won in the West. [German general Paul von] Hindenburg and [General Erich] Ludendorff wanted to win it in the East. The condition of Russia at the start of 1915 was such that it looked as if they might be right. Of the three major enemies, Russia seemed to be in the worst shape.

Russia in Disarray

By now there appeared to be widespread shortages plaguing the Russian economy and war effort. The traditional picture is of an emergent industrial state buckling under the heavy pressures of a massive war. This picture has recently been challenged as a self-serving one drawn either by postrevolutionary historians or by anti-revolutionary "White" Russian writers, seeking to justify their own failures to master their situation. More modern students have claimed that what Russia was experiencing was not a crisis of collapse, but a crisis of growth. In their view there were plenty of supplies in the country, both for the needs of the war and of the civilian populace, but they were unavailable because of government ineptitude, transportation shortages, poor communications, and unequal distribution. Soldiers at the front, for example, constantly demanded more artillery shells and complained that they were not getting them. One answer to this complaint is that there were plenty of shells in the depots and fortresses, but the officers responsible for them would not release them to combat units, because they knew that if they did so, the shells would simply be fired off wastefully instead of being husbanded for when they were really needed— really needed, that is, in the view of the supply officers, not in the view of the gunners at the front.

This may be no more than arguing that the shortages were apparent rather than real, a point which makes little difference to the person at the business end of them. If a consumer cannot buy flour, he is suffering from a shortage, whether it is because there is no wheat, or because some war profiteer is holding back his grain for a higher price. If an artillery battery has no shells for a barrage, it is laboring under a shortage, whether there are in fact no shells, or several million of them back in some supply depot behind the lines. Hungry people and shell-less soldiers are not in a position to weigh the semantic niceties of the situation in a philosophic light. As far as the soldiers were concerned, there were shortages, and they were crippling Russia.

It was undeniable that the government and the war machine were inefficient. At the front the soldiers could not help but be aware of their qualitative inferiority to the Germans. Russian staff work was less competent, Russian communications did not function as well, Russian tactics were costlier in casualties; experts have assessed the Germans as anywhere from five to fifteen times more combat effective than the Russians. The army of the Tsars had made great forward strides since the Russo-Japanese War [1904–1905] but it still had a long way to go, and for that difference the Russian soldier paid a heavy price.

Nor was such inefficiency confined to the military ranks. . . . [T]he ruling bureaucracy had not caught up with the burgeoning changes of twentieth-century society, and there was waste and weakness throughout the body of Russia.

There was also corruption. Unscrupulous businessmen, entrepreneurs, civil servants, and politicians amassed fortunes out of the war, visible fortunes that made the sufferings and the shortages of the multitudes all the harder to bear. There was unprecedented inflation, and while new fortunes were made old ones were wiped out. Foreign contractors tried, in some cases very successfully, to pick Russia clean. The government simply lacked the ability to put its own house in order under the heightened pressures of wartime— . . . and as the war progressed, the rumblings of discontent and the cries for reform grew increasingly strident.

The Romanovs and Rasputin

Eventually, and it did not take that long once the initial patriotic euphoria wore off, public anger focused on the royal family. The Tsar Nicholas and his wife, Alexandra, after all, were the father and mother of all the Russians; he was The Autocrat, and if things were going wrong, then it must be because Nicholas was not doing his job, or, equally bad, had fallen under evil counsels. One of the time-honored fictions of monarchical institutions is that monarchs can do no wrong— but they can be ill advised. It happened that Nicholas and Alexandra were peculiarly vulnerable on this score.

Nicholas had come to the throne in 1894 on the death of his father, Alexander III. The father had devoted his entire career to holding back the clock and preserving a rule of personal autocracy. Nicholas believed wholeheartedly in the system he inherited and tried unceasingly to resist the inroads of modernity on his government and dynasty. He was supported and sustained in this by his wife, who had been before her marriage a princess of the German principality of Hesse-Darmstadt. Indeed, with one exception, Nicholas' family line had married Germans for the last seven generations, which, for what it was worth, meant there was very little Russian blood in the Romanovs [Russia's royal family] by 1914.

Blood was one of their problems, and as time went on, it took their attention virtually to the exclusion of all else. Nicholas and Alexandra had four daughters, and then they finally produced a son, Alexis. He was the hope of their dynasty, and he had hemophilia. This peculiar disease, in which the blood does not clot properly so that a normally insignificant bruise or small cut endangers life itself, appears only in males, who inherit it through their mother. There was very little that could be done about it, and it drove the royal family nearly to despair. Regrettably, they chose to hide their affliction from the country, so that instead of eliciting the sympathy that they and the boy deserved and might well have received, their silence and rumors of strange events around the throne caused consternation and dissatisfaction and seriously contributed to the loss of support they suffered as the years went on.

The appearance on the scene of Gregory, Rasputin, aggravated the situation immensely. Rasputin, which is not a name but a nickname meaning "the drunkard," was a wandering character of a type not unfamiliar in Russia, part holy man, part mystic, part charlatan. One of the women of the Tsarina's court came under his influence and convinced her mistress that Rasputin, of whose dissolute life Alexandra determinedly knew nothing, might be able to help the child. The lady-in-waiting was right; Rasputin was the only person who could calm the Tsarevitch [tsar's son] when he was in pain, and this wandering reprobate came to have an absolutely predominant influence over the royal family. The outside world wondered what on earth was going on; vicious rumors swept the country that he was Alexandra's lover, or that she and he were in the pay of the Germans. What was a family and national tragedy was seen instead as a sordid affair, and all of it was further complicated by Nicholas' weakness and Alexandra's strength, invariably asserted at the wrong time and in the wrong direction. Whenever he faltered, as he often did, she bolstered him in his autocracy, telling him to be strong, that the Russians needed and loved the whip, and that he must not budge an inch. Since Russia still was an autocracy, since government ministers still were responsible to the Tsar, and since he and his wife remained absorbed in their family difficulties and politically trapped inside their own archaic view of monarchy, they were leading the country straight down the road to catastrophe. Weak men can influence history as much as strong ones.

Because of these problems at all levels of Russian society, the initiative in the war lay largely with the Germans. In the spring of 1915 they chose to exercise it.

Germany on the Offensive, 1915–1916

Even when the Central Powers had made a decision to fight in the East, there was still the problem of where specifically to do it. Hindenburg wished to move from the north . . . and drive in a southerly direction. Von Falkenhayn, who possessed the largest view of the general situation, wanted to overwhelm Serbia and, he hoped, open communications through the still-neutral Balkan States to Turkey. But Austrian pleas overrode German desires. Conrad von Hötzendorf wanted an attack out of the south-central front, between the slopes of the Carpathians [mountain range] and the upper reaches of the Vistula [River]. As the Germans looked over their situation, they concluded that Austria was weak and that the Russians quite possibly might have the strength to break over the Carpathian barrier in the summer. It was a case of beating the relatively weak Russians before they beat the even weaker Austrians.

To this end the Germans subordinated their entire strategy of the year. Hindenburg launched a smallish attack in Lithuania to draw Russian troops northward. That succeeded but eventually used up so many Germans that the comparative changes in strength ratios were minimized. Von Falkenhayn withdrew troops from the Western Front and fought the Battle of Second Ypres to mask their departure. Finally, around Gorlice and Tarnow [on Austria-Hungary's frontier with Russian-controlled Poland] the Germans built up a massive concentration of troops and guns, the whole group of armies under the command of Field Marshal August von Mackensen.

The attack opened on May 2, with a tremendous artillery barrage of an intensity previously unknown on the eastern front. The Russians were absolutely pulverized, troops driven crazy by the shellfire, units panicking, whole mobs of men wiped out or rushing to the rear. Within two days the Russian 3rd Army was completely annihilated, Mackensen had taken more than 100,000 prisoners, and his soldiers were into the open country and rolling to the northeast. The breakthrough compromised the entire Russian position in the Carpathians, and they had to go back all along the line. By the end of May they had retreated eighty miles, as far as the San and the Dniester rivers, and the immediate threat to Austria was lifted.

Early in June the German leaders sat down once more to decide what to do next. By that time Italy had declared war; [Austro-Hungarian general Franz] Conrad now wanted German troops for his new southern front, to protect him from the Italians. Von Falkenhayn would have liked to go back with reinforcements to France, but this time Hindenburg's arguments carried the day. Even though Austria had gained a temporary reprieve, the German eastern commanders had little confidence in her ability to maintain the war if German troops were pulled out. Russia was pushed back, but not defeated. Therefore, they should continue their drives as they were.

This line of reasoning appeared the more promising as the southern Russian withdrawal had now created a large salient in Poland, with Warsaw as its point. Mackensen was still pushing ahead; he had taken the fortress of Przemsyl, and Lemberg fell in the third week of June. If the Germans mounted a similar attack from East Prussia, driving south, it ought to be possible either to drive the Russians out of Poland altogether or, even more fruitfully, to trap and destroy them while they were still there. Though this was really little more than a rehash of Hindenburg's earlier proposal, the changed situation in the south now made it more attractive, so the plan was accepted.

Mackensen, further reinforced, turned the axis of his attack northward, aiming for Brest-Litovsk, about a hundred miles due east of Warsaw, and in mid-July the Germans began a complementary drive from East Prussia, heading for Warsaw itself.

The Grand Duke Nicholas Retreats

The Russians had, indeed, hoped to wreck Austria-Hungary this year, but they lacked the power to do it. Russia's overall field commander, the Grand Duke Nicholas, who was a nephew of Tsar Alexander II and therefore a cousin of Tsar Nicholas and who was also a soldier of considerable talent, had hoped to make it over the Carpathians and into the Hungarian plain. He had launched a limited offensive in the mountains late in March, but the Russians had run out of matériel by mid-April. Then before they could recoup, Mackensen's Gorlice-Tarnow offensive had hit them, and they had been backtracking ever since.

Faced with an obvious pincer attack on a large scale, the Grand Duke now responded wisely and courageously. He decided the time had come to give up Poland, and the Russians began to pull back. There were mistakes; on 1st Army's front they succumbed to the temptation of a fortress and threw themselves into Novogeorgievsk, where they were promptly surrounded, losing 1,600 guns and more than a million shells along with the garrison. The Germans brought in their experts from the Western Front and took the vaunted citadel, symbol of Russian power over the Poles, in a matter of days. Usually, however, the Russians pulled back in good time, and the Germans had to admit that their offensive gained less than they had hoped, more ground perhaps, but fewer Russians. By mid-August the salient was gone; the Russian line was back against the Pripet Marshes, and two weeks later Mackensen took Brest-Litovsk. Russian rule of Poland, which had lasted since the end of the Napoleonic wars through plot and revolution, was over— until 1944.

Russia: Bending but Not Yet Breaking

With fall in the air the Germans were still reluctant to stop. They spent September on the flanks, Austrians attacking south of the Pripet Marshes for little gain, and the Germans pushing farther out of the Baltic principalities. By the end of September the Russians had gone back yet another 100 miles, to a north-south line that ran through Pinsk, east of the Pripet Marshes. They had lost 2 million men, half of them prisoners. German casualties had been heavy, too, but not that heavy. The Austrians did not seem elated by the removal of the Russian threat; they still had far more men and officers reporting sick than they had incapacitated in combat, a sign that their morale remained low. It was the same old story: The front was too long, and the Tsarist Empire too big, to achieve a complete victory, and nothing short of that was meaningful. . . . The Germans were wearing themselves out killing Russians.

Still, even Russia was not inexhaustible. The difficulties at home and at the front might have been bearable if they achieved victory. It was that much harder to endure them when the news was always of retreats and casualties, battles lost and fortresses surrendered. The Russians might fight stolidly, and the Germans might praise their capacity in a crisis, but morale continued to sag through 1915. It was necessary to do something to restore public confidence, and late in August, Tsar Nicholas decided on such a move. As usual, it was the wrong one. He sacked the competent, popular Grand Duke Nicholas—so popular indeed with the liberals that in some quarters his name was whispered as a possible replacement for the Tsar himself. The Grand Duke could be succeeded only by someone whose name possessed even greater power and appeal, and there was only one who qualified; on September 1, Tsar Nicholas himself assumed the supreme command of the army.

The Germans were delighted, for in truth the move was disastrous. The Grand Duke at least had been a soldier. The Tsar had no understanding of the workings or the complexity of the military system; to advise him he appointed generals because he got along well with them, not necessarily because they were competent.

The effect behind the front was potentially even more harmful. With Nicholas in the war zone, Alexandra was free to meddle in the affairs of government and to follow Rasputin's advice as to who ought to get ministries and war contracts. Incapable of running affairs herself, she was equally incapable of letting anyone else run them. The Tsar, weak though he was, had at least exercised a moderating influence on Alexandra's authoritarian tendencies, but now they were given free rein. Finally, by his move the Tsar had tied the fortunes of the dynasty to the military situation. If he won, he would be the saviour of his country, and he would go down in history as Nicholas the Conqueror as his grandfather had been Alexander the Liberator. But if he lost, he might well go down as the last of the Romanovs. By the end of 1915, it did not look like a good gamble.

Slaughter: The Battle of Verdun

John F. Wukovits

Teacher and writer John F. Wukovits is the author of several books of military history. In the following selection he summarizes and dissects the bloody Battle of Verdun. Wukovits focuses primarily on two aspects of the battle: the record-setting, tragic loss of life on both sides and the importance of a handful of French officers in the French refusal to surrender to the Germans. This battle began when German forces attacked the historic and fortified French site in early 1916. The German goal was to trap the French army in a war of attrition in defense of Verdun.

a reduction of decrease in numbers, size, or strength

With the opposing armies in western Europe mired in trench warfare, military planners on both sides tried to craft battle plans that would turn the momentum in their favor. The British and French devised full-scale assaults against the Germans in the Somme region, while German general Erich von Falkenhayn promoted an intricate plan to remove France from the war and force Great Britain back to home territory. Similar to most operations yet conducted in the war, both strategies failed to achieve their purposes. However, the French would forever remember the valorous conduct of its soldiers in front of one of its most cherished locales—Verdun.

Target Verdun

Falkenhayn, commander of German troops, believed that if the proper target were selected for a new offensive, France would divert all its effort into halting the drive. Falkenhayn argued that if such a situation arose, his forces could decimate

Excerpted from *World War I*, vol. 3, *Strategic Battles*, by John F. Wukovits (San Diego: Lucent Books, 2001). Reprinted by permission of The Gale Group.

the French army and leave France so weakened that Britain would be left alone on the western front.

The German general outlined his proposal in a December 1915 letter to Kaiser Wilhelm. He claimed that the "strain on France has reached breaking point. If we succeed in opening the eyes of her people to the fact that in a military sense they have nothing more to hope for, that breaking point would be reached" and England would be on her own. He added that he had to center the offensive on a portion of France so revered that the country would have "to throw in every man they have. If they do so the forces of France will bleed to death."[1]

Falkenhayn chose the French fortress at Verdun as his target. Since the glorious days of the Roman Empire, Verdun held historic significance. Attila the Hun had once attacked the spot, and it was at Verdun in A.D. 843 that the heirs of Emperor Charlemagne divided the remnants of Charlemagne's empire into French and German sections. In the seventeenth century the heralded French military engineer Sébastien Vauban had fortified the town into a formidable bastion able to withstand the most determined sieges. During World War I, this fortification was used to shield Verdun and its nearby city of fourteen thousand citizens by surrounding the main fortress with a series of smaller forts, including Fort Vaux and Fort Douaumont.

To ensure victory, Falkenhayn assembled a frightening display of offensive power. One thousand guns capable of hurling 2.5 million shells at the French backed the 1 million soldiers who stealthily moved into camouflaged forward positions called *stollen*. Poor weather hampered French efforts to spot the buildup in front of Verdun, and as the opening barrage approached, the French defenders remained unaware that the area was about to explode.

Because most of the fighting in the west had occurred far from Verdun, the French in the region had been lulled to inaction. In light of the disastrous opening advance in 1914, when Belgian forts had been quickly neutralized, many of the largest French guns had been removed from the complex of twenty-five forts in the Verdun region. French battalions had been transferred from the lines to serve elsewhere, so that as the 1 million German troops moved into position, barely half that number opposed them.

Falkenhayn intended to launch his attack on February 12, 1916, but a miserable mixture of rain, snow, and sleet forced him to postpone the action. German soldiers waited uncomfortably in their unheated, damp *stollen* for nine draining days before Falkenhayn issued the command to go on the offensive.

The Hellish Barrage

French soldiers rested in their trenches in the quiet predawn moments of February 21, relaxing with a cup of coffee or grabbing a fast meal. Suddenly, the calm erupted in a titanic explosion of sound and fury as the first of 2 million German shells over a twelve-hour bombardment tore into the scenic countryside and smashed against French fortifications. One thousand guns across an eight-mile front hurled 1,667 shells into French lines every minute. In the war's heaviest bombardment to date, mounds of earth tossed up by the shells buried French soldiers alive before they could put down their coffee cups, destroyed communication lines and artillery positions, and uprooted trees. Seven thousand horses perished in a single day. French aviators flying overhead stared in awe at an uninterrupted line of fire belching out from the German positions.

Terrified French soldiers fled their trenches to avoid death, only to meet it in another spot. Hundreds rushed to nearby woods for shelter but were torn apart by falling tree fragments. Out of one group of twelve hundred soldiers, eleven hundred perished on this ghastly day. A corporal reported that out of every five men in his unit, "two have been buried alive under their shelter, two are wounded to one extent or other, and the fifth is waiting."[2]

Men cracked under the strain of the intense shelling. One French soldier recalled,

> When you hear the whistling in the distance your entire body preventively crunches together to prepare for the enormous explosions. Every new explosion is a new attack, a new

fatigue, a new affliction. Even nerves of the hardest of steel, are not capable of dealing with this kind of pressure. It is as if you are tied to a pole and threatened by a man with a hammer. First the hammer is swung backwards in order to hit hard, then it is swung forwards, only missing your skull by an inch, into the splintering pole. In the end you just surrender. There is even hardly enough strength left to pray to God.[3]

Falkenhayn's soldiers then rushed from their *stollen* toward the French, whom they expected to be either dead or wounded or completely demoralized from the stunning half-day barrage. German officers turned their hats around so French sharpshooters would not recognize them, then led their men forward. They met sporadic resistance, but most French soldiers could not fire their weapons because dirt from the barrage had filled the barrels and buried their ammunition and grenades. As a result, within three days the German army advanced three miles deeper into French territory.

French officers begged for help to stop the unceasing German attack. One lieutenant reported that "The commanding officer and all company commanders have been killed. My battalion is reduced to approximately 180 men [from 600]. I have neither ammunition nor food. What am I to do?"[4]

With the French army in disarray, German soldiers advanced everywhere along the right bank of the Meuse River. On February 24 the French outer line of trenches collapsed, and the next day Fort Douaumont, once considered the anchor of the French defensive line, fell when a solitary German officer worked his way into the fort and captured the remaining fifty-seven French defenders.

Bitter hand-to-hand combat flared in the village of Douaumont on February 28, where French and German soldiers battled with knives, bayonets, and fists as a blinding snowstorm engulfed the region. German units suffered horrendous losses to match those of the French—two thousand of thirty-five hundred men in one sector were killed or wounded. Finally, on March 3, the surviving French forces in the village surrendered, and the French fell back to the final hillside shielding Verdun itself.

The fall of Fort Douaumont and the nearby village ended
the battle's first phase, a portion totally dominated by the
Germans. Church bells rang in jubilation in Germany and
schoolchildren received a special holiday to mark the occasion. Newspapers in Berlin and other major cities boasted
that the French were on the verge of collapse. However, the
Germans did not count on the astounding resilience and
willpower of their foes who, with their backs to the wall and
facing dire threats to Verdun and France itself, stepped forward to halt the offensive.

"We Shall Bear Up"

Two soldiers typified French defiance. When the German
ruler Kaiser Wilhelm visited the front, he asked to meet Lieutenant Colonel Bernard, a French officer who had been captured in the battle's opening moments. Instead of a broken individual, the kaiser encountered a determination that would
become a trademark for the remainder of the battle. Bernard,
captured but not beaten, warned the German ruler, "You will
never enter Verdun."[5]

The other individual stepped into the maelstrom, reorga-
nized the confused French forces, and vowed that the Germans would be rebuffed. Led by a man who would become
a national hero, sixty-year-old General Philippe Pétain, the
French turned disaster into glory.

Pétain had been in command on February 25 barely one
hour before he informed his officers that the Germans had
taken the last piece of French soil. He ordered them to re-
take any territory already lost to the enemy, and announced
to one of his top generals, "I am taking over. Inform your
troops. Keep up your courage." Heartened by Pétain's optimism, the general replied, "Very well, sir, we shall bear up.
You can rely on us, as we rely on you."[6]

Pétain, later honored as the hero of Verdun, realized that
to stem the German advance, supplies and reinforcements
had to be rushed to the front. He declared the solitary road
leading into Verdun as a supply route, banned other traffic,
and organized an around-the-clock flow of supplies. Soldiers
marching forward had to exit the road and use adjoining

fields to make room for the torrent of trucks that breathed life into Verdun on a twenty-four hour basis. Pétain stationed thousands of soldiers along the road to quickly repair damaged portions and to throw dirt into holes; they shoved to the side any vehicles that broke down to allow the following trucks to pass. Pétain so efficiently organized the relief effort that two supply trucks arrived in Verdun every minute. In all, 190,000 reinforcements and 23,000 tons of supplies kept France's soldiers fighting at Verdun.

The Crucial Battle of the Hills

Falkenhayn faced another problem besides Pétain's determination. Falkenhayn had been concentrating his attacks on the right bank of the Meuse River while allowing the left bank to remain in French hands. As a result, French artillery inflicted heavy casualties whenever the Germans tried to move forward. Falkenhayn decided to launch a new offensive on the left bank to eliminate this threat, especially that posed by French defenders implanted on two hills—Le Mort Homme and Hill 304.

The drive, which opened on March 6, 1916, kicked off two months of combat in the most miserable conditions at Le Mort Homme. A seemingly endless cycle gripped the fighting: German attack would achieve minor gains before slowing, then the inevitable French counterattack would push them back to their original lines. Each time, fresh bodies lying atop the contested ground served as gruesome evidence of the repetitive slaughter. Artillery shells churned the dirt again and again, tossing decaying remains into charred trees and demolishing whatever semblance of trenches remained. Snow, torrential rain, and sleet transformed the region into a muddy morass that sucked the boots off soldiers' feet, halted movement, and immobilized the combatants. Wounded French and German soldiers, unable to crawl from shell holes, drowned as rainwater cascaded into their shelters.

Sometimes, one man made a difference. A French officer named Macker calmly directed his troops in a successful counterattack. Ignoring the German machine gun bullets that ripped into the ground inches from his feet, Macker, puffing a cigar and brandishing a cane, walked directly toward the German positions. Emboldened by this display of bravery, his men swarmed toward the enemy lines and forced the Germans in that area to retreat. Later in the day Macker and a fellow officer were chatting when machine-gun fire killed both. Demoralized by the absence of their leader, the French fell back in the face of a strong German counterattack.

The daily horrors of combat ground down even the sturdiest of men, causing an increase of insubordination and defection on both sides. Men refused to leave their shelters, and groups of soldiers surrendered rather than endure further misery. One German officer said "the front soldiers become numb by seeing the bodies without heads, without legs, shot through the belly, with blown away foreheads, with holes in their chests."[7]

On the other side of the lines a French soldier battled a sense of doom. "Soon the losses became more and more. Every soldier is simply waiting in quiet acceptance for the grenade that has his name on it. And everywhere there is screaming and moaning, sirens and crackle, dirt and blood, death and dying."[8] To keep his soldiers at the front lines and slow the rate of desertion, one French officer moved a machine gun near him in case he had to turn it on his own men.

The Germans launched a second major effort on April 9, but it, too, failed to achieve anything beyond additional death and destruction. Artillery shells blasted Hill 304 with such thoroughness that it removed six feet of dirt from its height, and officers recorded instances of men going mad under the strain. Pétain later wrote:

> My heart leapt as I saw our youths of twenty going into the furnace of Verdun. But how depressing it was when they returned. Their expressions seemed frozen by a vision of terror; their gait and their postures betrayed a total dejection; they sagged beneath the weight of horrifying memories.[9]

For two months the Germans mounted unsuccessful attempts to seize both hills from the French. Finally, near the end of May, the Germans stormed the summits and gained a glimpse down toward Verdun itself. Across the Meuse, other German units advanced on Fort Vaux and, after a fierce fight with French defenders, seized the fort.

The Germans acquired their objectives, but at a high price to both sides. Two months of combat cost the Germans eighty-two thousand deaths, while eighty-nine thousand Frenchmen perished defending Verdun. These locations represented the farthest advance made by Falkenhayn's forces. For the next six months the antagonists stood their ground and battled like two exhausted boxers trying to stay on their feet.

The Fatal Gamble

A change in command brought a change in French tactics. General Robert-Georges Nivelle succeeded Pétain, who had been ordered to a different sector to halt a new German drive. Nivelle, an artillery specialist, organized the most deadly concentration of artillery fire Verdun had seen. During May and June, 20 million shells disrupted German concentrations, demolished German positions, and stripped the land of most foliage. When Falkenhayn's forces still advanced closer to Verdun, Nivelle rallied both French soldier and citizen alike with the stirring order, "They shall not pass!"[10]

Again the opposing military entered a brutal slugfest that sapped life and drained hope. One French soldier, weary of the endless carnage, moaned, "Having despaired of living amid such horror, we begged God to let us be dead."[11] A German infantryman wrote that bodies bloated and decayed faster in the summer heat, requiring the survivors to stuff garlic in their nostrils to reduce the stench.

The Germans launched a final offensive against Verdun on July 11 in hopes of cracking through the French defenses. After bitter fighting, the French halted the drive, and although fighting still flared, both sides settled into a three-month lull.

The French carefully marshaled their forces to organize an October attack against the German lines. By early November they had shoved the Germans out of the fallen

French forts, and before year's end the French had regained much of the ground lost in the spring. The Germans, who could not commit the needed men or material because so much had been diverted to battle the British drive in the Somme region, realized their action near Verdun had failed.

Falkenhayn's gamble to capture venerable Verdun, sap French strength, and demoralize the enemy had instead produced catastrophic results for the Germans. Had Falkenhayn succeeded in capturing Verdun in the spring, he might have so demoralized the French that they might have asked for peace. This could have enabled the Germans to then rush their forces eastward to knock out the Russians, which would have left Great Britain standing alone. The course of the war could have been altered at Verdun in Germany's favor. Instead, momentum swung in favor of the French. Before the fighting at Verdun, Germany had a chance to win the war; afterward, it never again posed as significant a threat. As a result, Kaiser Wilhelm replaced Falkenhayn as commander.

The eight-month battle in front of Verdun ended with opposing sides back where they started and no end in sight to the interminable slaughter. In saving the nation's honor, France lost 542,000 men killed, wounded, missing, or as prisoners of war near Verdun, while Falkenhayn's plan cost the Germans 434,000 soldiers. In a war already notorious for its appalling death tolls, Verdun held the dubious distinction of producing the highest density of dead soldiers per square yard of any World War I battle.

In sad testament, a memorial plaque currently rests at Fort Vaux, mounted by a French mother and dedicated to her fallen son. The plaque bears the simple but powerful inscription: to my son, SINCE YOUR EYES WERE CLOSED MINE HAVE NEVER CEASED TO CRY.[12]

Berlin newspapers could no longer boast of victory, and German church bells failed to resonate with triumph. Since enemy forces still occupied much of their territory, the French could not be too boastful; they had merely shoved back an attack, not defeated a foe. More fighting and dying awaited before the outcome of the war would be determined.

What high-ranking officers might not comprehend, the common foot soldier did. Exasperated with the lack of progress, in spite of the killing and maiming, German and French soldiers gazed into a future that held little promise other than death or injury. One German soldier, on the verge of despair, wrote his family that the fighting would continue "until the last German and the last Frenchman hobbled out of the trenches on crutches to exterminate each other with pocket knives or teeth and finger nails."[13] The unheralded German accurately predicted the war's path as it wound its way out of 1916 and into 1917.

Notes

1. Quoted in John Keegan, *The First World War*. New York: Vintage Books, 1998, p. 278.

2. Quoted in Martin Gilbert, *The First World War: A Complete History*. New York: Henry Holt, 1994, p. 231.

3. Quoted in http://war1418.com/battleverdun/witness, p. 2.

4. Quoted in Keegan, *The First World War*, p. 281.

5. Quoted in Gilbert, *The First World War*, p. 231.

6. Quoted in S.L.A. Marshall, *The American Heritage History of World War I*. New York: American Heritage Publishing, 1964, p. 173.

7. Quoted in http://war1418.com/battleverdun/witness, p. 6.

8. Quoted in http://war1418.com/battleverdun/thebattleoftheflanks, p. 6.

9. Quoted in Marshall, *The American Heritage History of World War I*, p. 190.

10. Quoted in Marshall, *The American Heritage History of World War I*, p. 194.

11. Quoted in Marshall, *The American Heritage History of World War I*, p. 192.

12. Quoted in Alistair Horne, *The Price of Glory: Verdun 1916*. New York: Penguin Books, 1993, p. xv.

13. Quoted in Marshall, *The American Heritage History of World War I*, p. 192.

The Battle of the Somme

S.L.A. Marshall

In this selection, renowned military historian and journalist S.L.A. Marshall (1900–1977) focuses on the Battle of the Somme (July–November 1916). The British command believed that a massive British-led frontal attack on German defenses along the Somme River in northern France would lead to a decisive breakthrough and Allied victory. Instead the British suffered the greatest military losses in its history with a gain of territory of only seven miles. Here Marshall explains the tragic mistakes of the Somme offensive. He finds Allied generalship sadly deficient and too ready to sacrifice hundreds of thousands of soldiers' lives in futile attacks.

History offers the explanation that the Battle of the Somme had to be fought as it was by the British to save the French Army from the crucifixion of Verdun.

It doesn't wash. In a letter to Douglas Haig on December 30, 1915, Joseph Joffre first mentioned that a great battle would have to be staged on the Somme, when the change in seasons and the man power picture favored it.

Haig was all for mounting a great battle; but he was all against having it on the Somme front, preferring Flanders. The Somme sector had been quiet ever since First Marne, and the enemy had taken advantage of the inactivity. The German line extending both ways from the Somme River had been made impregnably strong, and the chalk hills overlooking the Allied trenches had become a catacomb. Massively timbered dugouts, rebutted with concrete and

Excerpted from *The American Heritage History of World War I*, by the editors of *American Heritage: The Magazine of History*, narrative by S.L.A. Marshall (New York: American Heritage Publishing Co.). Copyright © 1964 by American Heritage Publishing Co., Inc. Reprinted with permission from the publisher.

equipped with electric lighting, were serviced with an underground reticulation of laundries, aid stations, repair shops, and arsenals. Life was relatively good there. The Germans didn't wish to be disturbed and felt it would be folly for the Allies to try. It was.

The Big Push

Haig set his jaw to oppose Joffre, then retracted to agree, and in the end, by self-hypnosis, became convinced that the Somme was an open-sesame to final victory. He would cut the German Army in two, and do it in one day. He would have the Cavalry Corps under bit and ready to charge through the shell-cratered gap and "into the blue," as proof of his intent to crush the enemy. This was big thinking. By February 11 his plan was tentatively set. By late April a great part of Europe knew that the British were organizing the Big Push and the Germans would feel it somewhere soon. But by then, also, the German pressure against Verdun had slackened and the French were counterattacking. The improvement along the Meuse only made Haig more eager for the Somme and caused Joffre to strain harder in jockeying him on. When General Fritz von Below, whose German Second Army on the Somme front had only eight divisions, reported that he sensed a great attack coming, Falkenhayn told him it was a wonderful hope. Having splintered his own army by throwing it against the immovable object, Falkenhayn couldn't imagine that the enemy would be equally stupid.

The Somme, a tranquil river, meanders northwest through Picardy to the Channel. It is shallow and marsh-bordered, spreading five hundred yards or more from shore to shore; its banks and small islets abound with rushes, osiers, and poplars, the haunt of blackbirds, herons, and other wild fowl. The river split the Anglo-French forces set for the Big Push. General Marie Emile Fayolle's French Sixth Army extended south from the right bank. From the left bank to beyond Ypres, it was all British country. General Rawlinson's new Fourth Army was next to the French flank. Out of General Allenby's Third Army, one corps forming its right flank was also committed. Thus from flank to flank the great array measured fourteen British divisions attacking over an eighteen-mile front and five French divisions hitting on an eight-mile front. Fayolle had 850 heavy guns, so many that he could afford to lend one hundred of them to the British, who were still short of the hardware needed to crush heavy works.

Britain's army of the attack was shaped largely out of the new conscripts, half-formed soldiers who, never having seen action, eschewed the cynicism of the old sweats and truly believed that in their first go over the top they were bound for Berlin. But the more seasoned fighters present—officers and NCO's—noted that the earth-shaking bombardment that opened at dawn on June 24 still hadn't cut most of the enemy wire at month's end. There were some very shrewd soldiers eyeing preparations for the Somme, men like Majors Archibald Wavell and Bernard Montgomery. There was also a muster of poets: Robert Graves, Siegfried Sassoon, John Masefield, Edmund Blunden, and Mark Plowman. From what they heard and saw, came no new songs to sing. "Trees in the battlefield," said Blunden, "are already described by Dante." "Armageddon is too immense for my solitary understanding," cried Sassoon. "I gaze down into the dark green glooms of the weedy little river, but my thoughts are powerless against unhappiness so huge." The earth churned, the landscape shriveled, the noise deafened, the fumes stifled. In that vast barrage, 1,508,652 artillery rounds were spent. And at the end of it the German works and wire were still not battered and riven into disuse.

At 7:28 A.M. on July 1 occurred both ways from the Somme, what John Buchan . . . calls "the supreme moment without heroics and without tremor." The French and the British infantry climbed up from their trenches and jumped off into the exploding unknown. Like many British commanders a sedulous diarist, Sir Douglas Haig just thirty-two minutes later was making this entry: "Reports . . . [are] most satisfactory. Our troops had everywhere crossed the enemy's front trenches." All along the line his soldiers were falling in windrows to zeroed-in enemy machine gun and artillery fire. It was a catastrophe. By day's end more than 60,000 soldiers of the British Empire were corpses littering the field, dying men trapped in the beaten zone, burdens for the stretcher-bearers, or walking wounded. But not one pivotal plot of ground had been won. Here and there, sections of the German forward defense zone had been shallowly penetrated, that was all. Blessed by a more systematic bombardment and a more intelligent tactical design, Fayolle's French troops fared better. But they were in too few numbers to open a decisive gap. . . .

Bloodbath

Haig should have called off the Somme that night and cut his losses. But having failed, he was too bulldoggish to quit. In consequence, this hideous turmoil must be recorded as the most soulless battle in British annals. The Somme deteriorated into a blood purge rivaling Verdun. It was a battle not so much of attrition as of mutual destruction, and it continued until November 18.

Joffre wanted it that way. He was as demoniacal as Falkenhayn. He kept prodding Haig, insisting that the offensive be continued. At the same time, noting by the numbers (infantrymen were but digits to him) that his own army was fading away from the effects of Verdun and the Somme, Joffre was pressuring the War Ministry to call up the class of 1917 for training, though 1916 campaigning was hardly begun. If at this time his strategic reasoning had any end in view, it could only be that the side that could scrape up the last 100,000 men would win.

Sir Douglas was as willing as Joffre to feed more men to the fire. So more plans were drawn, the battle was reenergized, tracts of ground and rubble heaps that had once been villages were won now and then, and an army of hope-filled, promising young men perished vainly. By the end of the year, another 607,784 sprouts of the empire had been put out of action, the greater number falling on the Somme. The fact that Germany had suffered in almost equal numbers did not make less the pain and loss.

The Tanks Are Coming, but Not Enough

But one interesting thing happened. Britain had brought along a new weapon created to break the deadlock on the Western Front. Many minds contributed to the innovation but the main credit goes to Winston Churchill. While at the Admiralty, he had winked at regulations and made available the funds for developing a land battleship. Colonel Ernest D. Swinton had earlier urged the building of an armored fighting vehicle that could charge cross-country on caterpillar treads.

In this way was born the tank, sired by several geniuses, damned by the military hierarchy. The origin of the name is more curious. During development, the vehicle had to be kept secret. That was a problem. A large, mysterious object shipped around the country under canvas would surely whet public curiosity. How to camouflage the secret became the question. Someone suggested that it be called a "water carrier," with the attendant explanation that it was for use in the Sinai desert. One planner said: "We call everything by initials; I will not stand for being on anything called the W.C. Committee." The word "tank" was suggested as a compromise, and it stuck.

As the Somme battle carried on into autumn, the first platoon of tanks was coming out of the British plant. These weapons should have been stock-piled to at least brigade strength for the staging of a monster surprise. But Haig's desire to bull through was too great. He grabbed the first forty-two and threw them into a twelve-division attack on September 15. Considering that the tank crews had just arrived up front and that the vehicles were untried in war, the effects, if local, were sensational. The rumbling monsters seemed to scare German infantrymen out of their wits. The German High Command only dimly sensed the potential and fumblingly set about developing its own armor. Even so, a grand opportunity was frittered away.

Haig and Joffre, soldiers steeped in traditional prejudices, did not seem to comprehend such values. At just about the time of armor's debut, Lloyd George visited the two commanders on the Western Front. He mentioned that he saw little or no future use for cavalry in the struggle. These two great men-of-war told him off, reminding him that civilians did not understand military operations.

Consequences of the Somme Carnage

But Haig had one quality. Like the old Frenchman in the Revolution, he survived, weathering the storms that beat down his more celebrated contemporaries. Victor Hugo once said of Napoleon that he was through when God got bored with him. About Falkenhayn and Joffre it is possible to be more specific. On August 28 Falkenhayn was advised that due to Rumania's entry into the war, the Kaiser had summoned Field Marshal Hindenburg to consult on the over-all military situation. The Chief of Staff knew the difference between a snub and an invitation to remove himself. He therefore submitted his resignation and H-L returned to home base to run the entire war and what was left of the empire—Hindenburg as Chief of the General Staff, Ludendorff as First Quartermaster General. Joffre was kicked upstairs in mid-December, appointed technical adviser to the Government for the duration of the war. In his place, as Commander in Chief on the Western Front, arose General Nivelle, made luminous by Verdun. A strange choice, it was determined mainly by clerical and anticlerical factionalism within the French Army and Government. Nivelle was by blood half British and spoke perfect English; while that might have been a debit, his Protestantism made him highly acceptable. Foch was also relieved of field command at the same time as Joffre and for a long time his star was behind a cloud.

Simultaneously, there was a political tempest in Britain. Asquith, who had never taken firm hold of the war's problems, became more remote after his eldest son was killed on the Somme. But he wanted to stay on as Prime Minister. A cabal was formed among Lloyd George, Sir Edward Carson, Bonar Law, and Sir William Maxwell Aitken (later Lord Beaverbrook) to force Asquith to yield war powers to a council of three men. As Lloyd George put it: "We can't conduct our affairs through a Sanhedrin." In the maneuvering that followed, Asquith was forced from office on December 4, and George V, much as he regretted it, saw no choice but to call Lloyd George to form a new Government. No one expected him to stay very long.

In France, the Government was shaken up and reformed at the same time under Briand, with General Louis Lyautey taking the War Ministry and Admiral Marie Jean Lacaze the Navy. All of these changes flowed in due course from Verdun and the Somme, which cast long shadows. What wasn't in due course was that Haig was made a Field Marshal. Joffre, the other mangler of armies, was also given a baton. These ironies were little understood by the Allied peoples, who knew only what the High Commands wished them to know.

Tragedy at Gallipoli

William R. Griffiths

The Dardanelles, or Gallipoli, campaign of 1915–1916 arose from Great Britain's interest in opening a new front on the southeast flank of the Central Powers in light of the costly deadlock on the western front. The operation proved to be a bold but flawed maneuver to cripple Germany's ally, Turkey, which stood astride the narrow waterway—the Dardanelles Straits—linking the Mediterranean Sea and the Black Sea. Another Anglo-French aim in the campaign was to supply aid to embattled Russia by seizing the vital passageway from the Turks and opening a Black Sea route to Russia. British civilian and military leaders who favored this "indirect approach" were known as "easterners," as opposed to the "westerners" who advocated all-out pressure on the western front. In this selection, former West Point historian William R. Griffiths examines the Gallipoli offensive, a venture that quickly spread the war toward the Middle East.

As 1914 ended with a bloody stalemate in France, members of the British War Council, led by First Lord of the Admiralty Winston Churchill and First Sea Lord Admiral John Fisher, began pressing the Government to return to the traditional British strategy of the indirect approach. David Lloyd George, a shrewd Welsh politician who served as Chancellor of the Exchequer, agreed that Great Britain needed to apply its growing power away from the caldron of the Western Front and provide the public with victories to sustain morale. He was interested in defeating one of Germany's weaker allies—Austria or Turkey. This energetic group was given the support it needed to carry the

Excerpted from *The Great War*, by William R. Griffiths (Wayne, NJ: Avery Publishing Group, 1986). Reprinted by permission of the series editor, Thomas E. Griess.

day by the Secretary of State for War, Field Marshal Kitchener. He expressed the view that the German trench line in France could not be broken until the arms and munitions industries had begun to supply sufficient artillery to support trench warfare. Therefore, if the British were to succeed anywhere in the near future, it would have to be outside of Europe.

The final impetus to action against Turkey came from the Russians. The Russian Commander-in-Chief, Grand Duke Nicholas, was extremely concerned about the Turkish offensive in the Caucasus [mountainous region on Russian-Turkish border], and requested a British demonstration against Turkey to prevent her from reinforcing the Caucasus Front. Given Allied fears over Russia's strength following her massive defeat in East Prussia, the British Cabinet was disposed to honor the request.

Sending in the Fleet

Because there were no troops at hand, a naval operation was the only option that could threaten and perhaps breach the Dardanelles. Such an operation had been studied by the British Admiralty and the Imperial General Staff on numerous occasions prior to the war. These studies had concluded that a purely naval operation could not succeed, and that a joint army-navy amphibious operation was necessary.

On January 3, 1915, Churchill, anxious to act on the Cabinet's direction, cabled Vice Admiral Sackville Carden, Commander of Naval Forces in the Aegean Sea, to ask if his naval elements could force the straits with ships alone. Replying that the Dardanelles could not be "rushed," Carden submitted a plan for a methodical reduction of the Turkish defenses. He stated that large caliber guns on aging battleships could pound the forts guarding the straits while minesweepers cleared channels through the mine belts. Carden estimated that this method would allow the naval expedition to reach Constantinople within a month. Having heard what they wished to hear, Churchill and the remainder of the War Council ignored the findings of previous studies and supported Carden's plan. Another influence on this decision was the example of the German heavy guns that had reduced the sturdy forts at Liège and Namur.

Thus began the most controversial and frustrating campaign of the war. Operations against the Dardanelles would always seem just beyond the grasp of the Allies. With great hope for decisive results, more troops and resources would be drawn into the campaign, only to be squandered through inaction or lack of coordination.

On January 13, 1915, the British War Cabinet directed "a naval expedition in February to bombard and take the Gallipoli Peninsula with Constantinople as its objective." This ambiguous order revealed the Cabinet's lack of understanding of the capabilities of a naval force operating without supporting invasion troops. It also proved that the British underestimated the Turkish Army, expecting, or perhaps hoping, that it would crumble under only slight pressure. Both miscalculations would lead to the gradual application of military and naval power without success.

Tough Turkey and a Botched Operation

Under the skillful direction of German Lieutenant General Limon von Sanders, the Turkish Army had been revitalized since 1913. Following a disastrous performance in the Balkan Wars, it had been provided with subsidies for pay, furnished with weapons and equipment, and given training under German methods. Because of the increasing possibility of war, Sanders mobilized the Army to a full strength of 36 divisions by the end of September 1914. With the British Mediterranean squadron's casual bombardment of the defenses of the Dardanelles in November, the Turkish Army was alerted to the intentions of the Allies.

In command of an Anglo-French naval squadron of 12 predreadnought battleships, one new super dreadnought (the *Queen Elizabeth*), and auxiliary ships and minesweepers, Admiral Carden planned to destroy the Dardanelles' forts at Cape Helles on the Gallipoli Peninsula and Kum Kale on the Asiatic shore. The key to the campaign was the narrows, where the shores were only a mile apart and 20 forts were concentrated to guard the passage. During the three weeks it took to assemble the naval force, the Turks reinforced the forts, deployed mobile artillery batteries along the shore, and reinforced the belts of mines that extended across the straits.

As directed, the British commander opened the campaign on February 19, shelling the forts at Cape Helles at long range. When no fire was returned, the ships closed to within three miles of shore. Then, just as the British became convinced that the Turks had fled, shore batteries returned the fire, and the Allied squadron withdrew. The next day, storms set in, delaying the return of Carden's ships until February 25. This time they silenced the forts in two days and then sent Marine landing parties ashore to destroy enemy guns. Following this, the fleet sailed into the straits.

Although the methodical advance continued, it was ham-

Churchill's Case for a Flank Attack

In 1914–1915 famed British statesman Winston S. Churchill served as Britain's First Lord of the Admiralty (equivalent to U.S. secretary of the navy). In this postwar account, Churchill explains why the bloody deadlock on the western front required an imaginative flanking maneuver to improve Allied chances for victory. The Gallipoli/Dardanelles campaign was, to a great extent, Churchill's project.

No war is so sanguinary as the war of exhaustion. No plan could be more unpromising than the plan of frontal attack. Yet on these two brutal expedients the military authorities of France and Britain consumed, during three successive years, the flower of their national manhood. Moreover, the dull carnage of the policy of exhaustion did not even apply equally to the combatants. The Anglo-French offensives of 1915, 1916 and 1917 were in nearly every instance, and certainly in the aggregate, far more costly to the attack than to the German defence. It was not even a case of exchanging a life for a life. Two, and even three, British or French lives were repeatedly paid for the killing of one enemy, and grim calculations were made to prove

pered by bad weather, accurate Turkish artillery fire against the improvised wooden minesweepers, and enemy mine-fields. The British persevered, however, and planned to make a major assault on March 18 that would break through the Turkish defenses. On the eve of this assault, Admiral Carden suffered a nervous collapse and was replaced by Rear Admiral John de Robeck, who pressed the attack, thinking that all the mine belts had been cleared. Unknown to the British and French, however, a week earlier a Turkish minelayer had sown a new line of 20 mines parallel to the shore. The French battleship *Bouvet* struck this belt and sank immediately, with a loss of 700. Sailors watched in disbelief, thinking that a Turkish artillery round had exploded in the ship's magazine. Two hours later, the battle cruiser *Inflexible* hit a mine, followed in rapid succession by the battleships *Irresistible* and *Ocean*. Confused and fearing a barrage of free-

---

that in the end the Allies would still have a balance of a few millions to spare. It will appear not only horrible but incredible to future generations that such doctrines should have been imposed by the military profession upon the ardent and heroic populations who yielded themselves to their orders.

It is a tale of the torture, mutilation or extinction of millions of men, and of the sacrifice of all that was best and noblest in an entire generation. The crippled, broken world in which we dwell to-day is the inheritor of these awful events. Yet all the time there were ways open by which this slaughter could have been avoided and the period of torment curtailed. There were regions where flanks could have been turned; there were devices by which fronts could have been pierced. And these could have been discovered and made mercifully effective, not by any departure from the principles of military art, but simply by the true comprehension of those principles and their application to the actual facts.

Winston S. Churchill, *The World Crisis*, vol. 2. 1923. Reprint, New York: Charles Scribner's Sons, 1951, pp. 4–5.

floating mines or torpedoes, de Robeck ordered a retreat back to his base on the island of Lemnos.

More Mistakes: An Amphibious Landing

When the operation to force the Dardanelles had first been discussed, Kitchener had stated that he could not spare any ground troops. Later, however, he relented, conceding that a few divisions might be found. Designated and assembled, those divisions were in the process of being concentrated in Egypt and Lemnos while the naval operations were proceeding. Known as the Mediterranean Force, they were commanded by General Ian Hamilton, a Boer War favorite of Kitchener. Hastily briefed before leaving London for the Dardanelles on March 13, Hamilton had been instructed that his force was not to be used until the Navy had been thwarted in its every effort to force the straits. Hopefully, his troops might only be used to destroy already neutralized Turkish forts and batteries.

Hamilton had arrived at the Dardanelles just in time to see the costly March 18 assault. Concluding that the Navy could not alone force the straits, he so advised Kitchener on March 19. Although de Robeck seems to have intended to renew his attack after refitting, Hamilton apparently convinced him that a joint ground-sea effort would be necessary. By supporting this view in a message to the Admiralty on the twenty-third, de Robeck effectively undercut an aggressively confident Churchill, who then had to concede to the change in plans.

Hamilton and his small staff began feverish preparations in the face of difficult conditions. The quartermaster had no experience regarding amphibious supply consumption upon which to base his plans. Weapons were scarce. Naval intelligence officers had almost no information concerning the Turkish troop dispositions. Maps were practically nonexistent. There were not enough ships, and joint planning with de Robeck on how best to use the ones available began very late. Yet somehow Hamilton managed to get his entire force of 5 divisions into 77 ships and concentrate those ships at Lemnos by April 21.

The four-week lull following the naval attack had been

put to good use by the Turks. Because preparations for the landings were now obvious, Sanders sent seven divisions into the Dardanelles area, fortified defenses around the beaches, and intensified training. Although defensive operations would be severely hindered by the primitive road network and the inability to move by water, Sanders placed his forces in centrally located assembly areas where they could react as quickly as possible to any landings.

Odds Against the Allies

The task facing the Allied attackers was by no means new. Throughout history, armies have been landed by ship on hostile shores. Until 1815, armies had fought as compact bodies formed in ranks. The problem to be solved by an amphibious commander then was to pick a landing point where the enemy army was not formed in ranks on the beach and to unload his army and arrange it in battle formation faster than the enemy army could march to the landing beach and attack.

The British at Gallipoli were well prepared to solve this classic problem. A large supply of barges was on hand. These unpowered boats were to be towed by motorboats. The tows, each with a string of four or five barges, would in turn be towed by battleships to within 3,000 yards of shore. Guide boats would lead the tows to the correct beach. After discharging their troops, the tows were to move 1,500 yards out to sea. There they would meet trawlers and destroyers carrying the second wave, transfer the second wave, and return to the beach.

Unfortunately for the Allies, machineguns and barbed wire had altered amphibious warfare as much as they had land warfare. Armies no longer needed to be formed in ranks on a small piece of ground before offering effective resistance. A small unit with machineguns could delay and disorganize a landing force, and such small units could easily be placed at all likely landing beaches. Fire support techniques were not sufficiently developed to allow the landing force to direct naval gun fire against a target as small as a machinegun. Twentieth century amphibious warfare, then, posed two problems: the new one of overcoming initial resistance on the beach, and the old one of getting troops ashore faster than the defender could mass. Hamilton had solved only the old one.

The British amphibious plan called for a series of landings, feints, and demonstrations. The French division was to conduct a feint by threatening a landing on the Asiatic shore at Kum Kale. The Royal Naval Division was to sail up to the base of the peninsula in a demonstration against Bulair. The British 29th Infantry Division would conduct the main attack at Cape Helles, while the ANZAC (Australia-New Zealand Army Corps) was to land 12 miles up the peninsula and conduct a supporting attack.

The Main Attack Begins

On April 25, the attack began as planned. The French division and the British Naval Division achieved their goals of diverting enemy forces from the main attack. Although the ANZAC landed a mile farther north than planned, it initially met no opposition. As the troops began moving inland, however, they encountered General Mustapha Kemal's [Kemal would later be known as Atatürk, the father of modern Turkey.] division, which quickly reinforced the area and contained the invaders. By noon, the situation at ANZAC Beach had stabilized.

At Cape Helles, the 29th Division landed, dispersed across five beaches that were designated S, V, W, X, and Y. At three beaches—S, X and Y—there was only light resistance. But at W Beach on the end of the Cape, the defenders were well entrenched, the landing area was mined, and the beach was protected with barbed wire, which in turn was covered by enfilading [flanking] machinegun fire. The British infantry were towed in rowboats to a point just short of the shore, where they were cut loose to glide onto the beach. The Turkish defenders held their fire until the attackers were ashore, and then opened with devastating effect. Despite heavy casualties, small groups got through; and the British now had a toehold on W Beach.

On V Beach, which was to be the location of the main assault, an old collier [coal-carrying vessel], the *River Clyde*, had been converted into a crude infantry landing craft to supplement the towed boats. Two thousand infantrymen were to disembark through doors cut in the bow of the ship. But V Beach was skillfully defended by a dug-in company of Turks with four machineguns. As the landing craft beached and small craft were positioned to make a ramp to the shoreline, the defenders' machineguns opened fire. While trying to leave the *River Clyde* and reach the beach, 70 percent of the first 1,000 troops became casualties. By mid-morning, the landing at V Beach had collapsed; the few survivors huddled inside the *River Clyde* or under the heights, which remained dominated by the Turkish defenders.

Failure

Although he could clearly observe the slaughter and stalemate on W and V Beaches, Hamilton chose not to influence the operation by ordering the shifting of troops between beaches. In his operational plan, he had placed all the Cape Helles landings under the 29th Division commander, and now scrupulously refrained from interfering with the latter's conduct of the battle. Unfortunately, the division commander was handicapped by poor communications, and therefore could not exercise effective control. Nor did the lower level commanders display the necessary initiative required to link up the beaches and advance to the high ground against an enemy who was outnumbered 6 to 1. Thus, when the British attacked on succeeding days, they made only minimal gains against the defenders, who had been promptly reinforced in the interim. Lady Luck had smiled briefly on the British, but the key commanders had missed the opportunity to court her.

By May 8, the Gallipoli beachheads had coalesced into trench lines. As in France, maneuver was no longer possible. The troops were exposed to the elements, particularly the hot sun, and were very short of supplies. Lack of transport made it difficult to evacuate the wounded. Disease, spread by flies and fleas, soon began to take its toll of Allied soldiers, and hospital rolls mounted.

The failure of the landings and the subsequent stalemate were blamed on the principal architects of the Dardanelles operation. The Cabinet fell, bringing about a change in the British Government. Admiral Fisher resigned in protest over the weakening of the Grand Fleet in order to reinforce the Gallipoli area: Lloyd George became Minister of Munitions. Winston Churchill, having been relegated to an insignificant Cabinet post, went to serve in the army on the Western Front.

Renewed Assault, Defeat, and Withdrawal

Lord Kitchener, who had originally opposed the entire Dardanelles operation, now became its principal supporter. He told the Government that the troops would suffer up to 50 percent casualties in any evacuation attempt. Since a continuation of the stalemate was out of the question, he recommended that Hamilton be reinforced and that a new attempt to secure Gallipoli be undertaken. As if to emphasize the importance of this new theater, the War Council was actually renamed the Dardanelles Committee. As far as the British were concerned, Gallipoli remained the principal theater of operations throughout the summer. Five new British divisions were sent to Gallipoli, and Hamilton's command received priority on ammunition and supplies.

Hamilton planned to use his new forces to make a landing at Suvla Bay. This landing was expected to outflank the Turkish defenders to the south and draw them away from ANZAC Beach, from which the British would launch the main effort. Hamilton also ordered supporting attacks at Cape Helles to pin down the enemy. The ANZAC objective was the Sidi Bahr Ridge, which dominated those Turkish forts and artillery sites that controlled the Narrows.

The assault resumed on August 6. Although the secondary attack at Cape Helles made only minor gains, it did manage to immobilize the Turkish defenders. The ANZAC main attack was launched at night and became disoriented; resumed the next morning, it failed to reach the heights of Sidi Bahr Ridge. To the north, the supporting attack at Suvla Bay missed yet another opportunity to make the Gallipoli

Campaign a success. There, the British IX Corps landing surprised the Turks and was virtually unopposed. Unfortunately, the corps consisted of new units that were poorly led, and, as a result, did not capitalize on the enemy weakness. After two days of ineffective efforts, Lieutenant General Sir Frederick Stopford, the IX Corps commander, was ordered to move inland and seize the high ground. By then, however, Sanders had used the intervening two days to transfer two Turkish divisions south to oppose Stopford and prevent movement from the Suvla Bay front.

Although operations on Gallipoli continued for the next few months, nothing broke the power of the defense. In October, Hamilton was relieved by General Charles Monro. In November, Kitchener traveled to Gallipoli to assess the situation firsthand. He advised the Government to end the campaign and withdraw the Allied forces.

The evacuations of the enclaves began in December and continued through January 9, 1916. Surprised and slow to react, the Turks did little to interfere with these professionally conducted evacuations. Contrary to dire predictions, not one life was lost, nor one soldier left behind. This was the only well executed British operation of a campaign that cost both sides more than 200,000 casualties each. The question of the lost opportunities in the Dardanelles and Gallipoli Campaigns has been debated endlessly. Without demeaning the dedicated and effective defensive actions fought by the Turkish forces, it is fair to say that the British lost several very real chances of achieving victory through the lack of realistic planning, the failure to coordinate properly, and the mistaken attempt to apply force gradually.

The War in the Trenches: Guns and Gas

John Ellis

British military historian John Ellis has authored histories of the machine gun and guerrilla warfare as well as various works on World War II. In this essay, excerpted from his *Eye-Deep in Hell: Trench Warfare in World War I*, Ellis graphically depicts the horror of war in the trenches for ordinary soldiers. Heavy artillery barrages and deadly poison gas attacks made the lives of both Allied and German soldiers hellish in the extreme.

Though the soldiers hardly ever saw their adversary, they were continually made aware of his presence, even in the 'quietest' of sectors. Any unit in the trenches would always sustain casualties, whether ordered to go over the top or simply to stay put. [British soldier] Charles Carrington relates that in one spell of three front-line tours, eighteen days in all, . . . [his] battalion lost one third of its strength. Fifty of these were battle casualties and the rest were men taken sick. During two months in the Neuve Chapelle sector, in late 1916, the 13th Yorkshire and Lancashire lost 255 men though they had been on the defensive throughout the whole period. [British] General Headquarters made an estimate of the expected wastage of men over a typical twelve-month period. In six months of a large-scale offensive they reckoned on losing 513,252 men and in six months of 'ordinary' trench warfare, 300,000. The most common cause of battle casualties when in the trenches was enemy artillery fire. On almost every day at least some shells would fall on the trenches, killing, maiming or burying a few unfortunates. Nor were villages behind the line immune, receiving their daily quota of heavier shells. . . . Worse, no troops were entirely safe from their own artillery. A French general has estimated, though it is difficult to imagine on what evidence, that some 75,000 Frenchmen became victims of their own guns. . . . The Germans, too, had their problems in this respect. One particularly incompetent unit, the 49th Field Artillery Regiment, was known as the 48½th because its shells persistently fell short.

In quantative terms alone the artillery war staggers the imagination. During the war the British fired off over 170 million rounds of all types—more than five million tons. The expenditure on ammunition was particularly awesome. In one day in September 1917 almost a million rounds were fired. During the first two weeks of the Third Battle of Ypres 4,283,550 rounds were fired. . . .

Barrages were not always so intensive. In a light barrage, usually in the afternoon, one could expect about half a dozen shells to land in the immediate vicinity every ten minutes. In a big bombardment, often the prelude to an enemy assault, howitzers supplemented the ordinary field guns, and twenty to thirty shells would be landing in a company sector every minute. For every three to four heavy explosive howitzer shells there would be one shrapnel to make sure the troops kept their heads down. Suddenly the barrage would lift and then, five minutes later, start up again. As the evening wore on the intervals would get shorter and shorter and the almost continuous noise grow to a crescendo.

Terror and Fear Under Fire

To experience this type of bombardment was a physical and mental torture. Writers have used all kinds of similes and metaphors to convey their experiences. If in a deep dugout a bombardment was just about bearable, Captain Greenwell found that 'the main impression gathered from the depths of a dugout is of a series of noises never heard before, though faintly resembling what I should imagine a tropical thunderstorm at sea to be like'. Later on he qualifies this rather romantic image 'Modern warfare . . . reduces men to shivering beasts. There isn't a man who can stand shell-fire of the modern kind without getting the blues'. The noise could be fearsome. 'It was as if on some overhead platform ten thousand carters were tipping loads of pointed steel bricks that burst in the air or on the ground, all with a fiendish, devastating ear-splitting roar that shook the nerves of the stoutest'. Lieutenant Chandos of the 2nd Grenadier Guards wrote: 'If you want the effect of an 8.5 [artillery shell] bursting near you, stand at the edge of the platform when an express is coming through at sixty miles per hour, and imagine that it runs into a siding about twenty yards away'. Yet, as the same officer wrote 'The sensation of this sort of artillery fire is not that of sound. You feel it in your ears more than hear it, unless it is only about one hundred yards away'. Many

Mutiny in the French Army, 1917

Historian Jere Clemens King indicates the futility of offensives with huge casualty rates that continued into the fourth year of the war. The French army experienced major mutinies within its ranks that, fortunately for the Allies, the Germans failed to exploit because they remained ignorant of the events.

The best-kept secret of the First World War was the mutiny which flared in the French army in May and June, 1917. The seemingly endless prolongation of the war threatened to turn France into a charnel house [a building where corpses are deposited]. The foolhardy and disastrous campaign of Chemin des Dames, which was undertaken in April, 1917, by General Robert Nivelle, Joffre's successor, at last pushed the heroic but jaded army to the brink of revolt. Enormous casualties suffered by the Second Colonial Infantry Division in its attacks upon prepared positions at Heurtebise goaded the survivors into insurrection on May 3. Signs were posted on the walls of their billets proclaiming: "Down with the war! Death to those who are responsible!"

Within several weeks mutiny had tainted seventy-five regiments of infantry, twenty-three battalions of chasseurs, and other soldiers took up this theme of the barrage being more than mere sound, of a noise that was so continuous and so deafening that it was almost tangible. [French soldier and author] Henri Barbusse wrote:

> A diabolical uproar surrounds us. We are conscious of a sustained crescendo, an incessant multiplication of the universal frenzy; a hurricane of hoarse and hollow banging of raging clamour, of piercing and beast-like screams, fastens furiously with tatters of smoke upon the earth where we are buried up to our necks, and the wind of the shells seems to set it heaving and pitching.

An NCO [noncommissioned officer] of the 22nd Manches-

---

twelve regiments of artillery. Especially susceptible to disaffection were divisions scattered through the four armies which had been the most brutally repulsed in Nivelle's offensive. Demoralized troops openly defied their officers, drunkenly sang the "Internationale [a socialist anthem]," chanted demands for furloughs, discharged their rifles into the air, and committed acts of vandalism. By June no less than fifty-four divisions—half the divisions of the French army—were openly insubordinate. The mutiny spread until only two of twelve divisions in Champagne were considered reliable, and no division between Soisson and Paris could be trusted to obey orders. The outbreaks generally occurred when troops on leave were ordered back to the trenches; when troops were forced to go through tiresome, pointless "busy work" in repetitious training maneuvers; when furloughs were delayed; or when billets were intolerable or the food inedible. Under such provocations the mutineers gathered around their spokesmen, who were generally noncommissioned officers who harangued them. The troops were not entirely lacking in respect for their lieutenants, but they ignored their orders.

Jere Clemens King, ed., *The First World War*. New York: Walker, 1972, pp. 258–59.

ter Rifles described the bombardment on the first day of the Battle of the Somme:

> The sound was different, not only in magnitude but in quality, from anything known to me. It was not a succession of explosions or a continuous roar; I, at least, never heard either a gun or a bursting shell. It was not a noise, it was a symphony. And it did not move. It hung over us. It seemed as though the air were full of vast and agonised passion, bursting now with groans and sighs, now into shrill screaming and pitiful whimpering, shuddering beneath terrible blows, torn by unearthly whips, vibrating with the solemn pulses of enormous wings. And the supernatural tumult did not pass in this direction or in that. It did not begin, intensify, decline and end. It was poised in the air, a stationary panorama of sound, a condition of the atmosphere, not the creation of man.

A Canadian private recalled similar sensations during the barrage that preceded the assault on Vimy Ridge: 'One's whole body seemed to be in a mad macabre dance . . . I felt that if I lifted a finger I should touch a solid ceiling of sound, it now had the attribute of solidity'.

But much worse than the purely physical effect of the noise was the effect on the nerves, the feeling of powerlessness. . . . A Frenchman at Verdun wrote that the battle was so 'terrible . . . because man is fighting against material, with the sensation of striking out at empty air'. A German private cursed 'the torture of having to lie powerless and defenceless in the middle of an artillery battle'. It became difficult to hang on to one's sanity. Lance-Corporal Hearn of the Durham Light Infantry dreaded the 'horrible nightmare of bursting shells. Sometimes the terrible noise makes me nearly mad, and it requires a great effort to keep cool, calm and collected'. A French infantry sergeant gave a description of the mental anguish:

> When one heard the whistle in the distance, one's whole body continued to resist the too excessively potent vibrations of the explosion, and at each repetition it was a new attack, a new fa-

tigue, a new suffering. Under this regime, the most solid nerves cannot resist for long; the moment arrives where the blood rises to the head, where fever burns the body and where the nerves, exhausted, become incapable of reacting. It is as if one were tied tight to a post and threatened by a fellow swinging a sledgehammer. Now the hammer is swung back for the blow, now it whirls forward, till, just missing your skull, it sends the splinters flying from the post once more. This is exactly what it feels like to be exposed to heavy shelling.

Men gradually lost control of themselves as the strain mounted. They began to moan to themselves and whimper like helpless animals. An English doctor wrote: 'I remember . . . a private in one of the four crack French corps who was at Douaumont in the Verdun battle told his parents that by the ninth day [of the barrage] almost every soldier was crying'. In some cases, at the end of a heavy bombardment, when the enemy finally began to push forward, they would find their opponents apparently asleep in the trenches, comatose, utterly and totally exhausted by the strain. Even for those who remained partially alert, the end of a bombardment, or a temporary lull, did not lessen the sense of horror. A variety of sounds might be heard in the sudden quiet; the ghostly wail of a shell's screw-cap as it whizzed through the air after an explosion, the plaintive moaning of the men, the buzzing of great swarms of flies, disturbed by the bombardment, the high-pitched screaming of the rats, and, sublime absurdity, the singing of the birds.

Experiencing Chemical Warfare

One particularly horrible type of shell were those that released gas. It was also discharged from cylinders, though this made the wind direction a particularly crucial consideration. Gas was first used at the Second Battle of Ypres on 22 April 1915, and the victims were a regiment of French colonial troops, who panicked completely, throwing down their rifles and fleeing to the rear. After this both sides began to use gas and experimented with different types. At first chlorine gas was the most common but this was later superseded by mustard gas, the cause of the most casualties. In the American Army out of nearly 58,000 gas casualties, 26,828 were known to have been due to mustard gas. Its smell belied its effect. One 'doughboy' likened it to a rich bon-bon filled with perfumed soap. Chlorine gas, on the other hand, was rather like a mixture of pineapple and pepper, whereas phosgene had more the stench of a barrel of rotten fish. But each had its own ghastly effects. The chlorine gases led to a slow death by asphyxiation [suffocation], and even the hopeless cases often took days to die, remaining conscious to within five minutes of the end. 'There, sitting on the bed, fighting for breath, his lips plum-coloured, his hue leaden, was a magnificent young Canadian past all hope in the asphyxia of chlorine. . . . I shall never forget the look in his eyes as he turned to me and gasped: "I can't die! Is it possible that nothing can be done for me?" ' Wilfred Owen of the Manchester Regiment, the poet, wrote of a man exposed to phosgene gas:

> The white eyes writhing in his face,
> His hanging face, like a devil's sick of sin;
> If you could hear, at every holt, the blood
> Come gargling from the froth-corrupted lungs,
> Obscene as cancer, bitter as the cud
> Of vile, incurable sores on innocent tongues.

With mustard gas the effects did not become apparent for up to twelve hours. But then it began to rot the body, within and without. The skin blistered, the eyes became extremely painful and nausea and vomiting began. Worse, the gas attacked the bronchial tubes, stripping off the mucous membrane. The pain was almost beyond endurance and most cases had to be strapped to their beds. Death took up to four or five weeks. A nurse wrote:

> I wish those people who write so glibly about this being a holy war and the orators who talk so much about going on no matter how long the war lasts and what it may mean, could see a case—to say nothing of ten cases—of mustard gas in its early stages—could see the poor things burnt and blistered all

over with great mustard-coloured suppurating [pus-filled] blisters, with blind eyes . . . all sticky and stuck together, and always fighting for breath, with voices a mere whisper, saying that their throats are closing and they know they will choke.

Some sort of precaution was available almost immediately after the first gas attack. One division sent a sanitary officer hot-foot to Paris to commandeer all the ladies' veiling he could find. The first anti-gas drill consisted of men running round in circles, holding noses and gasping between their teeth . . . [compresses] soaked in hyposulphite and wrapped in ladies' veils. Within sixty hours 98,000 pads of cotton waste in muslin containers were available at the front, two million having been provided at the end of the first month. Another early expedient was to clasp pads soaked in urine to one's nose and mouth. Unpleasant an experience as this was the ammonia in the urine did help to neutralise the chlorine. Later in the year a larger block gauze pad was used. Tied with tapes it had an extra flap to cover the eyes. Troops were provided with a bottle of hyposulphite solution in which to soak the pad. The next expedient was a grey flannel hood with mica eye-pieces, impregnated with phenol. After this there followed two types of tube-helmet, so called, which were the same as the hood with the addition of a rubber-tipped metal tube, to be held between the teeth for exhalation, and better fitting eye-pieces. From late 1917, the famous box respirator replaced all these devices and was soon standard issue for troops at the front. All in all, some twenty-seven million gas-masks of various types were manufactured in Britain during the war.

Chapter 3

Russian Revolution, American Intervention, and German Defeat, 1917–1918

Turning|Points

IN WORLD HISTORY

Russia Leaves the War: Revolution

Martin Gilbert

In the following viewpoint, historian Martin Gilbert describes how czarist Russia's war effort collapsed during the revolution of 1917. Military blows by the Germans and internal revolution brought the Bolshevik Party (later, Communist Party) to power. As Gilbert explains, the Provisional Government of Aleksandr Kerensky tried but failed to revitalize Russia's commitment to the Allied war effort; Russia's collapse was too far advanced for this renewal of warfare to succeed. The Bolsheviks quickly sued for peace with Germany in order to focus on the consolidation of power within Russia. As Gilbert notes, this set the stage for Germany to shift large forces westward for the final 1918 offensive on the western front. Martin Gilbert, a prolific and respected scholar of twentieth-century Europe, has written significant studies of both world wars.

The Entente Powers met in Petrograd in January 1917 to discuss new offensives. They had cause for optimism. If a successful Anglo-French attack could be launched in the west, carefully combined with another Russian offensive, if Italy could put pressure on Austria and if France could drive the enemy troops from Macedonia [in the Balkans], the war might end in 1917.

In Russia itself the murder of the monk Rasputin on 30 December 1916 suggested that the pernicious influence at court of this shadowy figure was to be followed by a more attractive court life. But social discontent in Russia went deeper than dislike of court intrigues. Factory conditions were bad and wages were low. Strikes involving half a million workers broke out in 1915. Over a million workers struck in 1916. There was no improvement in the new year: strikes in January and February 1917 were widespread and violence rose to the surface when the government arrested the [working-class] factory representatives who sat on the Central War Industries Committee.

Soldiers coming home on leave swelled the ranks of the discontented. One general wrote in his diary on 10 March: "I am firmly convinced that the common soldier today wants only one thing—food and peace, because he is tired of war." Two days earlier Nicholas II returned to his headquarters at Moghilev and wrote to his wife: "I greatly miss my half-hourly game of patience [solitaire] every evening. I shall take up dominoes again in my spare time."

Overthrow of the Czarist Regime

These domestic thoughts were disturbed by news of street demonstrations in Petrograd. Extreme socialists and parliamentary liberals were cooperating to demand reform. Soldiers, called out to halt the demonstrations, had first fired on the crowds, killing indiscriminately, then fraternized with the marchers. Imperial authority could not be exerted; Petrograd was in the hands of revolutionaries.

The aim of the demonstrators was to end the autocratic rule of the Tsar. The Duma, or Russian parliament, had for many years sought greater control over the administration. At times Nicholas had heeded its liberal recommendations; at times he had ignored them. Once the war began the Duma was deprived of its control of financial affairs. But it continued to sit and to criticize the conduct of the war. When revolution came to Petrograd the Duma sought to lead it. When dissolved by the Tsar it refused to disperse. It urged Nicholas to abdicate but he decided to return to Petrograd and reassert his authority. At midnight on 11 March he entered his train. For six hours no movement was possible as the line was blocked. The line was cleared by morning and the train moved on, but in the afternoon it stopped again. It was said that a bridge was damaged. Nicholas suggested an alternative route. But the "authorities" refused to allow him to proceed. Nicholas had ceased to be the sole and undisputed source of power. Others were exercising authority. Others were saying where or where not the autocrat could go.

A deputation from the Duma reached Nicholas and demanded his abdication. On 15 March he agreed. Tsardom was dead; the Provisional Government ruled. At its side the socialist Council of Workers' and Soldiers' Deputies, a "parliament" of left-wing parties known as the "Soviet," made it clear that the wishes of the masses must be taken into account in all governmental decisions. The Soviet set up its own committees, passed its own resolutions, and even took up rooms in the Duma building.

Kerensky Tries to Revive the War Effort

The War Minister of the Provisional Government was Alexander Kerensky. He believed that Russia could still play its part in the defeat of the Central Powers. He was convinced that he could revive the shaken morale of the army and re-create the discipline which had been lost during the excitement of revolution. He looked forward to the day when the Provisional Government would become permanent, liberal, and respected.

On 4 June Kerensky appointed [Aleksei] Brusilov as commander-in-chief of the Russian armies. The more conservative officers looked askance [with disapproval] at their colleague's acceptance of command under a republican regime. Kerensky himself toured the front, endeavoring to create enthusiasm for the continuance of the war. Appealing to the radical sentiments of the troops, he said: "Our army under the monarchy accomplished heroic deeds; will it be a flock of sheep under a republic?" His speeches created some enthusiasm on the spot. The appearance of a Minister was a rare occurrence. But once he returned to Petrograd the men lapsed into lethargy.

Britain and France were delighted that the new Russia was to continue to fight. Many of Britain's liberals and

France's republicans had felt uneasy with an autocrat as an ally. They welcomed the support of a democratic Russia. They were not particularly worried by the arrival in Petrograd of Vladimir Lenin, the Social Democrat leader who had spent most of the war in Switzerland. Lenin rallied the Bolshevik [hard-line revolutionary] element in the Soviet to his policy of "No support for the Provisional Government." He spoke of the day when the Soviet would come to power, unfettered by a liberal regime. But the Bolsheviks were only a minority in the Soviet. There was no evidence that they could succeed in dominating that body and no chance that the other parties in the Soviet might agree to overthrow the Provisional Government. When, at the April Congress of the Soviet, Lenin demanded a further revolution, the overthrow of the Provisional Government, and the ending of the war, he was treated as a crank by the other socialists. At the

A Somber 1990s View of the Birth of Russian Communism

The events of the Communist seizure of power in Russia in November 1917 have long been controversial among scholars. Here British historian Orlando Figes, a specialist on modern Russia, offers a critical assessment of the revolutionaries. His viewpoint may reflect the dismal image of communism so common in the post-Soviet 1990s.

When the Bolsheviks took control of the Winter Palace [the Tsar's former residence], they discovered one of the largest wine cellars ever known. During the following days tens of thousands of antique bottles disappeared from the vaults. The Bolshevik workers and soldiers were helping themselves to the Château d'Yquem 1847, the last Tsar's favourite vintage, and selling off the vodka to the crowds outside. The drunken mobs went on the rampage. The Winter Palace was badly vandalized. Shops and liquor stores were looted. Sailors and soldiers went around the well-to-do districts robbing apartments and killing people for sport. Anyone well dressed was an obvious target. . . .

All this suggests that the Bolshevik insurrection was not so

Soviet's April Congress only 105 of the 1,090 delegates were Bolshevik supporters of this strange extremist.

On 1 July Kerensky launched his summer offensive. By a successful advance he hoped to raise enthusiasm for the Provisional Government at home and support for it abroad. But on [General Max] Hoffman's insistence Ludendorff transferred four divisions by train from the western front. At one point the Russians advanced sixty miles, only to be met by the reserves hurried from the west. The Kerensky offensive was forced back, becoming first a defensive action, then a rout. On 1 September the Germans entered Riga. The Russians fled at their approach. Nine thousand, finding the Germans close behind them, surrendered. Russian morale was destroyed. Kerensky dismissed Brusilov, but it was not enough. The war had lost its appeal. No new commander could rally the disrupted, weary troops.

much the culmination of a social revolution. . . . It was more the result of the degeneration of the urban revolution, and in particular of the workers' movement, as an organized and constructive force, with vandalism, crime, generalized violence and drunken looting as the main expressions of this social breakdown. . . . The participants in this destructive violence were not the organized 'working class' but the victims of the breakdown of that class and of the devastation of the war years: the growing army of the urban unemployed; the refugees from the occupied regions, soldiers and sailors, who congregated in the cities; bandits and criminals released from the jails; and the unskilled labourers from the countryside who had always been the most prone to outbursts of anarchic violence in the cities. These were the semi-peasant types whom [Russian writer Maxim] Gorky had blamed for the urban violence in the spring [of 1917] and to whose support he had ascribed the rising fortunes of the Bolsheviks.

Orlando Figes, *A People's Tragedy: A History of the Russian Revolution.* New York: Viking Penguin, 1997, pp. 494–95.

Russian Military Collapse and Bolshevik Seizure of Power

On 29 July Kerensky had convened an emergency Council of War. General [Anton] Denikin, commander of the western front, explained why the offensive had collapsed: "The officers are in a terrible position. They are insulted, beaten, murdered." Discipline had entirely collapsed. The Soviet had asserted the rights of the common soldier and encouraged disobedience. The death penalty for disobedience and desertion (abolished during the March revolution) was revived. But few could be found to accuse, to condemn, or to inflict punishment upon disobedient soldiers. On 8 September over 19,000 deserters were captured. How could they be tried? How could they be shot? It was almost impossible to find enough troops to guard them; punishment was out of the question.

The Kerensky offensive destroyed what faith was left in Russia in the usefulness of further war. Lenin's Bolsheviks gained innumerable adherents with a program of "immediate peace." On 7 November, after careful planning and with brilliant leadership, the Bolsheviks seized power. Kerensky fled the capital flying an American flag on his car to avoid capture.

Lenin fulfilled his promise to bring the war to an end on coming to power. Certainly any prolongation of the war was politically impossible. On 8 November Lenin issued his "Declaration of Peace," demanding "A just and democratic peace for which the great majority of wearied, tormented, and war-exhausted toilers and laboring classes of all belligerent countries are thirsting, a peace which the Russian workers and peasants have so loudly and insistently demanded since the overthrow of the Tsar's monarchy, such a peace the Government considers to be an immediate peace without annexations (i.e., without the seizure of foreign territory and the forcible annexation of foreign nationalities) and without indemnities.

"The Russian Government proposes to all warring peoples that this kind of peace be concluded at once."

On 16 December the Germans agreed to an armistice

[with the new Bolshevik government]. Britain and France were powerless to reverse Lenin's decision. In vain they referred to a Tsarist pledge that none of the Entente Powers would make a separate peace. In vain they encouraged the anti-Bolshevik Russians to overthrow Lenin and his peace party. In vain they themselves intervened, in an attempt to create an Entente force in the east that would continue to harass the Germans. But they could not force Russia to go back to war.

The Bolsheviks negotiated peace with Germany. The Treaty of Brest-Litovsk was signed on 3 March 1918. The Russians conceded vast territories to the Germans and released the German armies in the east for further battles in the west. In return they were themselves freed from the need to pay indemnities to the Germans. Prisoners of war were exchanged. The treaty fell harshly on Russia but left Lenin free to consolidate his new government. It fell more harshly on Britain and France, in the form of a sudden and successful German offensive in the west. But the Great War in the east was ended.

President Wilson's Decision for War

Richard Hofstadter

Pulitzer Prize–winning historian Richard Hofstadter (1916–1970) here examines the hard choices facing President Woodrow Wilson between his reelection in November 1916 and his appeal for a U.S. declaration of war in April 1917. Hofstadter explains how Wilson moved from neutrality and hopes for what he called "peace without victory" (based on U.S. mediation of the war) to full-scale intervention on the side of the Allies in April 1917. Wilson's struggle to avoid war, Hofstadter concludes, was undermined by his own administration's previous nonneutral acts, especially its heavy economic commitment to the Allies.

Like every president before him, [Democratic president Woodrow] Wilson hoped and worked for re-election. The 1916 campaign slogan: "He kept us out of war," was not of his devising; in fact, it frightened him. He seems to have developed a rather exaggerated sense of his powerlessness to live up to such a commitment. "I can't keep the country out of war," he complained to Josephus Daniels. "They talk of me as though I were a god. Any little German lieutenant can put us into the war at any time by some calculated outrage." Since the Republican Party was no longer split, the election was extremely close, but Wilson ran well ahead of the rest of the Democratic ticket. Now secure in office for another four years, with the submarine controversy in temporary abeyance [suspension], and the conflict with Britain at a relatively high pitch, he turned increasingly toward neutrality.

War seems never to have been farther from his mind than in the winter of 1916–17. Although he had not definitely ruled out the possibility of entering the war, it seems—so far as it is possible to understand him—that he had not reconciled himself to going in if he could see any other recourse consistent with his main objectives.

"Peace Without Victory" Falters

Just before Christmas 1916 Wilson sent a note to both belligerents calling upon them to state their peace terms, with the impartial observation that "the objects which the statemen of the belligerents on both sides have in mind in this war are virtually the same, as stated in general terms to their own people and to the world." On January 22, 1917, he made an address before the Senate in which he analyzed the consequences of a crushing defeat of either side and declared that a lasting peace must be a "peace without victory."

> Victory would mean peace forced upon the loser, a victor's terms imposed upon the vanquished. It would be accepted in humiliation, under duress, at an intolerable sacrifice, and would leave a sting, a resentment, a bitter memory upon which terms of peace would rest, not permanently, but only as upon quicksand. Only a peace between equals can last.

The appeal for terms and the call for "peace without victory" were bitterly resented by the Allies, who had been led to feel that the United States was thoroughly committed to them. [Presidential adviser] Colonel [Edward M.] House complained in his diary that the President had lost his "punch," that things were drifting aimlessly, that Wilson now stood for "peace at any price." When he once again brought up the matter of preparedness for war, Wilson said flatly: "There will be no war."

At this juncture notice was received from the German government that submarine warfare would be resumed—and in an unrestricted form, directed against neutral as well as belligerent shipping. In one instant Wilson reaped the whirlwind of unneutrality that he had sown in the first two years of the war. For the Germans, realizing that the United

States was already heavily engaged against them with its productive capacity, and assuming that she [the U.S.] could not otherwise intervene effectively before a fatal blow could be struck against the Allies, were calculating on American entrance into the war.

When [Press Secretary Joseph] Tumulty brought to Wilson the Associated Press bulletin bearing the news of Germany's decision, the President turned gray and said in quiet

Antiwar Dissent, 1917

Woodrow Wilson's call for war against Germany in April 1917 had strong support in Congress and the country, but also generated significant dissent. In the following speech of April 4, 1917, liberal Republican senator George Norris of Nebraska attacks the reasoning of the Wilson administration and American interventionists. Norris believed these proponents of war were tools of armament and banking interests.

We are taking a step to-day that is fraught with untold danger. We are going into war upon the command of gold. We are going to run the risk of sacrificing millions of our countrymen's lives in order that other countrymen may coin their lifeblood into money. And even if we do not cross the Atlantic and go into the trenches, we are going to pile up a debt that the toiling masses that shall come many generations after us will have to pay. Unborn millions will bend their backs in toil in order to pay for the terrible step we are now about to take. We are about to do the bidding of wealth's terrible mandate. By our act we will make millions of our countrymen suffer, and the consequences of it may well be that millions of our brethren must shed their lifeblood, millions of broken-hearted women must weep, millions of children must suffer with cold, and millions of babes must die from hunger, and all because we want to preserve the commercial right of American citizens to deliver munitions of war to belligerent nations.

John Braeman, ed., *Wilson*. Englewood Cliffs, NJ: Prentice-Hall, 1972, pp. 131–32.

tones: "This means war. The break that we have tried to prevent now seems inevitable." Still Wilson waited, as though hoping for some miraculous turn in events that would relieve him of any further decision. In the meantime the plight of the Allies was pressed upon him. Both belligerents were badly strained, in fact, but it was the case of the Allies that he knew. Russia had undergone the March [1917] revolution, and her future effectiveness as an ally was extremely doubtful. Morale in the French army was desperately low. ("If France should cave in before Germany," House warned, "it would be a calamity beyond reckoning.") The submarine war would soon constitute a dire threat to England's supply line and bring her to the brink of starvation. Not least, the Allies, their credit facilities exhausted, were facing an economic collapse from which it seemed that nothing short of American participation could save them. This situation [U.S. Ambassador to Britain Walter Hines] Page outlined in his famous cablegram to Wilson of March 5: "Perhaps our going to war is the only way in which our preeminent trade position can be maintained and a panic averted. The submarine has added the last item to the danger of a financial world crash." Should Germany win, it appeared, the United States would have the hatred of both victors and vanquished, its influence on the future of Europe and on world peace would be at a minimum, and all the gains of recent years would be lost in an armaments race. Finally, public opinion at home, newly aroused by the revelation of . . . [German foreign minister Alfred] Zimmermann's note, proposing an alliance of Germany, Mexico, and Japan and the annexation of Texas, New Mexico, and Arizona to Mexico, was well prepared for participation. Wilson could not face the consequences, as he saw them, of *not* going to war.

An Agonizing Choice for War

Still he delayed. Even after German attacks on American ships had begun, [Secretary of State Robert] Lansing came away from him feeling "that he was resisting the irresistible logic of events." At the end of March, House came to Washington and found him repeating desperately: "What else can I do? Is there anything else I can do?" He told his friend that he did not consider himself fit to be President under wartime conditions. Frank Cobb, of the New York *World*, one of his best friends among the journalists, visiting the sleepless President on the night of April 1, the eve of his war message to Congress, found him still unresolved. Again he asked: "What else can I do? Is there anything else I can do?" Should Germany be defeated, he feared, there would be a dictated peace. There would be no bystanders left with enough power to moderate the terms. "There won't be any peace standards left to work with." As Cobb remembered it:

> W.W. was uncanny that night. He had the whole panorama in his mind. . . .

> He began to talk about the consequences to the United States. He had no illusions about the fashion in which we were likely to fight the war.

> He said when a war got going it was just war and there weren't two kinds of it. It required illiberalism at home to reinforce the men at the front. We couldn't fight Germany and maintain the ideals of Government that all thinking men shared. He said we would try it but it would be too much for us.

> "Once lead this people into war," he said "and they'll forget there ever was such a thing as tolerance. To fight you must be brutal and ruthless, and the spirit of ruthless brutality will enter into the very fibre of our national life, infecting Congress, the courts, the policeman on the beat, the man in the street." . . .

> He thought the Constitution would not survive it; that free speech and the right of assembly would go. He said a nation couldn't put its strength into a war and keep its head level; it had never been done.

> "If there is any alternative, for God's sake, let's take it," he exclaimed.

But Wilson's war message lay on his desk as he spoke to Cobb, and on the following day he read it to Congress. "It is a fearful thing," he confessed, "to lead this great, peaceful people into war, into the most terrible and disastrous of all wars. . . ." But "the right is more precious than peace." Without rancor, without a single selfish interest, the United States would fight for the principles she had always cherished—"for democracy, for the right of those who submit to authority to have a voice in their own Governments, for the rights and liberties of small nations, for a universal dominion of right by such a concert of free peoples as shall bring peace and safety to all nations and make the world itself at last free."

Woodrow Wilson had changed his means before, but in accepting war he was forced for the first time to turn his back upon his deepest values. The man who had said that peace is the healing and elevating influence of the world was now pledged to use "Force, Force to the utmost, Force without stint or limit." Having given the nation into the hands of a power in which he did not believe, he was now driven more desperately than ever in his life to justify himself, and the rest of his public career became a quest for self-vindication. Nothing less than the final victory of the forces of democracy and peace could wash away his sense of defeat—and Wilson was conscious of defeat in the very hour in which he delivered his ringing war message in tones of such confident righteousness. Returning from the Capitol with the applause of Congress and the people still echoing in his ears, he turned to Tumulty and said: "My message today was a message of death for our young men. How strange it seems to applaud that."

The Failure of Germany's Submarine Gamble

Trevor Wilson

The struggle for naval supremacy was a vital aspect of World War I. Surface warfare between rival battleship fleets proved inconclusive. The greatest threat to Britain's survival and perhaps the Allied cause was the German submarine campaign, especially the unrestricted U-boat attacks launched after February 1, 1917. As Australian historian Trevor Wilson explains here, the integrity of Britain's ocean lifeline to its armies and foreign suppliers was a life-or-death matter for the island nation. Wilson describes the initial German successes with unrestrained submarine warfare against Allied and neutral merchant ships. Aided by the American navy, however, the British finally developed an effective antisubmarine strategy, the convoy system, which pooled merchant ships into compact fleets protected by destroyer escorts.

I

In January 1917 . . . the rulers of Germany determined that Britain should now become the adversary destined for swift elimination. This would not be done on land, given Britain's continued strength in manpower and in industrial resources. Instead advantage would be taken of Britain's acute vulnerability to naval blockade. Germany's enlarged submarine force would be employed to sink a large proportion of the merchant shipping approaching and leaving Britain's shores. This would have a double effect. Neutral vessels would soon refuse to run the U-boat gauntlet and so would cease trading with Britain altogether. And British shipping would become so depleted

Excerpted from *The Myriad Faces of War: Britain and the Great War, 1914–1918*, by Trevor Wilson. Copyright © 1986 by Trevor Wilson. Used by permission of Polity Press.

that it could no longer adequately supply the nation's civilian population, war machine, and expeditions abroad. The calculation was that the destruction of 600,000 tons of British shipping a month, combined with the total withdrawal of neutral shipping, would force Britain to sue for peace within six months.

The German plan depended on the adoption of unlimited submarine warfare. That is, every merchant ship of Allied or neutral origin, within a large area of sea, would be considered fair game. And no regard was to be had for the safety of their passengers and crews. Attacks would be carried out without warning and, where appropriate, from beneath the sea.

Germany's High-Risk U-Boat Campaign

Developments in the submarine war had, in any case, been pointing the Germans in this direction. The new U-boats that Germany was building had a considerably increased torpedo capacity, thus facilitating many more submerged attacks. And Britain's growing practice of arming its merchant ships . . . was rendering submarine attacks on the surface both more perilous and less rewarding. As long as the U-boat could strike from beneath the sea, the weapons of merchantmen . . . held no dangers.

Technical evolution, then, was directing German thinking towards the unrestricted use of the U-boat. What the country's rulers contributed was the calculation that the consequent sinking of neutral vessels would not be an unfortunate corollary [result]. Rather, it would be the most lucrative part of the whole campaign. For whereas attacks on British shipping would deprive Britain only of that proportion of its merchant fleet that actually went to the bottom, the campaign against neutrals would accomplish far more. It would drive all neutral shipping from Britain's shores.

Germany's leaders, of course, were not under the illusion that in adopting this course they had nothing to lose. The United States would certainly become a belligerent. President Wilson might be prepared to retreat from his stand on the *Lusitania* and kindred incidents, whereby he had refused to tolerate the sinking even of Allied passenger ships if American lives were thereby endangered. But he would never back down so far as to tolerate the course that was now being contemplated: the indiscriminate sinking of American-owned and -manned merchant ships. Nevertheless, the Kaiser's advisers calculated that this would not matter greatly. In their view, American industry and raw materials were already at the disposal of the Allies. So the only further contribution the United States could make was in manpower. But the USA had for the moment no army deserving consideration. Hence its intervention would signify [matter] only if the war went on long enough for the Americans to raise and train an army that they could then transport to Europe. If all went according to German plans, this would never happen. The U-boat campaign would ensure that the war ended much earlier. And anyway, by the time the USA possessed a considerable army, the shipping required to carry it to the battlefield would have ceased to exist.

II

Events from 1 February 1917 to the end of July would test the validity of the calculation that the U-boat could force Britain to sue for peace within six months. Two things rapidly became evident. The first was that Germany could now put to sea considerably more submarines than at any previous time. The second was that the U-boats, employing unrestricted methods, were capable of exacting a greater toll than at any earlier stage of the war. . . .

The British Besieged

[The] effectiveness [of the U-boats] rapidly became apparent. In January 1917, the last month of the restricted campaign, Britain had lost 49 merchant ships to enemy action, and its allies and neutrals 122. This made a total of 171 ships sunk, constituting a tonnage of about one-third of 1 million. . . . In February and March, with the opening of the unrestricted campaign, the total of ships destroyed rose dramatically—by not much short of 100 per cent. Britain lost 105 merchant ships in February and 127 in March, its allies and neutrals 129 in the former month and 154 in the latter. Total tonnage sunk was in excess of 500,000 in February and 600,000 in March.

Even these losses paled by comparison with the events of April, when the destruction of merchant shipping became a holocaust: 169 British vessels and 204 of other nationalities went to the bottom, constituting a total of 870,000 tons. This meant that in the third month of the campaign one-quarter of merchant ships leaving Britain's shores would never complete the round trip. The cargoes lost in consequence were heavy enough. But far worse was the depletion of vessels capable of carrying future cargoes.

Nor did the cost of the U-boat campaign to Britain end there. In April a further one-third of 1 million tons of world shipping was damaged by German action, choking the repair yards and ensuring a considerable delay before these vessels could be got back to sea. Again, the known proximity of U-boats was reducing the effectiveness of undamaged ships by causing them to shelter in harbour or to adopt evasive routing. Already from January the toll exacted by submarines in the Mediterranean was forcing merchantmen from the Far East to take the longer journey around South Africa. And some neutral shippers were refusing to run the U-boat gauntlet, so that in April the volume of neutral vessels calling at Allied ports fell to one-quarter.

In the next three months the number of U-boats at sea declined somewhat, as did their toll of victims, although hardly significantly. Total losses (British, Allied, and neutral) in this period were as follows: in May 287 ships of 600,000 tons; in June 290 ships of over 680,000 tons; and in July 227 ships of 547,000 tons. Hence in the half-year that the rulers of Germany had allowed themselves, they had destroyed 3.75 million tons of world shipping, had reduced the efficiency and so the carrying capacity of much that survived, and had persuaded a significant (although not constant) body of neutrals to shun Britain's shores. No one could doubt that it was an imposing—and, for Britain, deeply threatening—accomplishment. . . .

III
Britain Fights On, America Joins In

By mid-1917, therefore, there was no doubt that Germany's submarine offensive had achieved considerable success. But something else was not in doubt. This success had proved less than decisive.

Britain at the end of July 1917 was not suing for peace. Though its food and oil supplies were not secure, neither its civilian population nor its war industries were facing serious deprivation. As for British military operations, they were far from running down for want of supplies. On the contrary, the BEF [British Expeditionary Force] was on the point of launching a massive new offensive . . . [on the Western Front]. . . .

In every respect German calculations regarding the U-boat war were proving overoptimistic. Only in one of the designated six months (April) did the sinking of British merchant shipping approach the required total of 600,000 tons. As for neutral shippers, far from abandoning Britain's shores altogether, most of them were soon being prevailed upon—by '[d]iplomatic skill, hard bargaining and pressure exerted in various other ways'—to resume their service. So by July the volume of foreign ships supplying Britain was only 20 per cent below normal. And it was transpiring that Britain was better equipped to survive shipping losses than had been predicted. It was able to prune extravagances in military shipping, further restrict imports to absolute necessities, employ internal transport in place of coastal shipping, enhance the efficiency of its ports, and economize on sea miles. Thus the day of Britain's collapse was certain to be delayed well beyond its enemies' anticipation.

In this last matter of economizing on sea miles, the British authorities were greatly aided by what, for the Germans, was the supreme negative effect of the submarine campaign: the USA's entry into the war.

This development was ironical. During the second half of 1916 a decided deterioration had occurred in Anglo-American relations. Britain had stepped up its economic warfare against Germany in ways that deeply offended President Wilson. For example, the British authorities had issued a 'blacklist' of US and Latin American firms with which, on account of pro-enemy affiliations, British subjects were forbidden to deal. Moreover, Wilson was not pleased to discover, as he approached the presidential election late in 1916, that the British did not intend to call upon him to mediate between the warring powers. The ill-feeling engendered by these events was brought home powerfully to Walter Hines Page, the deeply Anglophile [pro-British] American Ambassador in London. In August and September 1916 Page was in Washington to confer on the situation. Five weeks passed before he was accorded a private interview with the President, and what transpired there gave him no joy. Page wrote in his diary: 'The P[resident] said to me that when the war began he and all the men he met were in hearty sympathy with the Allies; but that now the sentiment toward England had greatly changed. He saw no one who was not vexed and irritated at the arbitrary English course.

There was little likelihood that this cooling in Anglo-American relations would ever have led to actual conflict. But there was at least a possibility that the US Government would refuse clearance to British ships discriminating against the goods of the blacklisted firms. And, what was far more serious, by the beginning of 1917 Britain was ceasing to be capable of purchasing goods from American suppliers. The excellent credit position with which Britain had entered the war *vis-à-vis* the USA was now at an end, thanks to the vast purchases Britain had been making not only on its own behalf but also on that of its allies. On 5 March 1917 Walter Hines Page, now returned to London, sent his Government an urgent telegram. It warned that Britain had absolutely reached the end of its resources for securing credit in the USA, and that unless the US Government was prepared to guarantee a large loan, or itself supply the credit, the Allied war trade with the USA would cease.

By the time Page sent this message Wilson had already responded to the Kaiser's declaration of unrestricted submarine warfare by severing diplomatic relations with Germany. But the President hoped that this would be sufficient: that the Germans would realize he meant business and would back down. In short order British diligence in securing and deciphering German diplomatic messages helped to disillusion him. On 25 February the Foreign Office passed on to him the contents of the Zimmermann telegram. In it the German Foreign Minister [Arthur Zimmermann] proposed to Mexico that, in the event of war breaking out between Germany and the United States, the Mexicans should take Germany's side and receive a handsome reward in US territory. But not until 18 March did the President's last hope of preserving neutrality depart. On that day U-boats sank, without warning and with heavy loss of life, three American merchant ships. Six days later Wilson authorized his Secretary for the Navy to open conversations with the British Admiralty [equivalent: Navy Department], regarding the coordination of their naval operations. On 7 April the United States declared war upon Germany. At this moment the U-boat campaign was accomplishing, in a sense quite contrary to the intentions of its originators, its most considerable contribution to the outcome of the war.

Nor was it the case, as Germany's rulers had calculated, that America's intervention could be of no immediate benefit to the Allies. The struggle against the U-boat was straightway affected. In the first place, the American navy included a significant number of destroyers, and these were promptly diverted to anti-submarine warfare. Secondly, America's merchant shipping ceased to fall into the neutral category, so that there could be no question now that it might be scared away from trading with Britain. Thirdly, there was locked up in American harbours some half-million tons of German cargo ships. These were promptly seized by the authorities and employed in the Allied cause. Finally, the British Admiralty in deciding on cargoes and routes so as to make the best use of available shipping, no longer needed to be inhibited by economic considerations.

Some examples will indicate the weight of this last factor. Hitherto, for purposes of the balance of payments, Britain had devoted much shipping space to the importation of raw cotton and the export of manufactured cotton goods. Now, with American credit at its disposal, it felt obliged to do neither, so reducing its shipping needs. Again, Britain could now secure from the USA commodities that it had hitherto been importing from more distant sources. So, having purchased the whole of Australia's export wheat crop, the British authorities decided to leave it there. The length of voyage was plainly excessive once it had become possible to secure wheat from America without economic restraint.

The Allies Search for an Anti-Submarine Strategy

What all this meant was clear, but also what it did not mean. Germany's attempt to accomplish the defeat of Britain within a specified time had failed. The U-boat could not attain the required killing rate. Britain possessed greater resilience than its enemies had allowed for. And America's intervention was enhancing British resources.

But it did not follow that, on an adjusted timescale, Germany's expectations might not yet be fulfilled. If the toll inflicted by the U-boat between February and July 1917 could be repeated in the ensuing six months, and perhaps for a bit longer, the outcome would not be in doubt [a German victory]. A point must be reached when the number of merchant ships available to supply Britain would be inadequate to sustain the country's livelihood and war effort. The question confronting Britain was whether, before that stage was reached, the Royal Navy could master the U-boat.

In the opening months of the unlimited submarine campaign the response in the Admiralty and in [British] governing circles was less than adequate. . . .

Plainly, a different solution [than the unsuccessful search-and-destroy strategy] must be sought. If the submarine could not be found, then it must be denied victims. After all, it was not essential to destroy U-boats in order to thwart an underwater blockade of Britain, any more than it was necessary to sink Germany's battleships to prevent them from blockading Britain on the surface. A U-boat fleet unable to gain access to merchant ships would be of no more use to Germany than a [German] High Seas Fleet permanently confined to harbour.

No one doubted that, in most circumstances, there was a way of preventing submarines from attacking surface vessels. If a particular unit of the fleet were deemed important enough, it could be safeguarded from U-boats by the provision of a screen of destroyers—that is, by convoy. This practice has assured a large measure of immunity to the battleships of the [British] Grand Fleet and also to troopships. And since January 1917 it had been extended to the cargo ships serving the vital coal trade to France.

That the merchant fleet was essential to Britain's war effort, and indeed to its very survival, was evident enough. Hence the unrestricted U-boat campaign seemed to create an irresistible case for extending convoy to Britain's overseas trade. The chiefs of the Admiralty, however, judged that there was an overriding argument against this course: namely, that it was impractical. Three aspects in particular weighed with them. First, many owners and captains of cargo ships agreed that an aggregation of merchantmen simply could not keep station—that is, a convoy would soon disperse itself. Secondly, it appeared that convoying on a large scale must reduce the ports of Britain to chaos by producing gluts and dearths of vessels requiring servicing. Thirdly, the navy chiefs argued that they simply did not possess the numbers of destroyers and similar craft needed to safeguard the huge volume of shipping travelling to and from Britain. . . .

[It] was not a person that shocked the chiefs of the British navy into reconsidering their resistance to convoys. It was an event; or, more accurately, a succession of events: the massacre at sea in April 1917. This made it starkly evident not only that existing methods of combating the U-boat were failing but also that this deficiency would shortly encompass [bring about] Britain's defeat. Hence it became imperative to look with greater sympathy, and on a sounder basis of knowledge, at the only course of action still untried. Imminent catastrophe at last dispelled the prejudice against using ships of the Royal Navy as guardians for merchantmen. The statistics suggesting that there were far too many merchant ships coming from overseas to make convoys practicable had to be subjected to searching inquiry—whereupon they were found to yield a quite different message. As for the claim that merchant ships could not hold their place in convoys, it was at last recognized that this matter had better be put to the test—a proceeding that would soon ensure that no one in authority would make that claim again.

Allied Convoy System Counters the U-Boats

So at the end of April 1917 . . . the decision was taken to institute convoys as an experiment. On 10 May, a crucial day in the history of Britain's involvement in the First World War, a collection of 17 merchant ships with various escorts set out from Gibraltar [British base where Mediterranean Sea meets the Atlantic Ocean]. Their experience was instructive. Twelve days later every one of them reached port in Britain. The time of their journey proved to be two days less than it would have been had they sailed independently. And in the course of the journey not only did the enemy fail to make a kill but not a single U-boat was sighted. If there are such things as 'decisive events' in this war, the first Gibraltar convoy must rank high among them.

Time would pass before convoys could become fully operative. Their institution required a large feat of administration: the planning of routes, the diversion of naval craft from futile searchings after U-boats to this new protective role, the gathering together of merchant ships of like seagoing capacity to form a coherent entity, the reorganization of ports. While this was happening, the U-boats continued to find victims. In the second six-month period of the unrestricted campaign, from August 1917 to January 1918, 2.25 million tons of merchant shipping was sunk. But that was well short of Germany's minimum requirements. And it was a sum total that masked a steady decline: 211 ships went to the bottom in August, only 150 in January. Moreover, a large majority of the ships sunk were travelling individually, so that with every extension of the convoy system the potency of the U-boat declined.

Already by mid-1917 the merchant traffic of inward-bound ships across the north Atlantic was fully under convoy. In August and September the system was extended to traffic from Gibraltar and the south Atlantic, and also to outward-bound ships (whose losses had begun rising sharply). By the end of the year the Mediterranean trade had also come under convoy, to such noteworthy effect that shipping from the Far East, which had been driven to taking the longer route around South Africa, once more began using the Mediterranean. The accomplishment was remarkable, if not by any means complete. By the end of 1917 rather more than half of Britain's overseas trade had been brought under convoy.

What made the system so effective? It did not contribute significantly to the destruction of U-boats. Certainly, sinkings of enemy submarines were on the increase. But mainly these were due to such factors as the development (at last) of an efficient British mine and the more effective sowing of minefields as submarine traps; the action of patrol craft against U-boats operating ever closer to the British coast in the search for targets; and the use of British submarines against their German counterparts. By these means the destruction of U-boats reached a point where it more than equalled Germany's acquisition of new submarines.

The especial contribution of the convoy lay not in destroying U-boats but in rendering them ineffective. This it did by denying them victims. Increasingly from May 1917 U-boat commanders who earlier had looked out on seas swarming with merchant ships now found themselves gazing at empty oceans. Given the limited stretch of sea visible from a submarine, a convoy of 20 ships was not much easier to spot than a single vessel. And, of course, the convoy reduced drastically—to one-twentieth—the number of possible sightings. In addition, the Admiralty's wireless intelligence soon became effective in establishing the whereabouts of the enemy, either from messages sent by U-boats to their headquarters and to one another or from the distress signals of their victims. Convoys were diverted from these areas.

The effectiveness of the convoy went further. On the occasions when a U-boat did run in with this accumulation of ships it could make nothing like as many kills as when encountering the same number of merchantmen individually. In the daytime it could only risk an attack submerged; at night it might also attack on the surface using a torpedo. In either circumstance employment of the gun as the main instrument of destruction was out of the question. Admittedly, this form of attack had been declining anyway because of the increasing arming of British merchantmen. But that did not apply to neutral ships, which were never armed and so had hitherto been defenceless against U-boats. The convoy constituted the first, and a highly effective, form of protection available to neutral merchant shipping.

Again, the convoy did more than limit the types of attack that the submarine might employ against such ships as it managed to encounter. It seriously limited the number of attacks. By the time the U-boat had claimed one victim, or at the outside two, the remaining merchantmen in the convoy had departed the scene. The patrol ships with their depth charges were now occupying it. The U-boat might survive this hazard. But it had to remain well below periscope depth for so long that all contact with the convoy was lost.

What all this signified for Britain was not early appreciated. And confidence in the Admiralty, having been badly shaken by the gravity of the situation in April, continued low for the rest of 1917. The depredations of the U-boat seemed to be continuing on a large, even if diminished, scale. . . .

Yet notwithstanding these negative aspects of the war at sea, only one thing really signified [mattered] and that was most certainly positive. The threat confronting Britain of being strangled by a submarine blockade, having been held at bay in the first half of the year, was decisively surmounted in the second half. The U-boat, on whatever timetable being employed by the enemy high command, would not bring Germany the victory.

Peace with Victory: Wilson's Fourteen Points

John Milton Cooper Jr.

In his survey of American history from 1900 to 1920, University of Wisconsin historian John Milton Cooper Jr. discusses the background of President Woodrow Wilson's famous Fourteen Points address of January 8, 1918, outlining what amounted to an American liberal peace program. Pressure to end the war was building on all sides. Allied labor and Socialist groups were discontented with the conservative domestic and international aims of the war. War weariness and unrest also spread among labor and Socialist groups within the Central Powers. Finally, the Bolsheviks in Russia caused a sensation at this time by publishing the contents of "secret treaties" negotiated by the czarist regime and other Allied powers since the start of the war. As Cooper's account suggests, these treaties revealed Allied war aims to be as imperialistic as those of the Central Powers, and Wilson's influence over his fellow Allies was increasingly in doubt.

Any Republican [Party] role in foreign affairs was bound to stir conflict because [President Woodrow] Wilson had already advanced his own ideas about international order. As he had proclaimed in his war address, he was seeking "peace without victory," and in pursuit of this during the war, he maintained arm's length relations with the Allies and an emphasis on liberal, non-punitive war aims.

Diverging U.S. and Allied Aims

To the chagrin [annoyance] of the British, the French, and pro-Allied enthusiasts at home, Wilson insisted on calling the United States an associated power rather than an ally. The administration conducted cool, controlled relations with its co-belligerents and maintained diplomatic ties with all the Central Powers except Germany. In February and March 1917, Wilson tried to induce Austria-Hungary, Germany's faltering war partner, to make a separate peace. Though the Austrians severed relations with the United States in April 1917, America did not declare war against them until December. Wilson finally decided to go to war against Austria-Hungary to buttress Italy's flagging war effort and to encourage nationalist movements in [Austro-Hungarian] Central and Eastern Europe. The United States never did enter the war against the remaining two Central Powers, Bulgaria and Turkey, despite cries from [ex-President Theodore] Roosevelt for all-out common cause with the Allies. These actions sprang from Wilson's doubts, as he told [ex-President William H.] Taft in December 1917, about "the desirability of drawing the two countries [Britain and the United States] too closely together" because of "divergences of purpose." Wilson was referring to his suspicions about Britain's objectives in the war, especially regarding colonies in Africa and Asia, and postwar control of the seas. His suspicions went double for the French, especially regarding their colonial designs, and their desires to dominate the postwar European continent. The president's lack of warmth was not lost on the British and French. King George V once reputedly snapped, "Do we have a co-belligerent or an umpire?"

Pressures for Liberal Peace Aims

The Allies had both in Wilson, especially in regard to war aims. Wilson was not alone in his search for a middle course. In Europe left-wing parties and trade unions on both sides of the fight were critical of the war and reluctant in their support, insisting upon non-imperialistic purposes behind belligerency. And by 1917, bowing to war-weariness, the British government had begun to pay lip service to a non-punitive peace. The restiveness of the European left gave Wilson the opening that he sought for promoting his vision of a new world order. In 1917 he allowed [his key adviser] Colonel [Edward M.] House to form the Inquiry, a band of bright young men who included Walter Lippmann of the *New Republic* and the future presidents of Yale and Johns Hopkins. They were to study war aims, plan for peace negotiations, and cultivate sympathetic contacts on the other side of the Atlantic. In August 1917 Wilson stole a march on the Allies when he made a public reply to an appeal for an end to the fighting by Pope Benedict XV. The United States and the Allies, he avowed, "believe that peace should rest upon the rights of peoples . . . great or small, weak or powerful,—their equal right to freedom and security and self-government and to participation upon fair terms in the economic opportunities of the world,—the German people of course included, if they will accept equality and not seek domination."

After November 1917, as it started to move toward a separate peace with Germany, the Bolshevik government of Russia published the secret Allied treaties that had promised spoils of the war to Czarist Russia. The emergence of the Bolshevik challenge to the war aims of the Allies placed Wilson for the first time in a centrist role on the international stage, where he had to distinguish his positions on war aims from opponents on the right and left. Socialists, labor groups, and others on the left in Allied countries might prove receptive to calls from Russia to lay down their arms, in the belief that their governments fought only for imperialistic ends. On the right, traditional nationalists considered the war a fight for military, naval, territorial, colonial, and economic gains for their respective countries.

The Middle Way of the Fourteen Points

Wilson set out his middle course in his most celebrated and powerful foreign-policy declaration: a speech to a joint session of Congress on January 8, 1918, in which he proposed a numbered set of peace terms that were at once dubbed the "Fourteen Points." Those points included "open covenants of peace, openly arrived at"; free use of the seas; removal of trade barriers; reduction of armaments; fairness to Russia on territorial and economic issues as "the acid test" of a peace settlement; evacuation and indemnification of Belgium; restoration to France of the Alsace and Lorraine, which had been lost to Germany in 1871, new frontiers for Italy, territorial adjustments and national autonomy for peoples in the Austro-Hungarian and Turkish empires, and independence for Poland. The final point was: "A general association of nations must be formed under specific covenants [binding agreements] for the purpose of affording mutual guarantees of political independence and territorial integrity to great and small states alike."

The Fourteen Points speech was a diplomatic masterstroke. The Allied governments were grateful for Wilson's answer to Bolshevik attacks and to their own critics on the left. They muffled their reservations over naval and territorial questions and applauded the statement of war aims. Wilson had avoided commitments either to make peace with Germany on the basis of the Fourteen Points or to break up the Austro-Hungarian and Turkish empires, but he had clearly implied that those provisions might be essential parts of a post-war peace settlement. Wilson had also hoped to induce Russia not to leave the war, but in that effort, the Fourteen Points failed. Published on March 3, 1918, the Treaty of

Woodrow Wilson

Brest-Litovsk, in which the Bolsheviks submitted to humiliating peace terms, seemed an act of betrayal in Allied quarters, and it heightened already rampant anti-radical sentiment in the United States. Wilson himself momentarily succumbed to the mood of bitterness. "There is," he declared in April 1918, ". . . but one response possible for us: Force, Force to the utmost, Force without stint or limit, the righteous and triumphant Force which shall make right the law of the world and cast every selfish dominion down in the dust."

Such Roosevelt-like fervor did not last long. Wilson did not let anger at the Bolsheviks guide his policy toward Russia. Throughout 1918 British and French leaders, particularly Winston Churchill and Marshal Foch, strove to mount a joint intervention to aid counterrevolutionary forces in Russia in efforts to overthrow the new Bolshevik regime. Wilson would have no part in those ventures. He reluctantly permitted small-scale participation by 14,000 American troops alongside the European Allies at the Russian towns of Murmansk and Archangel, and with the Japanese at Vladivostok, but the commanders were under strict orders to limit their activities to guarding Allied property and to stay out of internal Russian affairs. Wilson believed that these moves might help marginally in winning the war by preventing supplies from falling into German hands, and perhaps by allowing pro-Allied Czech forces in Russia to be transported to the Western Front. At no time did he express sympathy with any plans for outside intervention to bring down the Bolsheviks. His attempts to intervene in Mexico had taught Wilson the hard way not to butt in on revolutions. "In my opinion," he observed about Russia in 1919, "trying to stop a revolutionary movement by troops in the field is like using a broom to hold back a great ocean."

The Fourteen Points and Ending the War

Having stated the Fourteen Points, Wilson began to lobby for their acceptance as a basis for peace. Quiet, informal contacts with liberal elements in Germany, and the CPI's [Committee on Public Information, the U.S. wartime propaganda agency] distribution of the Fourteen Points in translated leaflets, played a big part in undermining the Central Powers' will to resist. Bulgaria, Turkey, and Austria-Hungary dropped out of the war in September and October 1918. After the successes of the Allied counteroffensives in the summer and early fall, especially the American onslaughts at St. Mihiel and at the Argonne Forest, Germany's military leaders privately admitted that they could not hold out much longer. Instead of bearing the onus of defeat themselves, however, they stepped aside in October and let a new civilian government open negotiations for an armistice on the basis of the Fourteen Points. A tense, complicated set of exchanges followed. Wilson forced the Germans to accept terms that would prevent them from resuming offensive operations. He used Colonel House, who was already in Europe, to cajole the British and French into agreeing to an armistice based on the Fourteen Points.

Wilson also tried to keep the Allies from achieving, as he told House, "too much success and security" under the military terms of the armistice. Too strong an Allied position would, he believed, "make a genuine peace settlement exceedingly difficult, if not impossible." Yet at the final armistice negotiations, held in a railroad car in the forest of Compiègne in France, no American representatives were invited, and Marshal Foch imposed harsh terms which ended any possibility of even defensive German resistance. The elimination of a credible threat from the other side was already weakening Wilson's leverage over the Allies.

At an hour before noon on November 11, 1918, the Armistice took effect. A wave of euphoria sprang up among victors and vanquished alike. As the AEF [American Expeditionary Force] newspaper *Stars and Stripes* reported, "At the eleventh hour on the eleventh day of the eleventh month hostilities came to an end from Switzerland to the sea. . . . There followed then a strange unbelievable silence as though the world had died. It lasted but a moment, lasted for the space that a breath is held. Then came such an uproar of relief and jubilance, such a tooting of horns, shrieking of whistles, such an overture from the bands and trains and church bells, such a shouting as the world is not likely to see again in our day and generation."

The Central Powers Collapse

Keith Robbins

In this selection British historian Keith Robbins presents a thoughtful account of the dramatic defeat of Germany and the Central Powers in 1918. General Erich Ludendorff, the architect of German strategy, gambled on a massive offensive on the western front to win the war before American troops could become a decisive factor. The German bid for victory, however, exhausted its already depleted manpower and morale. After effective Allied and American counteroffensives, Germany sued for peace in the fall of 1918. Also hastening Germany's defeat were Allied military successes in Italy, the Balkans, and the Middle East in 1918. Keith Robbins has written extensively on modern British history and is vice president of the University of Wales.

At previous turning points, the war had resolutely refused to turn, but at the beginning of 1918 there did seem grounds for believing that it would prove the decisive, if not the concluding, year. The pressure seemed to be on the Allies. The Austro-Germans steadily consolidated their grasp over vast areas of Eastern Europe. The Russian empire was in process of dissolution. . . . Each week that passed saw the transfer of German divisions from the Eastern to the Western front. Russia was out of the war and it seemed that Italy was only precariously in it. Neither the British nor the French were in a position to mount offensives. [German *de facto* supreme commander Erich] Ludendorff believed that the time had come for Germany to launch a major attack in the West for the first time since 1914. Planning for Operation 'Michael' began in mid-November 1917 with a target of the late

---

Reprinted from *The First World War*, by Keith Robbins, by permission of Oxford University Press. Copyright © Keith Robbins, 1984.

spring for the decisive offensive. Ground conditions would then be favourable and it would be possible to achieve victory before the American presence was felt. . . .

The Americans were very much in the minds of the opposing European leaders. Although they had been in the war for some nine months, their military impact was minimal. The build-up of American divisions in the last months of 1917 had been slow, reaching a total of some 175,000 at the opening of the year. While they looked remarkably healthy and confident to European eyes, there was the knowledge that this confidence was based on inexperience. [General John J.] Pershing, commander-in-chief of the American Expeditionary Force was determined to establish a self-contained United States Army and not allow his men to be swallowed by the military appetites of the Europeans. The problems of constructing a major [American] army were considerable and it was vital for the Germans that they were not overcome before their offensive struck home. . . .

Ludendorff decided to strike the British on the old battleground of the Somme, with the main effort being made where the British and French sectors joined. The possibility of attacking the French to the south was considered, but rejected. They had too much space into which to retreat. The initial preferences were gradually elaborated and at a conference on 21 January Ludendorff came to firm conclusions. The main thrust would be between Arras and St Quentin. If the attack was successful, the British would retreat to the north-west to secure their communications to the [English] Channel ports and the French would retreat to the southwest in order to protect Paris. German armies would exploit this gap and encircle the British on their open right flank. Ludendorff also placed stress upon the tactics to be employed. He had ceased to believe in the efficacy [effectiveness] of the massive initial bombardment. Experience at Riga and Caporetto [sites of German victories on the Eastern Front and Italy respectively] suggested that an intense whirlwind barrage was the answer. Relying upon small and well-equipped infantry groups, the attackers would move across the field of battle with great speed.

It was apparent by early February that an attack was likely and the [Allied] intelligence assessments proved fairly accurate. Yet, despite the creation of the Allied supreme war council [in late 1917] there was little agreement on the appropriate reaction. After Passchendaele [a costly British offensive on the Western Front in late 1917], Lloyd George had been reluctant to increase British force levels in Flanders. . . . He also claimed that a German assault on the Western Front would be no more successful in bringing the war to an end than had been previous Allied efforts. He looked again at south-eastern Europe and the Middle East. Aware that he now had responsibility for forty additional miles of the front, [British general Douglas] Haig pressed for half a million more men. He did manage to reach an arrangement with [French general Henri-Philippe] Pétain to switch reserves if circumstances demanded it. It had the unfortunate effect of justifying the relative weakness of the most southerly of the British armies, that commanded by [General Hubert] Gough, where the attack was in fact to fall most effectively.

The Ludendorff Offensives

The massive but swift bombardment began early on 21 March over a sixty-mile line. The Germans pushed Gough's army back nearly forty miles by the end of the fifth day. . . . The position in the north was better initially but soon came under intense pressure. In the French sector, which was also now under attack, the Germans took Noyon. Pétain and Haig met late at night on 24 March to assess the position. Confronted by the collapse of the Fifth Army, which threatened to become a complete rout, Haig appealed for the reserves he had been promised. Pétain still feared that the main German attack had not yet come and reserves would have to be moved to cover Paris. Haig supposed that the Frenchman was willing to leave the British to their inevitable fate while he [Pétain] prepared, probably unavailingly, to defend Paris. He appealed to London stating that in this desperate situation a supreme commander had to be appointed. A high-level meeting was arranged. . . . Clemenceau, who had been prime minister since mid-November, remained a tiger in defeat. Haig and Pétain confronted each other. In an emotional session, [French general Ferdinand] Foch became the hero of the hour, showing a willingness to fight in front of, in and behind Amiens. He was appointed 'co-ordinator' of the Allied armies on the Western front, a post significantly short of commander-in-chief. . . . What was most important, however, was that reinforcements were shifted from the French front to help the British. In fact, the German momentum was already faltering and, in early April, despite another assault, Amiens did not fall. Ludendorff ended the attack. It seemed to have been successful since his armies had penetrated some forty miles on a front of the same length. They had captured many prisoners and guns and caused around 150,000 casualties, chiefly among the British. Their own losses were heavy but probably lower than that total. It was a successful but not decisive attack. The British army was still in the field and the British and French forces had not been separated and the vital wedge driven between them. It was not even the case that the territory gained was worthwhile. . . . He [Ludendorff] now again had longer lines of entrenchments to defend, and he did not have the men. Indeed, arguably, it was insufficient numerical superiority which prevented him from sustaining his advance and permitted the Allies to regroup and save themselves. And, as time passed, the spectre [an object of fear or dread] of the Americans increased. Their role in March was only marginal, but it was significant none the less. Pershing, at least temporarily, was prepared to let American troops serve under foreign command. . . .

Ludendorff did not delay long before making his next move. Still not abandoning hope of victory, he shifted his next attack to Flanders . . . against the British and the Portuguese. The German commanders had considerably fewer troops at their disposal and the front on which they attacked was much shorter, but nevertheless the initial assault was again successful. Haig rushed what reinforcements he could find to the scene of the breakthrough and begged Foch for some French divisions, initially without much success. There was talk of evacuating Calais [a key port], even of flooding the countryside. British troops fought tenaciously and the German impetus faded. . . . Even so, the attacks continued spasmodically [intermittently], culminating in fierce battles . . . in late April. His successes cost him dear and he was no nearer the decisive break-through which he sought. However, it still seemed tantalizingly close and he knew that the British had been badly mauled.

His third offensive was prepared in great secrecy. The area selected was the Chemin des Dames, the highway along the Aisne River, the scene of bitter struggles in the past. The French remained convinced that the attack would probably come at the junction of the British and French lines. After a massive artillery bombardment, German shock troops broke through on the morning of 27 May. They crossed the Aisne River and three days later they had reached the Marne [River] near Château-Thierry—a drive of about thirty miles and only some forty miles from Paris. There were signs of panic in the capital. Ludendorff's problem was that this attack had originally been designed to draw away reserves from the north prior to what he hoped would be a decisive thrust in Flanders. It now seemed so successful that it appeared madness to stop it. In this desperate position, Pershing again agreed to waive his insistence that American troops should only fight as an independent army. Units of the American Third Division joined French troops in throwing the Germans back in their repeated efforts to cross the Marne. Another American division had been successful a few days earlier in capturing the village of Cantigny in its first offensive of the war. And the US Second Division successfully blocked a determined German drive in early June west of Château-Thierry on the way to Paris. Over 275,000 American troops crossed the Atlantic in June, the highest monthly figure yet achieved, and after their performance in these battles their fighting quality could not be dismissed. The arrival of fresh troops was some compensation for the heavy Allied losses; the Germans had no such relief. Ludendorff, however, discounted the combat-readiness of most of these new [American] arrivals and still believed that he held the initiative—but he could not delay for long. The salient [part of the battleline projecting farthest toward the enemy] he had established was vulnerable, but to withdraw would damage the momentum of progress. Equally, if it was to be adequately defended, he would not be in a position to take away troops for the Flanders campaign. He decided to launch two more modest attacks beginning on 9 June but, partly because the French had advance information, this offensive ran into difficulties at an early stage. [French] General [Charles] Mangin's defence in depth was well-planned and a vigorous counter-attack, with American participation, led Ludendorff to abandon the operation in the middle of the month. German losses had been considerable and the numerical balance shifted against him. This final drive could not even be regarded as a tactical success.

Even so, Ludendorff had not given up. He still contemplated a final drive against the British in Flanders but decided to launch one more offensive against Reims with the ultimate objective of threatening Paris and drawing in Allied reserves. Foch again gained advance information of the impending attack and made adequate preparations—even beginning a bombardment of his own. Nevertheless, one of the attacking German armies made substantial progress and crossed the Marne. However, its progress was deceptive and the attackers encountered strong resistance at the second line of defence. Although, again, there was alarm in Paris, Ludendorff realized the strength of the forces now opposing him and on 17 July halted the attack, still hoping, despite the belief of many of his troops that they had been engaged in Champagne in the final *Friedenssturm* [German peace offensive], that the time was ripe for the Flanders campaign. However, the loss of morale among German troops was becoming apparent—the influenza outbreak over the previous few weeks had sapped many of them physically. And there was an even greater surprise in store which finally ended the Flanders dream.

The Allied Counteroffensive

On the morning of 18 July Foch ordered the counteroffensive to begin, with the objective of wiping out the German salient on the Marne. Tanks and infantry were used in successful combination and took advantage of surprise. The Americans joined in, Pershing at last able to form the First American Army. However, German forces safely recrossed the Marne and were able to regroup. . . . Nevertheless, the salient had been eliminated and Foch was promoted to marshal of France. . . . German losses since the spring now amounted to some 800,000. The Allies sensed that they were in the ascendancy, though no [German] collapse appeared imminent. It was decided to press ahead immediately with an attempt to reduce the Amiens salient. British, French, American and imperial troops, together with tanks and aircraft, took part in the successful onslaught on 8 August. German divisions reeled under the impact and some fifteen thousand German prisoners were captured. Ludendorff reported to the Kaiser that the German army had ceased to be a perfect fighting instrument. The Allies had a brief pause but on 21 August the offensive resumed on a much wider front. At the end of the month the Germans were back on the Hindenburg Line [a northerly defensive position]—their departure point five months earlier. The Amiens salient had been reduced. It was then the American turn to take the offensive—preceded by the customary argument between Pershing and Foch. In the end they attacked in Lorraine and cleared the St Mihiel salient in four days by mid-September.

It was now time to think in terms of master-plans which might end the war, though there remained a presumption that the campaigning would extend into 1919. Foch himself thought it might end earlier if he could disrupt the vital railway line running from Lille [in Belgium] to Strasbourg [in eastern France]. If he could capture certain crucial junctions the Germans would have difficulty in receiving adequate supplies. Isolated, certain sections of the German army could be defeated in a piecemeal fashion. Even if the bulk of it nevertheless succeeded in withdrawing into Germany, it would be compelled to leave a great deal of equipment behind. If all went well, Foch hoped to accomplish a pincer movement [simultaneous flanking manuevers to surround the enemy], with a Franco-British force attacking from the north-west and a Franco-American from the south. Belgian, Italian and Portuguese contingents would also join the attack. The German forces were now numerically inferior and about a quarter of their available divisions were under strength. Foch intended to throw as many different units into action in as many different places as possible.

The attack began in the south on 26 September as Franco-American forces struck in the direction of Mézières and Sedan. Three days later British, French, Canadian and Belgian forces attacked in the north-west. The co-operation between the armies in both of these attacks was excellent. However, criticism of the disappointing progress made by the Americans began to be heard. It was very easy to describe them as inexperienced and their casualties were particularly heavy. In fact, the attack in the north-west encountered comparable problems and progress in Flanders was slow. The Germans took advantage of their fortified positions to fight furiously but an increasing despondency on their side could not be disguised. The initiative was clearly with the Allies and in October they steadily consolidated their advance, unspectacular though it was. At this juncture, political calculation and military strategy increasingly intermingled. The Allied advance had not been as great as had been anticipated. The Germans were not surrounded and the natural obstacles to campaigning in Flanders in the winter were as great as ever. It did begin to look as though fighting would have to be resumed in 1919 if a substantial Allied military victory was to be achieved. By this point, however, Ludendorff had already decided that Germany would be best served by the conclusion of an armistice. There was a change of chancellor [prime minister] in Germany and President Wilson was informed in early October that Germany was prepared to negotiate for a peace on the basis of his Fourteen Points. Just over a month later, on 11 November, the armistice was signed.

More Allied Victories

Ludendorff's recommendation that Germany should seek an armistice was based as much on developments elsewhere as on the German position on the Western front. While that was grave, it was not yet catastrophic, but Austria-Hungary, Bulgaria and Ottoman Turkey were in dire straits. Germany's allies had all been expected to play their part in assisting the spring offensive in the West by their own efforts. Berlin would have liked Italy to be knocked out of the war so that Vienna could provide reinforcements for the Western front—German troops had already been withdrawn from the Italian front. In mid-June, with a small numerical superiority, the Austrians attacked the Italians and the five Franco-British divisions which had not been transferred back to the Western front. Perhaps because, in effect, two uncoordinated assaults were launched, they proved disappointing. . . . [Italian commander General Armando] was encouraged by reports that Austria-Hungary was on the point of internal collapse. The [Italian-led] attack was launched on 24 October—a year after the humiliation of Caporetto [major Italian defeat by Austro-German forces in October 1917]. The intervening months had been used for intensive preparations and Diaz had 57 divisions under his command including, for the first time, an American contingent. This initial fighting was fierce—the Austro-Hungarian forces were not as demoralized as had been assumed—but gradually the Italians pushed more and more troops across the Piave [River] and, after an intense struggle in the last few days of the month, the Austrian resistance crumbled and about half a million prisoners were taken. An armistice was signed on 4 November. The Italians had regained their military self-respect by their victory at Vittorio Veneto, although some of their Allies wanted this offensive to have come rather earlier.

The defeat of the Habsburg forces was not the only disaster. In July 1918 General Franchet d'Espérey was appointed commander of the Allied forces in Greece and began to make preparations for an attack northwards which would coincide with the Allied offensive in France. French and Serb divisions attacked on 15 September and, within days, the Bulgarians were retreating. Cavalry units covered nearly one hundred miles in a fortnight. In the last few days of the month, an armistice was discussed and then agreed. The army was to be demobilized and the country was at the disposal of the Allies for their future operations. The Serbs advanced through their own country and Franchet d'Espérey marched across Bulgaria and entered Romania shortly before the war came to an end. It was a modest achievement for an army of 350,000 men whose presence had not disturbed the supply line between Germany and Turkey for the duration of the war. And Bulgaria, by itself, had never been likely to tip the balance of the conflict.

In this final episode, British action had been concentrated against Turkey and formed part of a many-sided envelopment [surrounding] of the Ottoman empire. The capture of Jerusalem had been followed by the usual debate between those in London who believed that a further advance to Aleppo [in Syria] would lead to the collapse of the Turkish war-effort and those who believed it would not and who felt, in addition, that troops could not be spared for such a purpose, given the gravity of the position in France. The decision was taken to transfer troops from Mesopotamia [Iraq] and in the spring Allenby assembled his forces, only to find that he had to sacrifice a considerable number of men for France. The Turks, aided by a small German force, were now commanded by [German general Otto] Liman von Sanders. The encounters between the opposing forces were inconsequential—the British imperial forces became accustomed to crossing to and fro over the Jordan. [British officer T.E., "Lawrence of Arabia"] Lawrence, meanwhile, refined his raiding tactics and finally succeeded in making the Hejaz railway [in the western Arabian peninsula] useless and cutting off Medina. It was not until September that the imperial forces and their Arab allies were able to break through. The battle of Megiddo, fought in mid-September, was the best kind of victory—it was achieved with comparatively little fighting. Damascus was reached by British and Arab forces on 1 October in what was now a rapidly-moving campaign. Different units speedily captured the important towns—Beirut, Homs and finally, on 26 October, Aleppo. [Turkish general] Mustafa Kemal still hoped to make a stand north of the city but it proved impossible to check the British advance—tired though the troops were after travelling some 500 miles in just over a month. Turkish resistance was effectively at an end and an armistice between Britain and Turkey was signed on 30 October. This act did not prevent the Turkish commander at Mosul [in Iraq] threatening to continue the fight when British troops appeared before the city on the following day. A few days later, however, he bowed to the inevitable. Indian, Australian, British and New Zealand forces seemed to have secured the supremacy of the British empire in the Near East. Peace, in this sense, had arrived, though that did not prevent the continuance of skirmishing [in the Middle East]. . . .

Such unsettled conditions did not only obtain in the Middle East. German Baltic barons showed no great disposition to believe that the war had come to an end. Nor did the intrepid [General Paul von] Lettow-Vorbeck in East Africa. In ignorance of wider developments, he captured a small Northern Rhodesian town two days after the armistice had been signed in France. When this further development was drawn to his attention he agreed, after due deliberation, to surrender, concluding that to reverse the verdict in Europe might tax even his ingenuity.

Chapter 4

The Home Fronts

Turning Points

IN WORLD HISTORY

Mobilizing the Home Front for Total War

Gordon A. Craig

Waged both on land and at sea, World War I was a total war. In turn, the civilian home fronts of the warring nations experienced intense pressures and strains. In the following essay, distinguished historian Gordon A. Craig identifies key changes that affected the internal affairs of the belligerents: Both political power and economies were centralized as never before, and severe restrictions were also placed on civil liberties, even in countries where such liberties were well established.

On February 10, 1916, a panic broke out along the east coast of England because of a rumor that a German Zeppelin had appeared over the resort town of Scarborough; and public indignation over this outrage was so great in the weeks that followed that the government found it expedient to appease it by creating ten home-defense squadrons of the Royal Flying Corps.

The incident is worth mentioning because it illustrates the fact that World War I was the first total war in modern history, in the sense that its rigors were apt to be visited upon all citizens of the participating powers, however remote they might be from the battle area. In earlier wars— even in the protracted and enormously destructive wars against Napoleon—it was only occasionally that the average citizen at home felt the war's effects, and, for long periods of time, it was quite possible for him to forget that there was fighting in progress. In the war of 1914–1918 this kind of detachment was impossible. Citizens of northeast France or Belgium or Poland, whose countries were overrun, whose

Excerpted from *Europe Since 1914*, 3rd ed., by Gordon A. Craig. Copyright © 1971 by The Dryden Press. Adapted by permission of the publisher.

homes were commandeered as billets [military housing], and whose friends and relatives were sometimes held by the occupying forces as hostages to assure the maintenance of local order, knew the war as intimately as the troops who passed through their streets. But they were by no means alone. Crofters [small farmers] in the Scottish highlands, businessmen in Leipzig, Russian farmers in the Volga lands were all brushed by the touch of war, even when they did not attract a visit from a Zeppelin or were well out of range of guns like that notorious Big Bertha which the Germans used to shell Paris. The fortunes of war influenced or determined their freedom of action, their employment, their diet, and even what they were allowed to think and to say. It subjected every aspect of their lives to an increasing degree of control and regimentation. And the fact that it did so had effects which persisted even after the war was over.

Only three aspects of this total war need concern us here: the progressive centralization of political authority, even in countries where political centralization had long been suspect; the economic regimentation practiced by all governments; and the tendency toward thought control and restriction of civil liberties.

War and Political Centralization

In all of the countries that participated in the war, the beginning of the fighting elicited a wave of patriotism and a closing of ranks. Even political parties and organizations that had been the bitterest opponents of governments six months before the war rallied to the national cause in August 1914. In France, the anarchist Gustave Hervé, who had been the defendant in a sensational trial in 1912 in which he was accused of encouraging mutiny in the French army, now became the most ardent of patriots; and this attitude was symptomatic of the general attitude of French socialism and French labor. In the French Chamber there was a party truce and the creation of what was called a *Union sacrée* [sacred union], and this situation had its counterpart in Germany, where the parliamentary factions buried their differences and listened with sincere emotion to the emperor's words: "I recognize parties no more. I recognize only Germans!" In Great Britain, although Ramsay MacDonald resigned the leadership of the Labor party rather than support a war for which he believed Great Britain shared much of the responsibility, his action was repudiated indignantly by the majority of his party and by the trade-union movement as well. Similar evidence of political unity was manifest in other countries.

This recognition of the overriding importance of the national interest freed governments from the criticism to which a vigilant opposition normally subjected them and enabled them to indulge in practices and to make claims to authority that would never have been tolerated in time of peace. The result was an increasing centralization of power, which, by the end of war, had assumed the appearance of government dictatorship in more than one of the great European states. It is not too much to say that no country was entirely exempt from this drift toward totalitarian political methods.

It is, of course, not surprising that this sort of thing should have happened in Russia, Austria, and Germany, where the tradition of parliamentary government was weak; and it was, of course, in those countries that the tendency was most marked and most disastrous in its results. In Russia, what progress had been made toward the separation of political power and the sharing of political responsibility came to an end during the war. This was unfortunate, because the vigorous and useful criticisms of the weaknesses of the Russian war machine came from the Duma and from the zemstvos [local governments]. But, in September 1915, the tsar, who had already assumed over-all command of the armed forces in a quixotic [impractical] gesture in August, suspended the Duma for the duration. In effect, then, the affairs of a great country were left in the hands of the empress, her favorite Rasputin, and whatever bureaucrats were willing to be their pliable tools.

In Austria and in Germany, centralization was marked by a diminution of parliament's role and an increase of that of the military. Until the death of Emperor Francis Joseph in

November 1916, after which time the fabric of the empire began rapidly to dissolve, Austria was held together by the authority of bureaucrats and soldiers. This was even more marked in Germany. At the outset of the war, the new tone was set when the local army commands were given the right to intervene in certain aspects of local government and, in some cases, to supersede local-government authorities entirely. On the national level, military influence was pronounced in 1914 and predominant from September 1916, when Hindenburg became chief of staff, until the end of the war. The team Hindenburg-Ludendorff and the political bureau in the General Staff not only made military decisions but laid down the main lines of economic and diplomatic policy. Backed by a popular support that amounted to adulation [excessive admiration], they arrogated to themselves authority that properly belonged to the emperor and the chancellor and, when crossed, won their point by threatening to resign. It was they who were responsible for the decision to resume submarine warfare; it was they who forced the resignation of Chancellor Bethmann Hollweg in July 1917 because he had permitted the Reichstag to debate and pass a vague resolution expressing interest in the possibility of a negotiated peace; it was they who dictated the terms of the treaty of Brest Litovsk [harsh peace treaty imposed on Bolshevik Russia in March 1918], which did so much political disservice to their country. Until the armies collapsed in the summer of 1918, their dictatorship was virtually free of any control.

This degree of centralization was never reached in the countries of the west. It is worth noting, however, that even England was not free from either concentration of power in few hands or the growth of excessive military influence. England started the war governed by a loose coalition government and ended with a small, tight war cabinet dominated by Lloyd George, with powers infinitely greater than those enjoyed by any peacetime government. Moreover, Britain's soldiers, usually silent in peacetime, were far from being so during the war, and some of them showed a dangerous contempt for the "frocks" [civilian political leaders] and seemed to believe that military men could do a better job of directing the war.

In France, the government started the war by declaring a state of siege and, during the first year of hostilities, the major decisions were made by the High Command and put into effect by presidential decree. This was perhaps understandable, given the extent of the threat to France in the first months of the war; but, even after the danger of defeat had receded, the High Command was reluctant to give up the position it had won. Not until November 1917, when [George] Clemenceau became premier, was it reduced to its proper role, for Clemenceau was a man who believed that even war, let alone politics, "was too important a matter to be left to the generals." It should be noted, however, that if Clemenceau restored civilian authority in France, his government, by normal standards, was dictatorial in its own right.

In neither England nor France did parliament, in any sense, abdicate. For reasons of security or efficiency, however, certain areas of action commonly subject to parliamentary decision or review were now handled by administrative or executive agencies. The growth of executive authority and the expansion of government powers in areas formerly considered private did not go as far as it did in the countries of Eastern Europe and was not as disastrous in its results; but it was, nonetheless, marked.

Wartime Economic Controls

Two stories are often told to illustrate the naive attitude of European governments toward economic matters at the beginning of the war. The first is that the French government permitted the Renault motor works to cease production at the beginning of hostilities because it could foresee no military use for its products. The second is that when the German industrialist Arthur Dix sent a memorandum to Chief of Staff Moltke outlining the need of an economic general staff, he received the answer: "Don't bother me with economics. I am busy conducting the war."

It did not take many months of war to show how unrealistic these attitudes were. One of the rudest awakenings—and it was experienced by all countries—was the discovery that there were not enough shells to keep the war going and no present means of producing enough to keep up with the demand. In September 1914 Joseph Joffre informed the French government that he needed a minimum of 70,000 shells per day and that his batteries had less than a month's reserve. At the same time, the British commander, Sir John French, was pleading with his government for more ammunition, and soon ugly hints were appearing in English newspapers about troops having to go over the top with inadequate artillery preparation and being slaughtered as a result. In Russia in 1914 factories were producing only a third of the shells needed at the front, and infantry were forced to rely wholly on night bayonet attacks because the armies had neither artillery shells nor rifle ammunition. In Germany, where the army had been confident that its preparations were sound, experts were appalled at the rate at which ammunition reserves melted away in modern war.

The shell shortage in France was caused by the fact that the enemy's swift advance had robbed the country of its richest industrial areas; in other countries, it was the result of a feckless [careless] mobilization policy, which sent skilled workers in industries soon to be discovered as crucial to the front, and by a general failure of imagination. The crisis was too serious to be solved by normal methods. Instead, governments appointed what might be called munitions tsars—the Socialist engineer Albert Thomas in France, David Lloyd George in Britain, men of similar energy in other countries—with extensive control over all branches of production of munitions and related articles, with authority to grant or deny government contracts to private firms, with adjudicative [decision-making] powers in labor-management disputes, and with the right to exempt skilled metal workers from military service and return them to bench and lathe [metal-cutting machine]. From this beginning, the European governments gradually extended their authority over all aspects of their countries' economic activity.

In Germany, for instance, [industrialist] Walther Rathenau . . . persuaded Moltke's successor Erich von Falkenhayn that an inventory of Germany's material resources was a prerequisite of any effective war planning. With government authorization, Walther Rathenau established a War Raw Materials Department which conducted an extensive survey and determined that Germany's stocks of essential raw materials would last less than a year and that it was, therefore, necessary to impound and control existing stocks, to eliminate luxury production, to requisition strategically important materials in occupied areas and purchase them from nearby neutral states, to develop new techniques of production, and to encourage the introduction of substitutes and synthetics. Starting with a miniscule staff, [Rathenau's agency] . . . developed into a mammoth organization with subdivisions in all vital industries, each with authority to apportion raw materials to manufacturers with war contracts.

Simultaneously, the German government set up bureaus to control the import and export trade, the most important being the Central Purchasing Company, which had a monopoly of all purchasing abroad, and a War Foodstuffs Office, with subsidiary agencies, to control food supplies, regulate rationing, and encourage the use of substitutes. In November 1916, in order to solve the problems created by a growing labor shortage which had not been alleviated by extensive use of women, children, and foreign laborers (French prisoners, Belgians, and Poles), a Central War Office . . . was established under the direction of General Wilhelm Groener, with wide powers to adjudicate between management and labor. A month later, with the inauguration of the so-called Hindenburg Program, a National Service Law came into effect that provided for compulsory employment of all noncombatant Germans between the ages of seventeen and sixty-one, made arbitration of labor disputes compulsory, and made change of employment subject to the approval of boards under the chairmanship of a representative of the local army command.

In the other belligerent nations, similar steps were taken to mobilize economic resources, efficiently in Britain and France, less so in Austria, Italy, and Russia. In most cases, manpower laws were passed and normal labor activity was restricted. In England, for example, the trade unions agreed in March 1915 that there should be no strikes for the duration of the war, that contracts should be relaxed to permit longer hours, speeding up of production, and the employment of women and unskilled labor in the interests of the war effort. The government assured the unions that these concessions would not hurt their postwar position and that the old conditions would be restored with the peace. Even so, as the war proceeded, there was growing suspicion in labor ranks that the concessions had been a mistake and that the workingmen were being asked to make sacrifices not borne by the employers or other classes of society. Something of the same feeling began to permeate labor ranks in Germany and other countries in the last years of the war and was reflected in a rise in the number of strikes, although most of these were unofficial.

Mobilizing and Controlling Minds

The regulation of economic life placed restrictions upon the freedom of citizens to sell their labor or services as they wished and to spend their wages as they would normally have done. But the war placed more serious limitations upon their liberty than these, affecting their rights of assembly and speech, and even their freedom of thought. In all belligerent countries, special laws were passed for the internment of people suspected of being enemy agents or sympathizers, for the prevention of the dissemination of information that might be useful to the enemy, and for the prohibition of activities that threatened to spread defeatism among the population; and, since these laws were administered by tribunals that were not immune to the influence of local hysterias and often openly encouraged tale bearers and self-appointed guardians of the national security, injustice was often committed in the name of the law. The democratic nations were no more enlightened in this matter than the absolute monarchies. In England, the Defense of the Realm Act gave the government the right to do anything it pleased with citizens suspected of sins against the war effort. Houses were searched without warrant; the possession of any literature considered by some overzealous magistrate to be subversive made a person liable to legal action; despite habeas corpus, deportation and internment were not unknown; public meetings were prohibited by police without right of appeal; and speeches held to be unpatriotic were punished by prison sentences.

Newspapers were subject everywhere to a rigorous censorship. Items which might give aid or comfort to the enemy or weaken the population's determination to fight to total victory were deleted. Some of the censorship was private (when Lord Lansdowne sent a letter to *The Times* [of London] in 1917 urging the necessity of seeking peace by negotiation, the editors refused to print it), but generally it was imposed by the government, which inserted into the spaces created by its deletions official propaganda that often baldly misrepresented the facts, magnified national successes and depreciated those of the enemy, and recounted atrocity stories designed to arouse hatred of the foe.

Since these practices deprived the reader of any objective presentation of fact, they denied him true freedom of thought and imposed distortions and myths upon his mind. In some cases, official propaganda bred a confidence in victory that was disastrous in its result. The discovery that they were not, after all, going to win the war came with such a shock to the German people that they succumbed to despair and let the tide of revolution sweep over them. In other countries, there can be little doubt that wartime propaganda played a large part in creating the hatreds and the illusions that made the job of arranging a just peace so difficult.

Civilians at War: Blockades Test the Home Fronts

Arthur Marwick

Ordinary civilians suffered through shortages, rationing, strikes, and hunger during the war. In the following article, noted British social historian Arthur Marwick explains how the Allies prevailed in this test of strength. Germany's internal political and social divisions proved worse than the Allies and set the stage for eventual German collapse and defeat.

When war broke out, none of the great powers was really prepared or equipped to wage a protracted war in which the rival blockades would increasingly impose siege conditions on the domestic populations. France, though industrially under-developed, came nearest in 1914 to self-sufficiency, with forty-two per cent of her active population still employed in agriculture; but the balance was totally distorted by the German invasion which involved a loss to France of almost ten per cent of her territory and fourteen per cent of her industrial potential. What France thus lost had to be supplied from outside. As the war dragged on into 1917 the situation became more and more critical. There was little scope for bringing more land under cultivation, and agricultural productivity steadily declined as the soil grew tired and the men who once had worked in order to cultivate it were slaughtered.

Great Britain had been prodigal [wasteful] in her neglect of agriculture in the pre-war years, so that she had to depend on imports for four-fifths of her wheat and forty per cent of

From "The Home Front: Europe, 1917," by Arthur Marwick, in *History of World War I*, edited by A.J.P. Taylor (London: Octopus Books, 1974). Reprinted by permission of Peters, Fraser, and Dunlop, as agents for the author.

her meat, and relied on Austria and Germany for almost all of her beet sugar. For the island nation more than any other, trade was life: the unrestricted submarine campaign launched by Germany on 1st February 1917 threw the whole Allied war effort into dire jeopardy.

Submarine Warfare

Before the war Germany had efficiently developed her agricultural and industrial resources and in 1914 was producing two-thirds of her own food and fodder requirements. Through scientific inventiveness and the use of *Ersatz* ('substitute') materials she was able to overcome many immediate shortages. The initial advantage was Germany's, but as the war continued that advantage slowly, implacably [relentlessly], wasted away. It was as vital to Germany that her submarine campaign should achieve a quick kill as it was to the Allies to ward off that fate.

By Easter 1917 German submarines were doing such deadly business that one out of every four ships sailing out of British ports was doomed to destruction. Disruption in basic imports meant scarcity, high prices, profiteering, and austerity. Life in Great Britain and France took on the hue of battleship grey: 'Paris is no longer Paris,' a contemporary lamented; *l'année des privations* ('the year of privations'), was how another described 1917. Day and night were reversed. Once the streets had been filled, during the day, with breathless bustle; now they were deserted—for everyone had work to do, whether in a munitions factory or the local forces canteen. At night there was now complete darkness where once there had been a constellation of lights, and the sounds of steam-hammers and factory machinery where once there had been total silence. And the night was full of the noise of rumbling convoys and the long, ominous-looking trains that carried munitions or delivered the shattered bodies of soldiers straight to the sidings at the military hospitals.

Although the strain on civilian morale was severe, the crisis point in Great Britain was limited to a few anxious weeks in the summer of 1917 when it seemed likely that the entire war effort might founder. Then the last-minute adoption of the convoy system [fleets of Allied transport ships grouped together with war ships protecting them against U-boats] eased the situation. But in France hardship and social strains were more intense, and these, added to the terrible slaughter at the battle of Verdun, the previous year, created a condition in which a complete collapse of morale was always a possibility—a collapse which would have struck the foundations of the whole Allied effort.

Shortages Everywhere

The first real shortages, and first queues [lines of people] appeared in Great Britain in the early months of 1917. . . . Margarine, fats, milk, and bacon became very scarce. Sugar and butter were practically unobtainable. Even 'Government Control Tea'—often likened to sweepings off the floor—was very hard to get. Towards the end of the year there was a 'meat famine', followed by meat rationing early in the new year. Upper and middle-class families turned to substitute dishes. To them shepherd's pie [meat pie with baked potato crust] still seemed something of an outrage: 'but mummy, it's a particularly nasty piece of shepherd', lamented a little boy in one of the many cartoons which concentrated on the food situation. For working-class families the biggest hardship was the steep rise in the price of bread: to make matters worse, bread was 'Government Bread' whose various strange ingredients tended to go bad in warm weather.

Bombs, Strikes, and Scandals

To ram home the consequence of their submarine blockade the Germans unleashed the heaviest civilian [aircraft] bombing raids of the entire war: the underfed, war-weary citizens of London took to the tubes [subways] for shelter. Across the Channel there was little bombing in 1917 but in other respects France did not fare so well. During the harsh winter of 1916–17 coal supplies gave out. . . . In various parts of the country coal wagons were forcibly commandeered by members of the public. *Pâtisseries* [French pastry shops] were closed, and restaurant menus subject to severe restriction. Because of flagrant profiteering, the government encouraged the founding of co-operative and civic restaurants and industrial canteens with *prix fixe* ('fixed price') menus. The cost of living had gone up by at least eighty per cent since 1914, causing special hardship to the million or so refugees from the German-occupied areas scattered throughout the main centres of population.

Farmers and many small tradesmen were able to do well for themselves (American troops became a particularly good source of quick profit) but many bakers, adversely affected by government price control, went bankrupt. The salaried middle class suffered severely from the rising cost of living, while sections of the working classes, protected by government minimum wage laws, did not do too badly.

The February and October revolutions in Russia, by which eventually a major country was lost to the Allied cause, spread a tremor of excitement throughout the working-class movement in Great Britain and France, though war weariness and the high cost of living were probably sufficient to account for the great outbreak of industrial unrest which characterized 1917. In France there were 689 strikes involving 293,810 strikers (compared with only 98 strikes and 9,344 strikers in 1916). In Great Britain the 'May strikes [1917]', . . . caused such dislocation of war production that on 13th June the government appointed commissions of enquiry into industrial unrest. . . .

Other commissions noted food prices and profiteering as the main grievances. In Great Britain the political structure, reactivated by Lloyd George, just managed to survive the test, though there were bitter struggles between politicians and military leaders. In France there was a succession of political scandals, some dangerously tainted with defeatism. By the end of the year, three prime ministers had resigned. . . . Only the accession on 15th November of the seventy-six-year-old [Georges] Clemenceau gave promise of any restoration of leadership and stability.

The Razor and the Noose

In her use of submarine warfare Germany just failed to slash open the jugular vein of the Allied powers. But if the German weapon against the Allies was the razor, the Allies weapon against the Germans was the noose—and it was already applying slow strangulation. There were no bloodstains but the life was being squeezed from the German nation. As the war continued, so Germany's initial advantage disappeared: food imports from neutral countries came to a halt, and whatever requisitions [demands for foodstuffs] Germany might make from conquered territories these fell far short of redressing the balance. By the winter of 1916–17 the German people were already suffering hardships beyond anything endured in Great Britain or France. Yet, while the Allied press did occasionally carry stories of shortages and hunger in Berlin, they more usually concentrated on praising the thoroughness of Teutonic organization, setting it up as an example for the Allies to follow. In fact, ever since August 1916 when the dominion of General Erich Ludendorff (the new quartermaster general) and General Paul von Hindenburg (the new chief-of-staff) had been established, Teutonic [German] organization was not doing too well against the vested interests which were stronger in the loose confederation known as the German empire than in more homogeneous [united, uniform] countries like Great Britain and France. Part cause, more symptom, of Germany's troubles was the bad harvest of 1916: for all the pre-war advances farming was now in decay because of a shortage of farm workers and, thanks to the blockade, of a shortage of fertilizers and farm implements.

No Men, No Trains

The problem upon which the new military rulers concentrated was that of Germany's manpower shortage, staggeringly revealed in a census of 1916 which showed that although there were a million more women and thousands more children in employment, total numbers in productive employment were three-and-a-half million less than before the war. The 'Hindenburg Programme' of December 1916 was basically intended to surmount the manpower problem. Under the terms of a law of 5th December every male German citizen aged between seventeen and sixty not on active service, was to be drafted into 'Patriotic Auxiliary Service'. Because of the resistance of employers, who were as reluctant to employ women as they were to release their skilled men, and because there were many routes through which wealthier citizens could escape their obligations . . . the law was not very successful. The early months of 1917 revealed the 'Hindenburg Programme' to be falling far short of its targets. Manpower was the topic of the moment, rather as coal was in France and austerity food in Great Britain. . . .

Undue attention to manpower concealed the chaos which was developing in German transport. Before the war German imports had come inland from the North Sea ports by river and canal: now, with these ports blockaded, the main transport burden lay on the rail connections to the Ruhr and Silesian coalfields, to the iron deposits of occupied France, and to the food-stores of the east. Trains simply began to go missing as the various state and local authorities raided them for the provisions they needed. Close on the heels of the transport crisis there followed a widespread coal deficiency.

Poor German production figures—thirty to forty per cent less than before the war by 1917—revealed not so much inefficient leadership as the weariness of an underfed people. Etched deep into the German consciousness was the bitter 'Turnip Winter' of 1916–17 when in place of potatoes the people ate fodder beets—and there was not always a lot else to eat. For Germans it was not a question of the imposition of rationing—for two years they had had cards for bread, fats, milk, meat, and butter—but a question of whether the ration to which they were officially entitled would in fact be obtainable. . . . Total German consumption of meat in 1917 was one quarter of what it had been in pre-war years, and what was available was most inequitably distributed.

Throughout the year schoolchildren and women's organizations collected kitchen waste, coffee-grounds, hawthorn fruits, kernels of fruit, acorns and chestnuts, stinging nettles, pine cones, green leaves (as fodder), paper waste, rubber waste, cork and cork waste, tin waste, metals, parts of bulbs, bones, bottles, celluloid, rags and tatters, photographic silver residues, platinum (from discarded sets of teeth, or from jewellery), gramophone records, women's hair. Most notorious example of all of German thoroughness was the conversion of dead horses into soap. This prompted the Allied atrocity story that Germany was building 'corpse-conversion factories' to make soap from dead soldiers.

To the pains of hunger and squalor was added anger over profiteering and black marketeering. Price control, in the hands of over a thousand separate agencies, was totally inadequate. 'The black market,' said a speaker in the Reichstag [national legislature], 'has become the one really successful organization in our food supply system'. The famous memorandum from the Neukölln municipal council to the war food department, pirated in the left-wing press, revealed clearly what was happening. Big firms, using their economic power, or access to desirable commodities, were directly cornering food for their own employees; occasionally municipalities were able to do likewise, creating conditions of bitter local rivalry, and a complete breakdown of any pretence at food distribution. The memorandum predicted that from 'shortage and famine' the country would go to 'catastrophe'.

Even those allowed extra rations by virtue of their heavy manual work were getting less than half the necessary intake of calories. By late 1917 milk was practically unobtainable. Scarcity of soap brought a new menace: lice [parasites infecting human hair and skin]. The toll in disease and premature death was heavy. Death among those under five increased by fifty per cent in 1917; deaths from tuberculosis doubled. . . . Altogether nearly two million working days were lost [in strikes by German workers], compared with less than a quarter of a million in 1916 and 42,000 in 1915. In the German navy, bottled up in its own ports, frustration, privation, and bitterness were at boiling point. Sailors, as well as workmen and food rioters, participated in the second wave of strikes which broke out in June.

German Morale Crumbles

Social and industrial troubles, naturally, bubbled over into politics. The political crisis of July [1917] began with various vague promises of reform: if the workers had no bread, then they must have political rights—that was the argument of politicians. It ended with the resignation of the chancellor, Theobald von Bethmann Hollweg. But conditions got worse, especially for the farmers—who had earlier done reasonably well, but who were now subject to food searches, regulations, and enforced slaughter of their stock—officials, who in some cases were, literally, worked to death, and the salaried middle class. Relatively speaking the upper strata of the industrial working class did better, because in official circles the industrial worker was valued more highly than any other class in the community, except the military. . . .

The blockade, on both sides, brought home to the civilian populations some of the grim truths of war. From governments it brought, in a curious way, certain positive responses. Minimum wage laws and social welfare, designed to meet some of the grievances of the industrial worker were now seen to be as vital to the nation's survival as the man in the trenches. France was sorely tried. One more bloody reverse on the field of battle might well have been sufficient to let loose civil disorder. But on the whole civic loyalty in Great Britain and in France withstood the test. It was in Germany, apparently the efficient, disciplined nation, that the pressures of economic warfare exposed the selfishness of the employers, the jealousies of the different localities, the class antagonisms, and the hollow facade of the parliamentary structure.

In January 1918 Germany was hit by the third and mightiest wave of strikes. Subsiding before the priority needs of the last great German offensive [spring, 1918] it was, nonetheless, a clear sign that while Britain and France had, by a hair's breadth, managed to survive their worst year, 1917, the existing German system was approaching collapse and revolution.

Germany's Home Front Ordeal

Laurence Moyer

By 1916 the Allied naval blockade of Germany severely squeezed the German economy and civilian population. The following selection, by Connecticut-based historian Laurence Moyer, graphically portrays the growing hardships, including food shortages, inferior substitute foods, and inadequate wintertime heating in the cities. Germany's "turnip winter" of 1917 shaped a homefront mood of exhaustion and despair. Hungry and weary Germans confronted collapse and revolution by late 1918.

The potato harvest failed! A combination of wet weather, early frost, transport problems and shortage of field hands cut the usual fifty-million ton harvest to twenty-five million tons and the [German] home front felt the effects almost immediately. In early December 1916, in Berlin and soon thereafter throughout the country, food authorities informed citizens that in place of their usual ration of seven pounds of potatoes weekly, they would receive five pounds of potatoes and two pounds of turnips. Within a few weeks it became three pounds of potatoes and four pounds of turnips; by the middle of January 1917, it became five pounds of turnips and two of potatoes. In February, potatoes ran out completely in many parts of Germany. The nation found itself forced to survive the winter on a diet of turnips.

Food Shortages and the Turn to Turnips

This was the so-called "Swedish turnip" (*Kohlrüben*), a coarse, bland, tasteless, stringy root crop, unappetizing and unnutritious, suitable chiefly for animal fodder for which vast quantities had been planted. Cookbooks before the war

Excerpted from *Victory Must Be Ours: Germany in the Great War, 1914–1918*, by Laurence Moyer. Copyright © 1995 by Laurence Moyer. Reprinted by permission of the publisher, Hippocrene Books, New York.

contained an adage describing how serving such turnips would drive children from the dinner table. It was, in no sense, a satisfactory substitute for the potato.

This turnip also replaced potato meal and thus found its way into "stretchers" used in bread. In other guises it formed a major component in marmalade and a dozen other products. Homemakers sought ways to put them into soups, casseroles, baked and boiled dishes but nothing resembled anything appetizing. What made this nearly intolerable was the increased scarcity of almost everything else. Diminishing grain supplies forced a cutback in the bread supply. In shivering January weather, bakery store lines grew longer as newspapers spoke of a "bread calamity" when rations were not always available. Butter and other fats fell to two ounces per person a week which meant that fried foods were out; meals became a dreary succession of watery, boiled dishes or bone-dry baked offerings. Milk became ever more scarce and the beer shortage reached such dimensions that some Berlin breweries closed down and many inns served food only during restricted, reduced, hours. Most fruits and vegetables had become only a memory. It was an *Ersatz* [simulation] manufacturers paradise.

If turnips were genuine, they nonetheless left a distinctly unappetizing aftertaste both physically and psychologically. Yet it was the only edible food readily available. Thus most Germans learned to subsist on a steady diet of turnips plus, usually, seven ounces of turnip-stretched bread daily. Some coal miners and other heavy workers had to contend with ten-hour workdays on a diet of boiled turnips to which a potato or two had been added, supplemented only by a slice or two of dry, grey bread on which turnip marmalade had been spread. This "turnip winter" virtually destroyed any pleasure in eating. One went to bed hungry, woke up in the morning to face another day of tasteless turnips to sustain life. That winter, Albert Speer [Hitler's armaments czar in World War II] later recalled, although his mother cleverly devised many variations for turnip dishes, he became so hungry he consumed an entire bag of stone-hard dog biscuits which had been left over from peacetime.

In Berlin, an irreverent poet penned a new oath appropriate to the times:

> I believe in the Turnip, the Holy Provider of the German people, and in marmalade, its begotten son, conceived by the City Food Office, born in the War Nourishment Office, died with the hope of potatoes, buried and suffered under the price gougers and the farmers. Gathered up, pressed and processed, and risen again as Bread, from whence ye shall come to be a bread-spread for Germany's heroic sons. I believe in the Holy War, the universal society of price gougers, the community of foragers, the resurrection of taxes, the reduction of meat rations, and the eternal existence of the bread ration card.

A Berlin newspaper conducted a contest for the best recipes for turnips. The winning soup recipe (for 5 persons) consisted of two pounds of turnips combined with two beef bullion cubes and two potatoes. Its creator added, "it tastes better with the addition of some cabbage." This winter of 1916–1917 would turn out to be the worst winter of the war with respect to food supplies.

Mounting Problems for Civilian Germans

Nature had also decreed that this would be one of the coldest winters on record, made more unbearable because of immense coal shortages. In early February, Berlin registered an unusual seven degrees below zero (Fahrenheit) and in other cities the temperatures dipped even lower as waves of frigid arctic air swept across the continent, the cold wave continuing deep into March. In Nuremberg, thirty-five thousand homes ran completely out of heating coal before the winter ended, resulting in an epidemic of burst pipes. Most cities drastically cut back on electricity and gas in order to save coal. Streetlights in Berlin, Munich, and other cities fell dim or completely out at nighttime. Schools which ran out of coal closed down until the spring. At the end of January, more than half of Berlin's elementary schools had closed, its students crowding into those schools which still possessed a coal supply. At the very time when war production required ever greater quantities of coal, mining production declined. In 1913, Germany produced 190 million tons of coal; in 1916, this fell to 159 million tons.

Burst pipes became such an everyday occurrence that one observer compared Germany to the scene from Dante's inferno that described icy, frigid conditions. Railroads stopped heating coaches and some municipal authorities permitted central heating for apartments to be reduced from 66 degrees to 59 degrees Fahrenheit. "Now, one sees faces like masks, blue with cold and drawn by hunger" noted [a woman diarist]. . . . Toward the end of January, it began to snow in Berlin; for several days the snow descended in gale force and by the time it had finished, the city found itself brought to a standstill with clogged streets. But the sanitation force was at the front as were most of Berlin's horses. To free the streets for traffic, Berlin's military Commander, General von Kessel, ordered the citizenry to clear the streets themselves, forthwith. Fortified, no doubt, with a cup of turnip soup and some acorn *Ersatz* coffee, they shoveled the snow on to whatever carts were available and hauled it away to the river Spree.

But in ways that were more serious than mere physical exertion, the "turnip winter" began to take its toll on the nation's health. Teachers reported a tiredness and lack of vitality among their students. Adults in offices complained of lapses of memory and of making mistakes in calculations and workers were often reported to be apathetic at work. Physicians noted an alarming increase in cases of stomach and skin problems and serious digestive disorders. Ominously, health authorities registered a slight but disturbing rise in tuberculosis cases. These health problems, stemming as much from the accumulated impact of years of shortages and substitutes as from the turnips and winter cold, served warning that the nation could not continue to endure such shortages indefinitely.

And, if Karl Scheffler is to be believed, a spiritual and emotional exhaustion further beset the nation. Karl Scheffler, popular playwright and writer, assessed the mood of Christmastime 1916 and concluded that it was tormented with a sickness of the soul, a kind of spiritual sea-sickness or vertigo. He believed that the rush of unimaginable events both at home and on the front had become so overpowering as to disorient the psyche, too violent and catastrophic to be internalized, bringing in its wake a separation between internal equilibrium and external events. "The agony of wartime," he wrote, "is that the rhythm of external events varies so greatly with the rhythm of the soul as to be incompatible . . . bringing about a form of spiritual nausea."

Women, War, and Work

Gail Braybon

The home fronts of the nations at war witnessed an unprecedented entry of women into jobs important to the
war effort. Women were especially visible in wartime munitions factories, but they also entered many other jobs
such as transportation and white-collar service work tied
to the war. However, as British historian Gail Braybon
makes clear in this study of working women in the warring
nations, myths abound about the extent to which the
Great War transformed women's social status. Women's
wartime employment gains mostly failed to survive the
end of the conflict. Returning male soldiers soon replaced
female industrial workers, and economic and social inequality between the sexes prevailed in the postwar era.

Within months of the outbreak of war, journalists, politicians, social scientists, and other commentators across
Britain, France, and Germany began to talk of its impact on
'society'. With surprising rapidity, the idea took hold that
military and industrial mobilization would have a permanent, possibly radical, effect on class, sex, and familial relations. Debates on women workers' future were ironically fu-
elled by writers from widely differing political backgrounds.
Feminists sought to show that women's new skills must now
be recognized by all, and that they should be rewarded with
'the Vote'; the patriotic right [conservatives] (and government commentators) used 'women's wonderful work' as propaganda, proof that the nation was united against the enemy;
other writers, from a variety of backgrounds, warned that
women workers might not want to go 'home' after their experience of new jobs and higher wages, a fear played upon by

Reprinted from "Women, War, and Work," by Gail Braybon, in *The Oxford Illustrated History of the First World War,* edited by Hew Strachan, by permission of Oxford University Press. Copyright © Oxford University Press, 1998.

some trade unionists, concerned with the possible danger of cheap female labour. In many ways, women became a focus for both anxiety and hope amongst those who looked forward to the post-war world.

Myth and Reality

Contemporary interest in women's role was by no means surprising, given the essential nature of their war work, and their sudden visibility on the urban scene, performing a wide variety of tasks 'normally' done by men, from window cleaning to clipping train tickets. What is perhaps more intriguing is the extent to which so many recent social historians have also accepted the idea that the war was a social and political 'watershed' for women, and even that it marked the 'emancipation' of women. The enduring myth that women's wartime jobs led to dramatic social change can be summed up by this quotation, from a book about the war's impact on world history:

> The social behaviour and dress of women altered concomitantly with these changes of status. Women and girls frequented the night clubs that had sprung up during the war, and single women dined in restaurants without escorts. Women began to smoke in public, and their drinking increased. They took up the free use of cosmetics, the bobbing of hair, and the wearing of short skirts or slacks and uniforms at work. Their new social freedom encouraged freer sexual relations, the consequences of increasing promiscuity and illegitimacy.

This is patronizing, misleading, and so inaccurate as to be unworthy of further discussion, but it is a fairly typical piece of hyperbole [exaggeration]. There are two main problems with this kind of approach. The first is that it makes assumptions about 'social change' based solely on apparent changes in women's employment patterns—which, as we shall see, have been much exaggerated. Such generalizations do justice neither to the complexities of arguments about women's work, nor to the variety of women's wartime experiences. Secondly, it assumes 'Women' were some kind of coherent group, with a uniform set of aims, ambitions, and experiences. This was not the case. Women's wartime lives were as varied as men's; they were influenced by class, age, marital status, trade, geographical area. Such immediate issues as food rationing, fuel prices, rents, and even local censorship also had an impact. Consider the lives of the following individuals: an Italian peasant woman, running a farm on her own; a Russian nurse on the eastern front; a Scottish fish gutter, unemployed in 1914; a French car worker; a Berlin housewife, sewing uniforms at home; a Woolwich Arsenal [London] worker, forced to leave work because of TNT poisoning. These women had very different wartime experiences, and one can be quite certain that they had more on their minds than bobbing their hair, night clubs, and smoking.

Working Women Before 1914

The political and economic structures of Britain, France, and Germany were quite different, yet the role of women in industry before the war was strikingly similar. Most women workers were single, and they always earned considerably less than men, even when working on similar jobs. Usually, there were rigid demarcations between 'men's work' and 'women's work', and any skilled trade which required apprenticeship or long training was almost by definition 'men's'. It was widely assumed that women would leave work on marriage; this encouraged women themselves to view their work as temporary, and employers to under-utilize their skills. They were often viewed with suspicion by trade unions, which tended to cater for skilled men, and saw any suggestion of using female labour as a threat to wages, status, and jobs. Women were also said not to 'need' job security or higher wages, as they were not the primary breadwinners. In reality, however, many working-class wives did move in and out of work according to financial need, and their presence in industry was underestimated by official figures. They took in washing, went out cleaning, did childminding for neighbours, worked for a few hours in the corner shop, or took in lodgers. Middle-class wives, on the other hand, seldom worked after marriage. The rapidly expanding numbers of white-collar jobs in offices, banking, and government departments were taken up by young single women. There were also increasingly large numbers of women in teaching, though only up to a certain level, as they were still barred from many universities.

There was one big difference between Britain and mainland Europe, however, and this was the extent to which women worked on the land. France and Germany still had a large number of peasant farmers, including millions of women, while in Britain, with its large farms and extensive use of agricultural machinery, most rural workers were men.

Russia too had an enormous peasant population, but there were few similarities between this vast, under-industrialized nation and the other three countries. This was an autocratic and strongly patriarchal society, in which women's status was very low. In rural areas, they were completely under the control of husbands or fathers, and confined to hard and unskilled work. Domestic violence was both common and acceptable. Urban dwellers were a small minority—only around 3 million out of a total of 170 million worked in industry in 1914—but in Russia's towns and cities working conditions were worse than anything found in western Europe, where factory inspectors and limits on hours and night work went some way towards curbing the worst exploitation in major industries. All wages were low, but women's were far lower than men's, and those who campaigned for workers' rights risked imprisonment or exile. Housing conditions too were worse, with women factory workers often billeted in barracks attached to workshops. There were also few jobs available for educated women, as white-collar trades were not expanding as fast as in western Europe.

Two other facts are worth noting. The first is that all four countries had feminist movements, although these were of varying size, organization, and militancy. Britain's feminists were by far the most active, but there were high hopes for women's suffrage across western Europe—though Russia seemed to have little prospect of gaining democratic rights for either men or women. The second is that the largest single trade for women was still domestic service. Numbers were declining by 1914, as other job opportunities arose, but service remained the only waged work available for the majority of working-class girls. . . .

Industrial Mobilization of Women

As workers, women were newly 'visible' in the towns of Britain, France, and Germany from an early stage in the war, as they took over the jobs of fathers, husbands, and sons who had been called up, or volunteered. Within a few months it was common to see women road sweepers, lamplighters, delivery van drivers, or shop assistants. Their labour was also required across mainland Europe to bring in the harvests of the autumn of 1914. However, it was not until 1915 that the serious recruitment of women to major industries began. As casualty figures rose, more men were withdrawn from civilian life to replace the dead and maimed. A competition for men began between Europe's voracious armies and the war industries, now under pressure to deliver munitions on an unprecedented scale. Third in line for human resources were the civilian industries. Employers turned first to boys, old men, 'colonial' or foreign labour, and even prisoners of war— but in the end they had to accept that women would be necessary to keep both war and civilian factories operating.

The increase in women's industrial employment between 1915 and 1918 seems at first sight astonishing. In Russia, by 1917 it was estimated that women made up 43.2 per cent of the industrial workforce. In the German chemical industry alone, the number of women workers rose from 26,749 in 1913 to 208,877 in 1918; in the machine industry, numbers rose from 74,642 in 1913 to 493,374 in 1918. A single armaments firm, Krupps, employed only 2,000–3,000 women before the war, and 28,000 by January 1918. In France, it was calculated that women made up 33 per cent of the total labour force in munitions by spring 1918. Yet such figures can be misleading, as a closer look at the British statistics reveals. A contemporary analyst calculated that in 1914 there were around 3,276,000 women in full-time employment in industry, finance, and the professions, with another 1,600,000 in domestic service. This is certainly an underestimate, given the number of women in casual work, but is a useful starting point, giving a total of nearly 4.9 million women in waged work. By 1918, the same analyst estimated that there were 4,808,000 women in industry, and 1,200,000 in domestic work, a total of 6 million women workers. Two things are obvious. First, the total number of waged women only increased by about 1 million during the war, and secondly, a large number of domestic servants took the opportunity to find better jobs. (This shift was noticeable all across Europe—and indeed in the United States, where white domestic servants often found factory work, and many black women moved from the land to service in their place.) What seems to have happened in Britain was a transfer of women *from* low-paid 'women's work' *to* the war industries and transport, particularly trams and trains. Their reasons for taking such work varied. The jobs were usually better paid, they were often more interesting, and many women felt that they would like to 'do their bit' in supporting the troops as well. Numbers were further increased by girls entering work straight from school, and by married women—of all ages—whose labour was, for once, in demand. At this point, therefore, we can dispense with one of the most abiding myths of the First World War. Contrary to propaganda reports at the time, there was no enormous influx of non-working women into men's jobs: millions of working-class women in Britain moved into *different* trades when the opportunity arose. Furthermore, most women in industry and transport were working class. Although propagandists waxed lyrical about the idea of duchesses or colonels' daughters in the workshop, in reality there were few middle- or upper-class volunteers in the factories.

Working Women Face Job Inequalities

Women's move into industrial and transport jobs followed a similar pattern in France and Germany, although the amount of state interference varied from country to country. In Britain, the government managed many private factories for the duration of the war, as well as its own shipyards and arsenals. The introduction of women here was done with the co-operation of both employers and trade unions. Negotiations in 1915 culminated in a series of agreements about women's work on 'men's jobs' in munitions and engineering. It was to be temporary, they would not be trained up as 'fully skilled tradesmen'; and they would be paid equal wages on work 'customarily done by men'. In practice, women rarely achieved equal pay, even on very similar work, while in the [artillery shell] filling factories they were still classed as doing 'women's work' and paid accordingly, in spite of the risk of explosion or TNT poisoning. Women's wages in most jobs remained low compared to men's, but high compared to those in traditional women's trades like service or dressmaking. . . .

There was less government intervention [on behalf of women workers] in France and Germany [than in Britain]. It was usually left to employers and trade unions to sort out the terms on which women would be admitted.] But many employers, like those in Britain, were cynical about women's capacities, and anticipated laying them off as soon as the war was over. Certainly many trade unions maintained a hostile stance. To quote the French metalworkers' words of 1917: 'the systematic introduction of women into workshops is entirely at odds with the establishment and maintenance of homes and family life.' Yet in spite of much rhetoric about the health and welfare of mothers, future and actual, governments, employers, and unions paid little attention to the practical problems of women working in the war industries. Crèches [day nurseries] and canteens, though appearing later in the war, remained uncommon; regulations on the supply of nursing rooms in French factories were seldom followed, and no allowance was made for the time women might need to spend queuing for food. Protective legislation had been largely suspended in 1914, leaving women open to exploitation and exceptionally long hours in munitions. Industrial injuries occurred in all munitions factories in all countries. In France, for example, there were 69,606 reported industrial accidents in 1917, resulting in 59 fatalities, and thousands of permanent disabilities. It gradually dawned on each government that exhausted workers were inefficient workers, and the eight-hour shift returned in the later years of the war—although there was always overtime to add on. Women in civilian industries like transport often fared better, earning improved wages but facing fewer risks to health.

This much, women had in common. But at the same time there were major differences between the experiences of women in different areas of Europe. For example, in Britain the increase in domestic food production during the war years was achieved largely without additional female labour—older men, boys, prisoners of war, soldiers, and machinery were enough. The Women's Land Army arrived late in the day, and offered some skilled support in ploughing, gardening, and milking, but employed only a few women in farming. In contrast, the peasant farms of mainland Europe depended heavily on women's labour, often leaving younger girls to take care of the housework. Yet even peasant women's experiences were not uniform. In France, farm incomes rose, and women experienced a new level of prosperity in nearly all regions. Incomes were further raised by the state allowances paid to soldiers' wives and parents (which many Italian or Russian peasant women, for example, did not have.) Local observers frequently commented on the positive effects of this small extra guaranteed income. A schoolmaster reported: 'Never before has the wife of a day labourer, the mother of three children, received 82.50 F [francs] per month, the amount of her allowance. . . . More than one mother of a family, whose husband has been called up, is now able to buy things she had wanted a long time.'

As always, there were also those who disapproved of women earning more money than usual, complaining of women's 'profligacy, laziness and drunkenness', or even their 'debauchery' as a result of such untold wealth. While many rural areas prospered, food prices rose in towns, causing bitter complaint, yet there were no real food shortages in France—or in Britain.

Women Workers and Hardships of War

In contrast, Germany, suffering from the effects of the allied blockade, was increasingly short of food (and fuel) from early in the war. The average daily calorie input for a civilian adult dropped from around 1,500 in 1915 to below 1,000, in the winters of 1916–17 and 1917–18. Life for urban dwellers became increasingly miserable with even turnips, acorns, and horse chestnuts rationed. . . .

Rates of pneumonia and tuberculosis increased, and the death rate per thousand women went up from 11.2 in 1914 to 17.8 in 1918. The situation in Austria was similar. These deteriorating conditions had a dramatic effect on women's willingness (and ability) to do a great deal of industrial work. Not only did women have to queue for food on a daily basis, but at the weekend thousands of them took trains into the country in search of black market supplies. Many wives took in homework (poorly paid as usual) but would not work full-time in munitions, needing time to search for food instead. Ironically, the separation allowances paid to soldiers' wives actually discouraged women's full-time work by topping up part-time wages. This in turn exacerbated labour shortages. . . .

Russia's wartime factory conditions were inevitably even worse, given how little protective legislation was in force, and the fact that workers had no rights at all. Women carried a major burden in both town and country, yet had to survive on the lowest wages in Europe.

In these deteriorating circumstances, existing divisions in society—between town and country, between classes, and certainly between government and governed—grew wider. Britain and France managed to maintain a relatively united home front during the war, aided by good food supplies and maintenance of trade with the rest of the world, in spite of the German naval threat. Strikes, over wages and rents, increased as war-weariness spread, but morale never really plummeted. In contrast, the working classes of both Germany and Russia grew ever more desperate. It is no coincidence that so many strikes were led by women in 1917, and that looting of food shops was often done by mothers and children who had little to lose. (This happened in Italy too, where threats to send strikers to the front could hardly be used against women.) As a German military commander commented, the women's behaviour in 1917–18 was understandable: 'they are supposed to work and cater for their hungry families and see that they are powerless to do so.' . . .

The Aftermath of War

At the end of the war, there was a general desire that life should return to 'normal'—in so far as this was possible for victors or vanquished. (Clearly there was no possibility of 'normality' in Russia after the 1917 revolutions.) Women's task, in this post-war world, was to rebuild the homes of Europe. In Britain, women's ostensible [apparent] 'reward' for their work was suffrage for those over 30, though in truth the extension of franchise had probably been delayed rather than accelerated by the exigencies [demands] of war. In France, the feminists, who had been so convinced that they were on the verge of winning changes in the civil code and franchise, were now told that 'While women did give immense service to France during the war, they did so for love of *patrie* [country], not in the expectation of reward: it would be an insult to pay them for their patriotism.' Although the Chamber of Deputies passed a bill granting women's suffrage, the Senate voted against. It was in France that women bore the brunt of 'pro-natalist' legislation. Their role now was 'to give birth and give birth and give birth once again. A woman who refuses to bear children no longer deserves the rights she enjoys.' In 1920, a law was passed against the dissemination of information about birth control, and this was followed three years later by anti-abortion legislation. Penalties were large fines and imprisonment. In spite of much talk about encouraging motherhood, no other country was so aggressively pro-natalist—though significantly, the French birth rate remained low.

In the new post-war climate, women industrial workers were dismissed with alacrity. Even legislation was widely used to remove them from 'men's jobs'. They were supposed to go back to their old jobs, or their husbands—if these were still alive. A notice on the wall of one French munitions factory advised that, 'Now you may best serve your country by returning to your former pursuits, busying yourselves with peacetime activities.' Many women were shocked by the treatment they received, after years of being told that their labour was essential to the war effort. As one wrote to the French paper *La Vague*: 'My husband has been in the army for the last six years. I have worked like a slave at Citroën [armaments manufacturer] during the war. I sweated blood there, losing my youth and my health. In January I was fired, and since then have been poverty-stricken.'

Those still in work encountered abuse in the streets and criticism in the papers for their selfishness, while the unemployed faced a concerted effort by labour exchanges [employment bureaus] to get them back into 'women's trades'. One German exchange reported in 1919 that 'the reluctance to accept positions in domestic service has not diminished', and another confirmed that it was 'extraordinarily difficult to return these groups to their earlier occupations or to re-educate them to new circumstances'. These words were echoed by officials in France and Britain. The 1920s were to prove difficult years for many women workers. Married women were often barred from both white-collar and industrial jobs, and female workers were nearly always first in line for short-time working or redundancy [layoff]. Some said that life was harder than it had been during the war, when at least work was easy to find.

Although women strongly resisted the pressure to return to domestic service (and numbers never returned to pre-war levels) it was clear by the early 1920s that the old patterns of male and female employment had reasserted themselves. White-collar trades and light industrial work continued to use increasing numbers of female workers, but these trends had been established before the war. The world, it seemed, had not been turned upside down by the millions of women who worked in munitions factories, or on trams and trains.

Yet although one might conclude that the war's influence on women's employment prospects was broadly neutral, this fact should not be allowed to overshadow the importance of the war's wider effects—good or bad—on women as individuals. Furthermore, as we have seen, women's work cannot be viewed in isolation: their feelings about their work were inevitably influenced by the social, economic, and political environment in which they lived. There were those, particularly in Britain, who felt that these were the most exciting years of their lives, giving them a sense of purpose and companionship, with the added bonus of good wages. There were others, particularly in Germany, for whom the war marked a new level of poverty, hunger, anxiety, and exhaustion. In Russia, meanwhile, memories of war were soon overtaken and dwarfed by revolution.

Furthermore, the progress of the war itself affected women deeply, often pushing all thought of work or ambition into the background. For many of them, the most important thing was whether the men they knew survived. We know that there were millions of war widows, many of whom were young, and had children. We cannot even guess at the numbers who lost fathers, brothers, sons, and friends. Nor was death the only legacy of the war. Other women had to learn to live with men who returned mentally or physically scarred, including those too ill or badly injured to work again. This experience did not end in 1918.

Anti-German Hysteria in the United States

Meirion Harries and Susie Harries

As the United States desperately mobilized for war after entering the conflict in April 1917, the Wilson administration launched a national propaganda program not unlike Britain's. President Wilson's worries in March 1917 that U.S. intervention might unleash a "spirit of ruthless brutality" throughout American society proved sadly correct. British authors Meirion Harries and Susie Harries portray here the hysterical anti-German campaign that Wilson's Committee on Public Information encouraged and ultimately could not control. Merely being a German American was dangerous by 1918, as the following excerpt from the Harries' history of the American experience in World War I shows.

The failure of Woodrow Wilson and his war managers to unite the country behind the war did not mean that the CPI's [Committee on Public Information, Wilson's propaganda agency] gigantic effort had been without effect. What the [CPI] propaganda had done was intensify many of the pressures that had been building up within American society before the war, to the point where an explosion was inevitable. The war effort, as much as the fighting itself, was inflicting damage on the American psyche that in some ways was irreversible. This became most obvious in the summer and fall of 1918, a period of mass paranoia to rival the later [1950s] McCarthy era, when hatred, mistrust, and hysteria would grip the nation.

Mobilizing Hate

With the prime motivations of any war—the threat of invasion and the fight for survival—missing from the American matrix [situation], Wilson's propagandists had concentrated on two main themes: hatred for the enemy and loyalty to the flag. The one was far easier to inspire than the other, as Wilson himself had predicted before the fighting had even begun. "Once lead this people into war," he had told newspaper editor Frank Cobb in March 1917, "and they'll forget there ever was such a thing as tolerance. To fight you must be brutal and ruthless, and the spirit of ruthless brutality will enter into the very fiber of our national life, infecting Congress, the courts, the policeman on the beat, the man in the street."

It was not hard to generate hate for the Hun [derogatory term for Germans, World War I era], particularly after American soldiers began to be killed. But Germans were not just an external enemy, they were woven into the fabric of the [American] Republic itself; for decades they had been a solid, successful, integral component of communities across the nation. Then the machinations of Dr. Hexamer and the National German-American Alliance in the neutrality years had helped place a question mark over their loyalty—and now, everywhere, the hate [CPI propaganda chief George] Creel stirred spilled over them.

At the outset, the CPI insisted on a degree of calm and atrocity stories were outlawed. But as the temperature of the war effort rose, cool reason dissolved. "It is difficult to unite a people by talking only on the highest ethical plane. To fight for an ideal, perhaps, must be coupled with thoughts of self-preservation."

Propaganda Films and Pamphlets

In April 1918, the CPI began screenings of its most famous hate movie, the film "that blocked Broadway": *The Kaiser, the Beast of Berlin*. This epic portrayed the burning of Louvain [historic Belgian city] and the agony of the *Lusitania*, and depicted the Kaiser telling the American ambassador that he would "stand no nonsense from America after the war." In

Omaha, Nebraska, 14,000 people saw the film—"the largest number that ever saw a motion picture in Omaha in one week."

In print, one of the CPI's most popular publications, *Why America Fights Germany*, picked up the theme of invasion so skillfully exploited by prewar preparedness campaigners. Having made a successful landing on American soil, the Hun advances until he reaches Lakewood, New Jersey. There the apostles of *Kultur* [German civilization] demand wine, beer, and money. "One feeble old woman tries to conceal $20 which she had been hoarding in her desk drawer; she is taken out and hanged. . . . Some of the teachers in the two district schools meet a fate which makes them envy her. The Catholic priest and Methodist minister are thrown into a pig-sty while the German soldiers look on and laugh." Then, inevitably, the invaders get drunk and "robbery, murder and outrage run riot. Fifty leading citizens are lined up against the First National Bank and shot. Most of the town and the beautiful pinewoods are burned, and then the troops move on to treat New Brunswick in the same way."

The British had used atrocity stories shamelessly to aid their propaganda, most notably in the Bryce Report on German atrocities published at the time of the sinking of the *Lusitania*. In November 1917, Creel's committee issued its own report, *German War Practices*, and urged the Four-Minute Men [CPI patriotic speakers used at movie theaters] to arouse their audiences with choice examples of *Schreck-lichkeit* ("frightfulness"). Some duly responded with calls to string up "Withered Willie" from the tallest tower in the Wilhelmstrasse and to keep "those goose-stepping, baby-killing gorillas" away from U.S. shores.

Popular Paranoia Unleashed

Rumor was an effective catalyst of hatred. Germans, it was whispered, were putting ground glass into food, poison on Red Cross bandages; there was sympathy for the Hun in high places (Attorney General Gregory had to defend his wife's German antecedents). Spy fever reached epidemic proportions: the flashes of light refracted from the stained-glass windows of William Randolph Hearst's apartment on Riverside Drive [in New York City] were read as being signals to German submarines skulking in the Hudson River below.

Across the country, all things German came under attack. Beethoven's music was banned in Pittsburgh. King George III was lambasted anew in American history lessons, but now for his German origins. German Americans anglicized their names (as had the current King of England). Frankfurters [became] . . . "Liberty sausages," dachshunds became "Liberty dogs," sauerkraut (where it continued to be served) was "Liberty cabbage," hamburgers were "Salisbury steak."

The New York Times put German publications into intellectual quarantine: "Any book whatever that comes to us from a German printing press is open to suspicion. The German microbe is hiding somewhere between its covers." The eminent publisher Irving Putnam signed a pledge, declaring, "I am opposed to opening the markets of America to the products of Germany for the next 25 years, and I will knowingly buy and use no German-made goods during the said period of time." . . . German-language teaching was banned in many schools and the books burnt, in fear of the insidious threat of cultural slavery. "Behind the chair of innumerable teachers we have seen the shadow of the spiked helmet," raved one speaker at a conference of the League to Enforce Peace.

Coercion and Violence

Festering through 1917, paranoia deepened after Ludendorff's 1918 offensives and now more often erupted into violence. Gangs of vigilantes ransacked German Americans' homes and daubed yellow paint onto the walls; they tarred and feathered the men and made them crawl down the main streets of cities. The Cleveland *Plain Dealer* reported that in Willard, Ohio, on March 28, a Mr. and Mrs. Zuelch "were taken by a crowd of men to the city hall and there before a crowd of 200 persons compelled to salute the American flag and then kiss it. A flag was given to Zuelch and he was commanded to display it in front of his cigar store. It was waving there tonight."

Other mobs were not so restrained. Early in April, a young man named Robert Prager, a drifter with an argumentative manner and vaguely socialist views, fell foul of a group of miners in Maryville, Kentucky. Prager was German by birth, but as soon as America had entered the war he had taken out his first papers applying for citizenship and tried to enlist in the U.S. Army; being blind in one eye, he had been rejected.

The miners now jeered and hustled him and paraded him through town as an enemy spy. The next day, Prager posted a characteristically disputatious document demanding his rights. That night a mob of about seventy-five men left the saloon and made its way to his house. They pulled off his shoes, shirt, and trousers, draped him roughly in a flag, and made him march through the streets singing a patriotic song. Police officers extricated him and escorted him to the police station, but the mob forced its way in. They took him to the outskirts of town, where they put a tow rope around his neck. Prager asked to write a letter to his parents in Dresden, telling them he was about to die. Then he said, "All right, boys, go ahead and kill me, but wrap me in the flag when you bury me." Half an hour after midnight, they lynched him. The ringleaders of the mob who hanged Prager were themselves put on trial. At their trial, the mob leaders wore red, white, and blue ribbons in their buttonholes. As the jury acquitted them, one of the jurors cried, "Well, I guess nobody can say we aren't loyal now."

Chapter 5

Peace and the Legacy of World War I

Turning Points
IN WORLD HISTORY

A Troubled Peace

David Thomson

Noted Cambridge University historian David Thomson (1912–1970) argues in this selection that Allied statesmen shaped a postwar peace settlement based on compromises that reflected the instability of the postwar world. The peacemakers, especially in the eastern European settlement, often faced difficulties with ethnic groups in new nation-states like Poland and Czechoslovakia.

Representatives of 'the allied or associated belligerent powers' met at Paris in January 1919 to lay down the conditions of peace. They included spokesmen not only of the main Allies and succession states [nation-states succeeding the collapsed central and east European empires], but also of those powers which had, in the later phases, broken off diplomatic relations with the enemy powers. These were Bolivia, Ecuador, Peru, and Uruguay. China and Siam, having at the last moment declared war, were included amongst the allied belligerents. Former enemy states were excluded, so all the treaties except that of Lausanne with Turkey in 1923 were dictated and not negotiated.

Conflicting Aims of the 'Big Three'

The conduct and the main lines of the settlement were determined by the 'Big Three'—President Wilson of the United States, Georges Clemenceau of France, and David Lloyd George, the Prime Minister of Britain. Japan and Italy were at first included in the inner circle of leading powers, but their representatives soon absented themselves. Wilson's chief aims were to ensure the application of the general

Excerpted from *World History from 1914 to 1968*, 3rd ed., by David Thomson. Copyright © 1969 by Oxford University Press. Reprinted with permission from Oxford University Press.

principles he had enunciated for a just peace, and to set up the League of Nations. In order to get general agreement to the League he was driven to compromise on the application of his general principles in the territorial settlement, and consoled himself with the reflection that parts of the territorial and political settlement which he disliked could in time be improved, at more leisure, through the working of the League as an agency of conciliation and peaceful change. The actual settlement was, in consequence, a series of bargains and compromises between the high-minded but often unrealistic desires of Wilson, the nationalistic and intensely realistic demands of Clemenceau, and the somewhat unstable and opportunistic aims of Lloyd George.

The settlement, and particularly that part of it included in the Treaty of Versailles made with Germany, has often been criticized for being such a patchwork of conflicting purposes. Yet it was not necessarily the worse for that. What else was so large an international conference for, if it was not to find the highest common measure of agreement among states whose aims and interests in many ways conflicted? Wilson's general principles, had they been applied consistently, would have had disastrous and often absurd results: yet his enormous personal prestige and his persistence did succeed in infusing some wider vision into the arrangements. The exaggerated demands of Clemenceau and Lloyd George, had they not been moderated, would have resulted in a Carthaginian peace [harsh, like the terms ancient Rome imposed on Carthage]: yet they did serve to remind Wilson of the grimmer realities of European politics. A more serious criticism is that the settlement was not only a patchwork, but that it was harsh in the wrong places and lenient in the wrong ways. How far this criticism is valid may best be judged from the main arrangements made and from the degree of permanence they proved to have.

The German Settlement

Belgian independence was restored, and the provinces of Alsace and Lorraine were returned to France, from whom Germany had taken them in 1871. This was indisputably just.

France also gained ownership of the Saar coalfields, and the area was to be administered for fifteen years by a League of Nations' Commission. In 1935, after the prescribed plebiscite [vote] among the population, it was returned to Germany. This arrangement, again, worked reasonably well. The Rhineland was to remain in allied military occupation for fifteen years, as a guarantee that Germany would fulfil the Treaty. This was a compromise, and from the French viewpoint a most unsatisfactory one. Clemenceau, urged by [French general Ferdinand] Foch, had at first demanded indefinite control of the Rhine bridgeheads as a military guarantee of French security. The United States and Britain refused to agree, and persuaded the French to accept instead a joint Anglo-American guarantee to support France immediately if she were again attacked by Germany. But when the Treaty was not ratified by the American Senate this guarantee lapsed on the United States' side, and Britain then claimed that this invalidated her part of the bargain. France, in consequence, felt that she had been tricked into surrendering her material security for what now proved to be a worthless diplomatic assurance. Hence her feverish quest throughout the interwar years for more firm safeguards of national security. The fifteen-year occupation of the Rhineland proved equally illusory: it meant that allied forces would be withdrawn just after the interval of time which Germany needed to revive her ambitions and regain her military strength. It can certainly be contended that the material securities exacted from Germany were in these ways too slight.

On the other hand, the attempts to insist on German acceptance of the so-called War Guilt Clause were quite unrealistic. A sense of moral responsibility could not be created by including a statement of it in a document which German representatives were compelled to sign: and the demand for reparations for war-damage inflicted by the German armies, which was made to hinge upon this statement, was pitched in astronomical figures without any serious consideration of how it would be economically possible for Germany to pay or for the Allies to receive such wealth. No figure of reparations was fixed in the Treaty, although vast claims were made by France, Belgium, and Britain. A Reparations Commission was set up to fix the amount to be demanded and to arrange for the methods and time of payment. In this way the unavoidable difficulties were shelved, and left to be a recurrent source of rancour [bitter hate] during the next decade. Immediately, however, other forms of reparation were exacted. Germany was deprived of all her colonial possessions and most of her fleet. Some plants and goods were requisitioned, as was most property owned by German citizens abroad. The fleet was mostly scuttled by its crews at Scapa Flow [British naval base]. Military conscription in Germany was forbidden, and her army was limited to 100,000 men. She was forbidden to have heavy artillery, aviation, or submarines. She could not have afforded to build such weapons anyhow for some years after the war, and by the time she could afford them there were ample ways of evading the watchfulness of disarmament commissions. Meanwhile, since her small army had to be a voluntarily recruited and professional army, the power of the officer caste was preserved and it was allowed to plan the rapid expansion of German military strength as soon as possible. This whole series of punitive and compensatory measures was ill-devised and impracticable. They served to consolidate German national resentment without taking any watertight securities against her capacity to express that resentment in action.

Eastern Europe and World Settlement

The settlement in eastern Europe, embodied in the four other treaties drafted and concluded by the conference, was mainly concerned with redrawing the political map and seeking some protection for the national minorities which, even after the most ingenious map-drawing, were still left on the wrong sides of frontiers. It was here that endless compromises and refinements had to be made in applying the doctrine of 'national self-determination'. The Southern Slav movement was broadly satisfied by the amalgamation of Serbia, Slovenia, and Croatia into Yugoslavia, although Italy, as promised in the secret treaty of 1915, was given Trieste and some Dalmatian islands. Poland was reconstituted as an independent state, and was given an outlet to the sea through the 'Polish Corridor' of Posen and West Prussia. These areas contained German minorities and their bestowal upon Poland had the effect of separating East Prussia from the rest of Germany. Rumania was enlarged by the addition of former Russian and Hungarian territories. Greece was enlarged at the expense of Turkey. A new composite republic was created in Czechoslovakia, including Czechs, Slovaks, Ruthenians, and Sudeten Germans. The Baltic nations of Finland, Latvia, Lithuania, and Estonia were recognized as independent states. Austria and Hungary became tiny landlocked and separated states. Turkey eventually became a strong new state under [soldier-statesman] Mustapha Kemal, but confined to Constantinople and Asia Minor. Syria and Lebanon were entrusted to French administration, and Palestine, Trans-jordan, and Iraq to British, as mandated territories. This meant that they were administered by these countries who were responsible for them to the newly set up Permanent Mandates Commission of the League of Nations. Former German colonial possessions were distributed on a similar basis, German South-West Africa going to the Union of South Africa, her other African colonies being divided between Britain, France, and Belgium. The northern Pacific islands were mandated to Japan, German New Guinea to Australia, and German Samoa to New Zealand.

Achievements and Failures of the Peacemakers

Criticism of the wisdom of these arrangements must be distinguished from criticism of the peacemakers at Paris. There were many matters in which they had no real choice. Before they met the new states of eastern Europe were in existence, and the most that could be done in Paris was to ensure that the new frontiers should be reasonable ones. Similarly, the powers concerned were already in occupation of the territories now mandated to them, and to stipulate the conditions under which they should be administered was the most that the conference could do. They could not have restored the pre-war Empires even had they wished to do so, because they had utterly disintegrated.

Nor can the peacemakers be blamed for the continuance of large troublesome national minorities in eastern Europe. There were now fewer people living under what they felt to be an alien rule than there were before [the war]. The novelty was that the roles were usually now reversed, and it was Germans and Hungarians who lived as minorities under Polish, Czech, or Italian rule. Benefit of the doubt might more often have been given to the defeated nationalities, but otherwise things could have been arranged little differently. The systematic transplanting of minorities to different sides of the frontiers was rightly ruled out as bringing suffering and hardship to a war-stricken area: though some migrated spontaneously, and the flight of Greek minorities from Turkey and the removal of Turkish minorities from Greece in 1923 served this purpose. There was nothing inherently unjust in leaving peoples of different nationality within one state, so long as they were then treated with justice by the dominant majority of that state. The succession states, as the new creations were called, signed treaties with the allied powers undertaking that national minorities would not be subjected to disabilities: though this well-meant device, giving an aggrieved minority the right to petition against its government to an external authority which had little means at its disposal to protect them, did not prove to be a good way of reconciling groups within a multi-national state.

Most attacks upon the [peace] settlement during the following twenty years arose from the disparity between the excessively high hopes that men had pinned upon it and its tangle of uninspiring compromises. These compromises inevitably arose in any attempts to apply rational or moral principles to the fragmented territories of Europe. Justice in such matters could never be other than relative: yet the mood of men was perfectionist. It was simply impossible to satisfy the needs of Poland for an outlet to the Baltic [Sea] . . . and at the same time the demands of Germans that East Prussia must not be territorially separated from Germany. There was no satisfactory impartial solution to the rival claims of Jews and Arabs in Palestine. There was no humane way to remove the minorities problem from Balkan politics. Such conflicts of national interest have always been solved, in the end, by the use of force or by a long process of habituation and healing which makes them cease to matter. They could not be solved, in terms of absolute justice, by a single peace conference. Yet that was just what the peacemakers of Paris were, by so many, expected to achieve. Considering the passions aroused by more than four years of war, the intractability [severe difficulty] of the problems themselves, and the unknown aftermath looming ahead, the makers of the settlement achieved more than should have seemed probable when they first met.

How World War I Led to World War II

P.M.H. Bell

P.M.H. Bell, a historian at the University of Liverpool, explains how World War II (1939–1945) might be viewed as an inevitable outcome of World War I. Bell makes the case that the interval between the two wars was so troubled by the consequences of World War I that the entire period 1914–1945 might be called a new Thirty Years' War (the first Thirty Years' War was a religious conflict in the seventeenth century). Bell explains how Europe was deeply damaged—politically, economically, and psychologically—by World War I. The harsh terms of settlement imposed on Germany; continuing upheaval in Russia; new, weak small states in Eastern Europe; and the U.S. retreat from peacetime international responsibilities all led to European disorder and eventually another war.

In 1939 and the following years there was a powerful and general sense that men were engaged, not in a second war, but rather in the second phase of a Thirty Years War, another round in a struggle against the German domination of Europe. Since 1919 Europe had moved so rapidly through an attempt at reconstruction and stabilization into a time of renewed tension and conflict that it was hard to recognize anything which could properly be called peace. The mood was caught, lightly but exactly, by Nancy Mitford in her novel *The Pursuit of Love*, when she made her heroine Linda remark: 'It's rather sad to belong, as we do, to a lost generation. I'm sure in history the two wars will count as one war and that we shall be squashed out of it altogether, and people will forget that we ever existed.' The somewhat

From *The Origins of the Second World War in Europe*, 2nd ed., by P.M.H. Bell. Copyright © Addison Wesley Longman Limited, 1986, 1997. Reprinted by permission of Pearson Education Limited.

featherbrained Linda was in some very weighty company. The formidable Marshal Foch, generalissimo of the Allied armies in France in 1918, had said of the Treaty of Versailles, 'This is not peace. It is an armistice for twenty years.' Churchill, in the preface to the first volume of his memoirs of the Second World War, wrote: 'I must regard these volumes as a continuation of the story of the First World War which I set out in *The World Crisis*. . . . Together . . . they will cover an account of another Thirty Years War.' . . . In a more straightforward way, any Belgian over the age of twenty-six in 1940, seeing the German Army marching past his doorstep for the second time in his life, could have had little doubt that a nightmarish film had got stuck, and the same events were coming round once more.

In retrospect, such views have continued to carry a good deal of conviction. Europe was indeed wrecked by the First World War. The peace settlement which followed it had grave defects. Germany did try twice in thirty years for the domination of Europe. Taking all this into account, a school of thought has developed which regards the Second World War as the culmination of a disintegration of the European order, begun by the First World War and continued by the abortive peace, which left the Continent in a state of chronic instability. The main lines of this interpretation will be set out in this chapter. . . .

A Thirty Years War?

The basic premise of the 'Thirty Years War' thesis lies in the disruptive impact of the First World War, which shook the political, economic, and social systems of Europe to their foundations. The political and psychological damage was probably greater than the physical. It is true that casualties were very heavy: 8.5 million dead among the armed services is a generally accepted estimate, without trying to count the civilian casualties, direct and indirect. Yet, except in France, where the war losses struck a population which was already barely reproducing itself, the blow in purely demographic terms was absorbed and recovered from with less difficulty than was expected. The more lasting damage was to the mind and spirit. Many old certainties, traditional beliefs, and habits fell casualties in 1914–18. It was well said of the . . . [pre-1916 all-volunteer] armies raised in Britain that it took generations of stability and certainty to produce such a body of men; and their like would not be seen again. By 1918, there was a profound weariness and disillusionment pervading the armies of Europe which was a far cry from the fire and enthusiasm of 1914. The question repeatedly asked in German units by August 1918 was 'Wozu?'—'What's it all for?'—and this found its echo everywhere.

The economic disruption caused by the war was also severe. There was material devastation in the areas of heavy fighting, especially in the battle zones of north-east France and Belgium. All over Europe there was unusual wear and tear, arising from the working of industry, agriculture, and transport under heavy pressure and without adequate maintenance. The men and women who did the work, often for long hours and with insufficient food, were also worn out— the European influenza epidemic of 1919 told its tale of exhaustion and lowered resistance. The end of the war saw the breakdown of transport over much of central and eastern Europe, and shortages of both coal and food, caused partly by falling production and partly by problems of distribution. Financial and monetary problems were less immediately obvious than the material destruction, but were more lasting and insidious [dangerous] in their effects. Britain and France were forced to sell substantial quantities of their foreign investments to pay for the war; and other investments (notably French) were lost in the Bolshevik revolution in Russia. The Germans had their investments in enemy countries confiscated, and lost the rest of their foreign holdings at the peace. Britain borrowed heavily from the USA, and France and Italy from the USA and Britain; all ended the war with a new and heavy burden of foreign debt. There was also a great increase in internal government debts, because most war expenditure was met by loans rather than taxation. In many ways the most profound economic problem was that of inflation, the dramatic rise in prices and fall in the value of money which took place all over Europe during the war years. (In Britain, retail prices rather more than doubled between 1914 and 1918; and the position in some other countries was worse.) The confusion caused by this was the more marked after a period of generally stable prices before 1914; and the social effects spread out in all directions, to the benefit of those who could keep pace with or profit from inflation, and to the severe detriment of those who had to live on fixed incomes. In all this, it was the material damage that proved easiest to repair. Even the great scar across France and Flanders [or Franco-Belgian border], where the battle-line had run for four years, was patched over by 1925–26 with towns and villages rebuilt and land brought back into cultivation. It was the removal of the landmark of a stable currency which had the most lasting effects, psychological as much as material.

The political effects of the war were similarly far-reaching; and again were the more shocking because they came after a long period of comparative stability. In the whole of central and eastern Europe at the end of 1918, no government remained as it had been in 1914; and over large areas there was no effective government at all. The dynasties and empires of the Habsburgs in Austria-Hungary, the Hohenzollerns in Germany, and the Romanovs in Russia had all fallen; and the regimes and states which sought to replace them were struggling to come into being amid sporadic fighting and a fog of uncertainty. Three great autocratic empires had collapsed, and the parliamentary democracies of western Europe, along with the greatest of democratic powers, the USA, were intact and victorious. But if in this sense the democracies had won, the liberalism and individualism of the nineteenth century had clearly lost during the war years. The whole nature of the war meant that state control, state initiative, and state interests had all had a field day [golden opportunity]. The individual had been subordinated to the state—in Britain, the greatest symbol of this was the introduction of conscription for the armed forces, for the first time in British history. Paradoxically, this process was accompanied by a revulsion felt by many people against their own state, caused often by disillusionment, in some cases with the war and its pretences, in others with defeat or the inadequate rewards of victory. In either event, men turned away from their own state or form of government and looked elsewhere—often to communism on the one hand or fascism on the other.

By the end of the war, Europe seemed on the verge not only of political chaos but of revolution. In Russia in 1917 there were two revolutions, with the Bolsheviks precariously established in power by the end of the year. There was a revolution of sorts in Germany at the end of 1918. The hope of revolution for some, the fear of it for others, were widespread in Europe, with Bolshevik Russia as a beacon light or a menacing glare according to one's viewpoint. In the event, both hopes and fears proved much exaggerated. The new German republic turned out to be a mild form of social democracy, with large chunks of the old regime firmly embedded within it. Elections in Britain in 1918 and France in 1919 produced substantial right-wing majorities. Yet the revolutionary atmosphere had been real enough; it was not forgotten; and it had its effects later.

On this view, the war shook the foundations of Europe to an extent that was virtually irreparable. When the peacemakers gathered in Paris in 1919, they faced an impossible task; and . . . they proceeded to make the situation worse rather than better. The 1919 settlement, and particularly its centre-piece, the Treaty of Versailles with Germany, was criticized at the time and for the next twenty years for its harshness, its economic errors, and its inherent instability.

A Victor's Peace?

The accusations of harshness referred both to the terms imposed upon Germany and to the manner of their imposition. Germany lost territory. In the west Alsace and Lorraine were annexed by France (or, as the French said, were restored after wrongful seizure in 1871). . . . In the east, Germany lost Posnania and parts of East Prussia to Poland; and the port of Danzig became a free city under League of Nations administration, with special rights for Poland. Plebiscites [direct votes] were to be held in various other areas to determine whether or not they should remain part of Germany. . . . In all, Germany lost about 65,000 square kilometres [about 40,000 square miles] of territory and nearly 7 million inhabitants. She also lost all her colonies, which were handed over to various of the victorious powers under the cover of League of Nations mandates. All this was not unexpected after a country had lost a long and bitter war; and it compared quite favourably with the treatment meted out by Germany to defeated Russia in March 1918. But the Germans found it harsh. They resented handing over any territory to the Poles; and they claimed that plebiscites were used arbitrarily, and usually when there was a chance of them going against Germany; they were not used at all in Alsace-Lorraine or in most of the territory lost to Poland. Moreover, when in Austria a series of unofficial plebiscites showed overwhelming majorities in favour of union with Germany, the treaty laid it down firmly that such a union was forbidden. The victorious Allies had claimed loudly that they were fighting for democracy and self-determination, but they applied these great principles selectively, or even cynically. The Germans could thus claim unfair treatment; and after a time their claims found an attentive audience in western Europe.

The harshness was also claimed to lie in the severity of the disarmament provisions imposed upon Germany. The army was limited to 100,000 men, with no tanks or heavy artillery; the navy was to have no warships of over 10,000 tonnes, and no submarines; there was to be no military or naval aviation. Not least, the German General Staff, the brain and nerve centre of the army, and for long a separate centre of power within the state, was to be dissolved. These were unusual provisions in a peace treaty, specifically designed to paralyse German strength and to break the customs and attitudes that the victors called 'Prussian militarism'. The ostensible [apparent] purpose of the disarmament clauses was 'to render possible the initiation of a general limitation of the armaments of all nations'; and when no such limitation followed, the Germans could again claim to have been unfairly treated.

The same was true of two other aspects of the treaty whose impact was more psychological than practical. The first was the clause put at the head of the reparations section of the treaty, by which Germany was compelled to accept 'the responsibility of Germany and her allies for causing all the loss and damage to which the Allied and Associated Governments and their nationals have been subjected as a consequence of the war imposed upon them by the aggression of Germany and her allies'. This was almost universally referred to as the 'war guilt' clause of the treaty; though it does not use the word guilt, and it may be that its drafters did not intend to convey a moral judgement on Germany. Such niceties were of no importance. The clause aroused deep resentment in Germany, where it was thought that equal (or greater) responsibility for the outbreak of war could be found in the actions of other countries. German historians [of the 1920s and 1930s] worked hard to undermine the validity of this clause, and their claims found a ready acceptance among 'revisionist' writers in France, Britain, and the USA. Germany's case against the 'war guilt' thesis grew steadily stronger. The other aspect was the section of the treaty which provided for the trial of the former Kaiser, Wilhelm II, for 'a supreme offence against international morality and the sanctity of treaties.' . . . Little followed from this. The Kaiser was safe in the Netherlands, whose government would not extradite him. . . . But again, most Germans did not believe that their own leaders had behaved worse than those of other countries; they were merely being subjected to the spite of the victors.

To all this was added the claim that the Versailles Treaty was a 'dictated peace'. In one sense, this merely stated the obvious. The whole object of winning the war was to impose upon Germany terms which she would never accept voluntarily. Again, the claim referred more to the methods adopted than to the substance of what happened. At the Paris Peace Conference, the German delegation was simply presented with the Allied terms on a basis of take them or leave them; there was not even a show of negotiation, still less any real chance for Germany to influence the contents of the treaty while it was being prepared. The German complaints about this procedure reached a wide audience and it soon came to be thought (especially in Britain) that terms imposed in this fashion were not morally binding.

Second Thoughts About the Versailles Treaty

The significance of these claims about the harshness of the treaty lay less in their objective fairness (if there be such a standard), or in comparative justice when Versailles is matched against other peace settlements after great wars, but in the widespread and lasting impression that was created. It was natural enough that Germans should resent the fact of defeat, especially when for so much of the war they were sure that they were winning; and it was natural too for this resentment to attach to the peace settlement which registered their defeat. What was less to be expected was the extent to which the same view took hold among the victors. This was especially true of Britain, where it spread rapidly across the whole political spectrum. In France its hold was strongest on the Left. . . . The stability of the settlement thus came to be undermined by both vanquished and victors alike.

The accusation of harshness was particularly levelled at the reparations section of the treaty; and this may be best considered along with general assertions about the economic errors of the peace settlement. It was not unusual for cash payments, or indemnities, to be imposed upon the losing side in war; and a substantial indemnity was imposed on France as the defeated power at the end of the Franco-Prussian War in 1871. At the end of the First World War the victors renounced the idea of an indemnity, but claimed the right to exact 'compensation for all damage done to the civilian population of the Allied and Associated Powers and to their property'. The treaty itself set no figure for these 'reparations'; but it did establish the headings under which claims could be made, including not only material destruction (under which both France and Belgium had important claims), but also payment of war pensions, an almost unlimited demand which was inserted at the request of Great Britain. The task of producing a figure for reparations, and of deciding how they were to be paid, was delegated to the Reparations Commission, a body established by the victorious allies. In May 1921 this Commission arrived at a figure of 132,000 million gold marks [about $33 billion]; though at the same time the debt was divided into three sections, represented by A, B, and C class bonds, and the C class bonds were to be held by the Commission until Germany's capacity to pay had been established—which amounted to indefinite postponement of about 80,000 [about $20 billion] millions, or rather under two-thirds of the total.

Keynes and the Treaty's Economic Blunders

In 1919 the young John Maynard Keynes, then at the outset of his career as the outstanding economic theorist of the twentieth century, resigned from the British delegation at the peace conference and wrote at high speed a brilliant book, *The Economic Consequences of the Peace*. With a clarity, vigour, and skill which commanded attention . . . Keynes attacked the principles on which reparations were being imposed. He argued that the figures put forward by the victorious powers were too high in relation to the actual damage they had suffered; that Germany would not have the capacity to pay the amounts envisaged, especially when she was losing territory, resources, and population under other sections of the treaty; and that the problems of transfer (the actual means of payment, whether in kind, in gold, in German securities held abroad, or in foreign exchange earned by Germany) would prove to be insuperable. Keynes maintained that reparations, on anything like the scale being considered, could not work. They would place an impossible strain on the German economy; and involve Germany in permanent balance of payments difficulties, because she would be furnishing exports for which she was not paid, or earning foreign exchange which was not for her own use but for the purpose of making reparations payments.

In such circumstances, Keynes argued, the reconstruction of the European economy and financial system, which before 1914 had functioned as a smoothly working unit, would be impossible. The system could not be restored if one of its vital parts (and Germany remained the foremost industrial power in Europe) was permanently dislocated. This situation was made worse by the entanglement of the reparations question with the problem of war debts. During the war, the European belligerents borrowed very large sums to sustain their war efforts. Russia borrowed from France and Britain; all the European belligerents borrowed from Britain; and everyone borrowed from the USA, which in the course of the war had been transformed from a debtor to a creditor country. The position at the end of the war may be represented in a diagram.

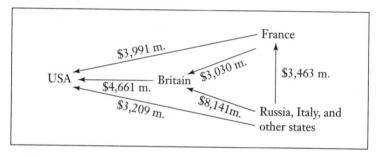

Tangled War Debts and Reparations

In a strict sense, these debts had nothing to do with the peace settlement or with reparations. But not unnaturally the victorious west European powers (Britain, France, Italy, and Belgium) wished to link their debts to the USA with their reparation payments from Germany: as Germany paid reparations, so they would pay their war debts; and since the debts had been incurred in the struggle against Germany, this seemed not only convenient but just. But the USA would not agree. Having declined to ratify the Treaty of Versailles, the Americans were not receiving any reparations from Germany; and on straightforward commercial grounds they expected to be repaid their loans by the various Allied states—in the famous phrase of [President, 1923–1929] Calvin Coolidge, 'They hired the money, didn't they?' Eventually, the British government, which was owed sums almost as large as those owed to the USA, announced (in the Balfour

Note of 1 August 1922) that since the USA insisted on the re-payment of war debts, Britain must do the same, but would only insist on payment up to the level of British debts to the USA. (This would mean Britain renouncing over half her debts.) The Americans for their part set about negotiating separately with each of their debtor governments, offering flexible terms which took into account ability to pay.

War debts were also linked with reparations because they involved a transfer problem—the means by which they were to be paid. They made another distorting element in the structure of trade and payments and added to the balance of payments problems of the debtor states. They also added to the anxiety of those who were owed reparations to ensure that they were paid.

Quite apart from its general distorting and complicating effects, the reparations question also brought about a very sharp international crisis, with far-reaching consequences. In 1923 France and Belgium seized upon a German failure to make deliveries of reparations in kind to occupy the industrial area of the Ruhr, with the object (certainly as far as the French were concerned) either of making the Germans pay, or of inflicting serious damage on the German economy—contradictory aims, doubtless, but either of them satisfactory from a French point of view. The occupation of the Ruhr involved the use of force (invasion, the Germans claimed; police action according to the French) and helped to precipitate the catastrophic German hyperinflation of 1923. This inflation had little direct connection with reparations payments themselves, but a great deal to do with the way the German government chose to subsidize industry and to pay the costs of the passive resistance to the occupation by extravagant use of the printing press. Inflation was already running strongly in 1922: in June 1923 the mark stood at 100,000 to the dol-lar; in November at 4,000 million. A pay-packet was worth-less before a worker got home; and anyone with assets tied to the mark (which meant anyone with savings, insurance poli-cies, or a fixed income) saw their value vanish absolutely. The effects of this in terms of individual lives and collective con-fidence were far-reaching; and they later contributed to the appeal of Nazism. The Ruhr occupation and the German hyperinflation were not inevitable consequences of the reparation clauses of Versailles; but as events turned out, they were among the actual results.

Europe's Dangerous Power Vacuum

Going deeper than claims about the harshness of the peace settlement or its economic errors is the judgement that it was inherently and disastrously unstable. This instability was apparent in a number of ways. The war destroyed the pre-1914 European balance, and the peace could put nothing adequate in its place. A profound shift in the pattern of power occurred while the war was in progress. French losses and weariness were such that France became dependent, even by 1916, on the help of the British Empire; and by 1918 both were dependent on the USA, which alone could provide the economic resources and the fresh troops to defeat Germany. It was the steady flow of American doughboys, raw but enthusiastic, and with limitless reserves, that brought home to the Germans with mathematical certainty that they must lose. Before this, Germany had fought four major European enemies to a standstill, and totally defeated one of them, Russia. The lesson was that Germany was so strong in terms of population, industrial resources, organization, and not least willpower, that four other European great powers had barely the capacity to hold her at bay; and an entirely new force from outside Europe [the USA] was necessary to tip the balance.

This bleak outlook stood revealed by the facts of war. What could the aspirations of peace do to soften its outlines? It was plain by as early as 1920 that the answer was, very little. The USA, having done so much to win the war and shape the peace treaties that followed it, withdrew her strength and activity back across the Atlantic—not into 'isolation', which is altogether too absolute a term, but into an indifference towards the European balance of power which came only too naturally to a people who found the phrase itself distasteful. The British, surveying with a grievous sense of loss the cost in lives of commitment to a Continental war, thought it best to turn back to empire and the more hopeful patterns of former centuries, or to turn away from all power politics into some form of pacifism. Russia stood transformed by revolution, weak in armed or industrial strength, but powerful in menace to ordered bourgeois society.

No country felt this change more than France. In 1914 her position against Germany rested on her long-standing alliance with Russia and her *entente* [understanding] with Britain. In the crisis of a German invasion, both came to her help, and in 1914 the Russian attack on East Prussia helped to check the German offensive in France. By 1919–20, Russia was gone, powerless and in any case unreliable, and Britain was anxious to diminish her European commitments. It was possible that the newly created League of Nations might be turned into an organization capable of restraining German power; but this was by no means certain. The situation of France in 1919, and the severity of French attitudes towards Germany, can only be properly comprehended by grasping the facts of French weakness in comparison with 1914.

There was no European balance in 1919–20. Indeed, the precarious nature of the new creation was immediately apparent. General [Jan Christian] Smuts, a member of the South African delegation at the Paris Peace Conference, wrote to Lloyd George, the British Prime Minister, in March 1919 that the peace treaty then being prepared would be utterly unstable. Notably, he held that Poland and Czechoslovakia, new states coming into existence in eastern Europe, would not be viable without German goodwill— and he was right. In the coming storms, he predicted, they would be the first to go under—and (except for Austria) they were. Germany remained in the centre of Europe, with (even after her losses of territory) a population and industrial resources which were bound, if allowed free play, to give her a predominant position on the Continent. The peace settlement had been harsh enough to infuriate the Germans, but not so crushing as to render them powerless. Machiavelli once advised: 'If you see your enemy in the water up to his neck, you will do well to push him under; but if he is only in it up to his knees, you will do well to help him to the shore.' The peace treaty did neither.

The Perils of Peacemaking in a War-Torn World

Robert H. Ferrell

American historian Robert H. Ferrell has written extensively on American foreign relations as well as on President Harry S. Truman. In this excerpt from his study of Woodrow Wilson and World War I, Ferrell portrays the clashing personalities of Wilson, David Lloyd George of Britain, and Georges Clemenceau of France—the "Big Three" leaders who shaped the Paris Peace Conference of 1919. He captures the confusion and disorder of the conference that led one diplomat to describe the assembly as a "riot in a parrot house." Ferrell notes that the failure at peacemaking in Paris had deeper results than temporary bickering. European civilization suffered permanent damage, with a terrible cost in human lives and lasting hatreds.

Leading delegates at the Paris Peace Conference of 1919 could not, unfortunately, look far beyond their own time, and took the moment for what it was—the opportunity to end World War I. In the presence of hundreds of top-hatted diplomats and bemedaled soldiers, they signed the German treaty in the Hall of Mirrors at Versailles on June 28, 1919. The day was overcast, but before President Wilson reached the palace grounds the sun broke through the clouds. Guns boomed, airplanes dipped, and for the first time since the war, the fountains outside the palace played; water rose high in the air and splashed into surrounding pools. After the ceremonies the Big Three strolled outside, and crowds burst through the cordon of troops and bore in on them, shouting *"Vive* Clemenceau!", *"Vive* Lloyd George!", *"Vive* Veelson!" For a moment they swept the leaders along the terrace, top hats bobbing uncertainly, until a platoon of the Garde Republicaine came up and rescued them, preserving decorum during this final moment at Versailles.

Personalities of the Peacemakers

Looking back on the Peace Conference in long retrospect, one wonders what went wrong at Paris, what kept the Treaty of Versailles from being a longer-lasting document and thereby preventing World War II. Could it have been flaws in the principal negotiators of the German treaty, the Big Three? The Italian prime minister, Orlando, did not count in the equation, for he was an inconsequential statesman. His concerns were territorial, his emotions tearful. While in attendance he stood apart from much discussion because he did not understand English. Clemenceau, admittedly an important negotiator, appeared as too much the protector of his country. An old man, he had been a reporter during the last days of the American Civil War, and married an American girl, Mary Plummer, from whom he long since had separated. He lived in the past, and no event had touched him more than France's surrender to the Germans in the war of 1870–71. He had been in Paris during the Commune [an uprising by radical Republicans soon after France's defeat] and never forgot the spectacle of Frenchmen fighting each other in the presence of Germans. The 1914–18 war had redeemed France, but he distrusted his countrymen, feared the future, determined to do what he could to keep Germany down. The flight of the Emperor [Kaiser Wilhelm] and announcement of the Weimar Republic [Germany's new Republican government, begun at the city of Weimar] did not impress him; the Germans would try again.

Lloyd George also had a point of view based on history, but it was a much shorter history. He had become prime minister late in 1916 after his predecessor, Asquith, proved incapable of leading Britain to victory. He took over when his country approached defeat, and with energy and administrative force pulled it back, with help from the Americans. Unsure of what the United States wanted from the peace, willing to appease anyone—Frenchmen, Americans, even Germans—to prevent another war, he trusted to his ability to talk adversaries around. He was aware of his hold on the British electorate, demonstrated in the so-called khaki election of December 1918, held while many Britons still were in uniform. . . . "He is slippery as an eel," Wilson told [his physician Cary T.] Grayson, "and I never know when to count on him." And again: "He is the most unsteady individual you can imagine. . . . He is unstable. He is constantly turning somersaults. He is an impossible, incalculable person to do business with."

As for Wilson, observers of the Peace Conference long remembered how Clemenceau's sarcasm had produced several versions of perhaps an original remark that focused on the negotiating inability of the President. "God gave us the Ten Commandments, and we broke them. Wilson gave us the Fourteen Points. We shall see." Or, "How can I talk to a fellow who thinks himself the first man for two thousand years who has known anything about peace on earth?" Or, "Wilson talked like Jesus Christ but acted like Lloyd George." A few years after the Peace Conference, [Wilson adviser] Charles Seymour was talking about peacemaking with Colonel House, who emphasized that Wilson was up against the two most skillful negotiators he, House, had ever seen. No one in the United States compared with them. Unlike Wilson, they understood personal appeal in conducting relations. Wilson always felt that if he had logic on his side, that sufficed. But to be right, House insisted, was only a small part of politics. Wilson had hypnotized himself by the beauty of his words and the effectiveness of his presentation, but this did not affect Clemenceau and Lloyd George, who probably did not even listen.

Within a few months of the treaty's signature, [British economist John Maynard] Keynes brought out *The Economic Consequences of the Peace*, the book about the Peace Conference that dealt principally with finance, with which he was familiar, but it was his portraits of the Big Three statesmen in the book's opening pages that caught the attention of readers. Clemenceau, he said, was an intense, clearheaded old man whose first and last thought was the safety of France, whose understanding of foibles and poses was so large that in an instant he saw through deception and super-ficial concern, concentrating on his purpose. Lloyd George he drew as a Welsh witch, a sorcerer, whose long blade flashed and skewered, a man with a sixth sense of what people had in mind, possessed of powers no human imag-ined. Wilson was an old Presbyterian "bamboozled" (the American word intrigued him) by flattery who needed to be debamboozled. The latter effort he said was impossible.

The personal appraisals were interesting, almost believ-able, even to individuals who ought to have known better, and [South African statesman Jan Christian] Smuts in 1948 told Keynes's biographer Roy Harrod that "the portrait of Wilson was absolutely truthful, but Keynes should not have written it; after all Wilson was our friend."

Larger Obstacles to Lasting Peace

Perhaps the conference failed not because of personalities but because of atmosphere. Here again Keynes described the scene, as in a nightmare; everyone, he said, was morbid, cat-astrophe overhanging frivolity [silliness], "the futility and smallness of man before the great events confronting him; the mingled significance and unreality of the decisions; lev-ity, blindness, insolence, confused cries from without,—all the elements of ancient tragedy." Seated amid the theatrical trappings of French salons, he wondered if the visages of Wilson and Clemenceau, with their fixed hue, were "really faces at all and not the tragic-comic masks of some strange drama or puppetshow."

Years later Keynes's countryman Harold Nicolson pub-lished an account of the conference that, if not so tragic, was equally critical. Nicolson beheld confusion as the problem—lack of organization, of procedure. However gifted the par-ticipants, they could not bring their purposes into focus be-cause staff work was poor.

Literary descriptions of ineptitude, morbidity, and confu-sion have the advantage of single issues, and in the hand of a skillful writer each becomes convincing. Yet all have the fault of simplicity. Failure at Paris occurred because of world forces too large for simple literary analysis. One of these forces was economic. Long before 1919 the spread of the Industrial Revolution out of England, where it first appeared, into Germany and the United States, and the beginning of industrialization in other countries, skewed the power balance of nations. Hence some of the miscalculation that brought World War I. The cause of World War II was similar miscalculation, refusal to anticipate the Great Depression of the thirties. Forces that brought the depression were so novel—economic changes that reached back into the nineteenth century, disarray caused by World War I, financial excesses of the twenties—that the men at Paris perhaps could not have anticipated them. In any event the Peace Conference dealt largely with territorial and military matters and barely touched economic. The reparations clause made no real economic sense, and the tangle of debts and reparations did not help. In this respect Keynes was right. But he himself did not understand what was to come and after the American stock market crash in 1929 at first described it as a minor readjustment of the marketplace. The crash tipped over the economies of Europe and brought Hitler to power and so palsied [paralyzed] the wills of Western democracies that the [Hitler's] Third Reich passed from triumph to triumph and nothing stopped it short of World War II.

The second force that the Peace Conference failed to deal with was what Wilson, employing a then new psychological term, described as the "war psychosis [psychosis: major mental disorder]." The President liked to talk about it, and believed it a major problem in world affairs. He never had admired military solutions; although he disliked Germany and favored the Allies, he looked with horror on the coming of war. He feared the sights of war; when he went to the Peace Conference he believed that this "war psychosis" might overwhelm him if he toured the battlefields, as Allied leaders, his advisers, and Pershing urged him. Eventually he went for a day or two.

The President was correct in sensing the war psychosis, but as an American he could never fully appreciate it. The war had gone on too long—battle losses had mounted, and hatreds with them, until clear thinking about peace had become almost impossible. Wilson could only sense what the war had done to Europe, a war in which Germany suffered thirty-six times as many deaths in battle (1.8 million) as did the United States (50,300), Russia thirty-four times (1.7 million), France twenty-eight times (1.4 million), Britain nineteen times (950,000). The American population was 35 million larger than Germany's, twice that of Britain, more than twice that of France. Not a town or village or rural area in Western Europe but young men failed to return. After the war great battlefields like Verdun became cemeteries; at Verdun the French government constructed an ossuary [memorial] for 100,000 men. Churches placed long lists of names on plaques; towns put up monuments. The village of Kreuth near the Tegernsee in Bavaria erected a monument that displayed village losses in wars beginning in the early eighteenth century, and listed as many men dead in 1914–18 as in two centuries of preceding wars; World War I names on Kreuth's monument showed several groups of brothers. For Europeans the war of 1914–18 was impossible to forget; bitterness made peace unlikely.

World War I and the Rise of Totalitarian Dictatorships

Jack J. Roth

American historian Jack J. Roth argues in the following essay that World War I was a turning point in modern Western history in that liberal democracy faltered badly and was transformed by the intensity of the war. Totalitarian regimes, whether of the left (Soviet communism) or the right (Italian fascism and German Nazism) built on the World War I experience of mobilizing for "total war." Roth maintains that the Soviet regime under Stalin and the total warfare state of Nazi Germany owed greatly to World War I models.

The war ended the ascendancy of European liberal democracy. This is not to say that the European world was completely "liberal" and "democratic" before 1914. Nor does this mean that liberal democratic goals had, in fact, been anywhere attained—only the states of western Europe approached them. But before the war, almost everywhere, the major currents of change had seemed to contemporaries to be working in the direction of these goals. After the war, even where the war had been won, this was no longer the case.

Liberalism Under Siege

Even before the war there were signs of the weakening of liberal democracy. An insidious anti-intellectualism which received apparent support from the scientific and intellectual achievements of the age undermined the individualism, rationalism, and humanitarianism that underlay liberal conceptions. Particularly ominous was the appearance of

Excerpted from the Conclusion, by Jack J. Roth, to *World War I: A Turning Point in Modern History*, edited by Jack J. Roth. Copyright © 1967 by Roosevelt University. Reprinted by permission of the McGraw-Hill Companies, Inc.

revolutionary movements that cultivated, organized, and propagated beyond previous limits a variety of hatreds—class, nation or race hatred. *Raison d'état* [reasons of state, power politics] progressively became the guiding light of statesmen and patriotism assumed a more and more aggressive and militaristic form. Even in the most favorable of national environments, where the apparatus of liberal democracy—civil liberties, universal manhood suffrage, party politics, parliamentary institutions, ministerial responsibility—was most solidly grounded, it sometimes failed to function. [Prewar] Liberal England could not avert suffragette, Irish, or labor violence. Republican France was shaken to its foundations during the Dreyfus Affair [unjust treason trial of a French Jewish military officer; later declared innocent] by the unsuspected depths of antisemitism. Still, on the eve of the first world conflict it is the persistence of liberal democracy that should be stressed. . . . The vast majority of Europeans, certainly in the most advanced parts of Europe, believed in . . . its methods and the desirability of its goals.

The war opened a new and difficult era for liberal democracy even where, it was asserted, the war was being fought in its name. The closing of ranks, such as the *Union sacrée* [sacred union] in France, freed governments from the criticism to which they were ordinarily subjected. They now made claims to authority that in peacetime would have entailed the risk of rebellion. . . . As the liberal bourgeoisie [middle class] abdicated, the soldiers and organizers took over. Freedom of thought, which with few exceptions had been respected for half a century in Europe, went by the board. And yet, distinctions must be made. Although Britain was seriously threatened by the submarine menace and northeast France was under German occupation during the entire war, parliamentary institutions continued to function, however imperfectly, and no serious danger of military dictatorship arose. Clemenceau's quip that war was too important to be left to the generals was significant. In Germany the wartime mobilization not only emasculated [weakened] the Reichstag and the civilian government generally, but culminated in a military dictatorship to which the Kaiser himself was obliged to submit. In Russia the liberal Provisional Government gave way to the Bolshevik dictatorship.

The postwar environment was not conducive [contributing] to the successful operation of liberal democracy—the Soviet regime, moreover, was a disturbing innovation. And yet, 1919 appeared to be the high-water mark of liberal democracy. The victorious powers viewed the outcome of the war as confirmation of their own faith in democracy and eagerly sought to resume "normal" life. Self-determination and parliamentary government succeeded the multi-national autocratic monarchies: The new regimes looked to parliamentary Britain or republican France for inspiration.

But all of democratic Europe found itself in serious difficulty in the immediate postwar years. The German republic—weakened by the unpopularity of Versailles and the pressure of domestic problems and threatened on all sides by extremist movements—was obliged to fight for its life. The Weimar regime [postwar republican government, 1918–1933], for the moment, survived, but Italian democracy did not. Though on the side of the victors, the conviction that the peace had been "lost" and the accumulated social distress aggravated by the war resulted in the breakdown of the [Italian] parliamentary regime. In 1922 it fell victim to Mussolini's legions. Moreover, the lesser states, such as Hungary, Poland, and Yugoslavia, soon demonstrated little capacity to deal with postwar problems within a democratic framework. Still, in the twenties one could easily persuade oneself that neither the Soviet nor the Italian development was conclusive and that the problems of the newer states might also be temporary.

With the Great Depression, however, liberal democracy once again began to lose ground rapidly—by 1938 only ten of the twenty-seven countries of Europe retained something of the apparatus and spirit of democratic government. Even Britain and France fell into a quagmire. The methods of liberal democracy were too slow or too feeble and the difficulties were compounded by expanding extremist movements. That much of the liberal democratic tradition was saved was due to the employment of measures rather similar to those of the wartime [1914–1918] emergency—"fronts" or coalition governments, high taxes and massive government intervention—and when necessary, rule by decree and banning of hostile organizations. What emerged here were the outlines of the "welfare state." But elsewhere in Europe the roots of democracy were planted in very shallow soil. There were no sizable groups that possessed a material interest in defending democratic institutions. The effects of the Depression, of the Nazi accession to power, and of the Anglo-French weakness were to undermine the basis of both internal and external stability. As experiments with democratic institutions failed, the new regimes turned to Italian Fascism or German Nazism for guidance. The democracies had won the war militarily; by 1939, they had lost it ideologically and institutionally.

Postwar Trend Toward Totalitarianism: Russia and Germany

The war greatly expanded and gave new vigor to movements with inclinations toward "total solutions." But not all such movements came to power and not all that came to power were able to establish totalitarian regimes. Totalitarianism was favored where an experiment with liberal parliamentary institutions had failed and where long-standing autocratic, military, and bureaucratic traditions survived—where the "welfare state" was ruled out, the "warfare state" got its chance.

The elements essential to totalitarianism already existed before the war, though in fragmented and disparate form. . . .

Europeans were provided with their first taste of totalitarianism in total war [World War I]. The new mobilization had required the combination of the prewar elements that already pointed in this direction. Nowhere, however, was the organization for war as comprehensive or as effective as in Germany where it was undoubtedly facilitated by the military tradition. . . . The German experience was to have far-reaching consequences. Revolutionaries of all persuasions could see clearly for the first time the extraordinary energies that could be released in the modern social order and the almost unlimited powers at the command of the modern state.

The first opportunity to employ the European but especially the German experience with total war came with the . . . dissolution of the [Czarist] Russian state. The collapse of the autocracy in 1917 left a void that could be filled only by a party prepared to employ extreme measures. What the Bolsheviks believed necessary to hold power was already implicit in the way in which they took it on November 7—the seizure of the power stations, telephone and telegraph exchanges, and railroad terminals. But to the extent that they used any model at all for maintaining power during the civil war and intervention, it was German *Kriegssozialismus* [War Socialism]. "We must organize everything," wrote Lenin, "take everything into our hands. . . ." The Bolsheviks appropriately labeled this period of the Soviet regime "War Communism." It foreshadowed the full totalitarian system that was to be introduced a decade later.

The war and its consequences furthered prewar totalitarian tendencies. In Russia the war, by favoring extremist and autocratic solutions, not only gave the Bolsheviks their chance, but determined in large part the character of the new regime. . . . Lenin himself observed in September 1917, "War is inexorable and puts the question with unsparing sharpness: either perish or catch up and overtake the advanced countries." Domestic chaos during the period of War Communism, however, did not permit the construction of an order of any permanence. Relaxation of the dictatorship was, in fact, necessary . . . [later] to stabilize the regime and to determine its future course. It was not until the introduction of the first Five-Year [economic] Plan in 1928 that the decisive step was taken. The wartime collapse and the danger of the renewal of war weighed heavily in the Soviet decision. Moreover, the war experience indicated how industrialization might be brought about. The problem the Soviets faced was not one of operating a working industrial system, but of creating one. It was in the name of industrialization that the totalitarian machine, the rudiments of which already existed, was perfected. Not the peacetime economies of the advanced countries, but the economy of total war—of rationing, of inflation, and of planning under centralized state control—was deemed appropriate. Also deemed essential was the exhilaration of battle, the *patrie-en-danger* [endangered nation] psychosis, either real or contrived. The First Plan began with a "war scare," spy trials, and a program of military preparedness. In justification, Stalin in 1931 virtually repeated Lenin's argument of 1917. . . .

Nazi totalitarianism, as well as Soviet, was a direct descendant of the war. The German breakdown, though not as precipitous as the Russian, also began during the war. The [German] imperial government gave way to a military dictatorship in 1917 and the monarchy collapsed in 1918. But the breakdown continued after the war with the middle-class debacle [collapse] in the inflation of 1923 and the collapse of the parliamentary republic in 1931–32. Both the French occupation of the Ruhr that led to the inflation and the Depression that reduced the Weimar government to impotence brought home to Germans the *fact* of defeat which the events of October 1918 had somehow failed to do. It was the Ruhr crisis, moreover, that brought the Nazis to national prominence and the Depression that brought them to power. Few Germans had been tempted by Hitler until the Depression revived the anxieties and fears produced by the defeat of 1918.

The Nazi movement, however, was not only a product of the breakdown produced by the war, it was itself rooted conceptually in the war experience. Hitler in *Mein Kampf* and even in his "conversations" during the Second World War was constantly preoccupied with German defeat in the first. The mobilization of 1917–18 had not gone far enough—if only he had been at the helm. "If I'd been Reich Chancellor [then] . . . I'd have cut the throat of all obstruction. . . ." Nazi writers were especially struck by General Erich Ludendorff's critique of the German domestic scene during the war and his proposal for an "armed state" without politics, prepared to conduct a future total war. What the Nazis aimed at was a militarized pan-Germanism, a regime that bore none of the weaknesses of the wartime mobilization. But their concern was with the permanent organization of the nation, in peace and in war. Totalitarianism was not a means to an end;

it was the end itself. The need for rapid industrialization, as in the Soviet case, did not exist. Germany already possessed the most modern industrial plant in Europe. . . . The totalitarian features of the new regime were most pronounced, however, in the radically new conception of the nation as a biological entity engaged in a struggle for survival. Whether or not Nazi leaders believed in the race doctrine is irrelevant. What is relevant is the purpose the doctrine was to serve. For the Nazis, both domestic and international politics was warfare. For German "national socialism," the Jewish "race" could be effectively depicted as the enemy—Communist or capitalist, domestic or foreign.

In sum, the problem of the First World War as turning point would appear to be basic to the meaning of contemporary history. With the spotlight on the events of 1914–18, both the prewar and postwar worlds are illuminated. Although the illumination is necessarily selective, what emerges are the very outlines of our time.

The Scars of Total War

Jay Winter and Blaine Baggett

Cambridge University historian Jay Winter and television documentary producer Blaine Baggett explain some of the lasting social and psychological effects of World War I on postwar Europe. The authors present a moving account of the massive human costs of the war. The war's destructiveness forever dashed romantic images of war still common in 1914. As Winter and Baggett suggest, the war "democratized suffering." Hundreds of thousands of mutilated veterans, together with their shocked and grieving families, found postwar adjustment extremely difficult.

The Great War, a leap into the modern age, unleashed an avalanche of the unmodern. This paradox has given the twentieth century its characteristic form. The war accelerated the ascent to a world dominated by machines of unparalleled power, and at the same time precipitated the descent into a world of unparalleled brutality. The trajectory of human progress was fractured: technical change leaped forward yet political life moved backward into a new age of cruelty, made worse than the past by the new and more efficient machinery of degradation and death.

The recognition that something terrible, something overwhelming, something irreversible had happened in the Great War explains its enduring significance for those born after the Armistice. For this war was not only the most important and far-reaching political and military event of the century; it was also the most important imaginative event.

New identities emerged during the war: new nations, new commitments, new solidarities. The United States emerged as an economic world power, although for a generation it withdrew from the political responsibilities that followed industrial pre-eminence. The ideological conflict between Communism and capitalism came out of this war; so did the European state system, the boundaries of which were set at Versailles in 1919. Seventy years later, Communism as a political system collapsed. Germany was reunified, without threatening the peace of Europe. In the 1990s the national boundaries created after 1918 began to disintegrate, either through the centripetal [centralizing] pressures of the European Community or through the centrifugal [fragmenting] pressures of ethnicity and nationalist movements.

The Great War established not only the political framework of our time, but also many of the fundamental assumptions to which we turn in trying to understand it. Above all it normalized collective violence, the signature of our century.

At some time between 1914 and 1918, virtually the whole world put on the clothes of war. In terms of outlook, of pessimism, of fear, few have completely shed them since. For war has entered our imaginations, our mental landscape, as a permanent feature of the world we inhabit, both the world we see, and the world of dreams and nightmares our desolate century has created.

The Scars of Total War

The face of war was transformed during the Great War. Nineteenth-century frontal assaults by massed infantry made no sense against the twentieth-century weaponry, yet more than a million men died in the first year of the war before generals began understanding the new nature of war.

Even then the lesson was not entirely learned: not at Verdun, not at the Somme, not at Passchendaele [a bloody, unsuccessful British offensive in 1917], or not even in the last year of the war when a desperate German Army launched its final offensive in an effort to win the war before Germany collapsed. All these hideous failures help to account for the fact that the successful Allied offensive in the last months of the war has largely been forgotten. It was a remarkable achievement, but this military feat has been obscured by the shock of earlier offensive failures.

Those who had seen war for what it was knew that older romantic illusions about war were inadequate, absurd or obscene. In order to absorb the shock, language itself changed, taking a more terse and realistic tone.

It is not surprising, then, to know that the men who endured combat were no longer the happy warriors of nineteenth-century romanticism. In 1927 Philippe Pétain, the hero of Verdun, inaugurated the giant ossuary [monument to dead soldiers] at Douaumont. It was, as Antoine

---

The Lost Generation of World War I

UCLA historian Robert Wohl explored the impact of the Great War on Europe's young intellectuals in his study The Generation of 1914. *The following excerpt suggests how the war and its consequences created a lasting image of a disillusioned postwar younger generation.*

Generation of 1914—close your eyes and a host of images leaps to mind: of students packing off to war with flowers in their rifles and patriotic songs on their lips, too young, too innocent to suspect what bloody rites of passage awaited them; of trenchfighters whose twisted smiles and evasive glances revealed their close companionship with death; of pleasure-seekers in the 1920s, cigarettes hanging from the corner of their mouths, defiance and despair showing in the directness of their stares and the set of their faces; of Communists, heads bobbing in a sea of masses, prisoners of the movement they claimed to guide; of Fascists, tight-lipped, stiff-postured, without pity for others or themselves; of pacifists campaigning belligerently against war; of veterans unable to forget the grandeur of the trenches; of wasted women who had become widows before becoming wives; of a generation missing, sacrificed, decimated, destroyed "for an old bitch gone in the teeth, for a botched civilization."

Robert Wohl, *The Generation of 1914*. Cambridge, MA: Harvard University Press, 1979, p. 1.

Prost has put it, 'a kind of cemetery of cemeteries'. Pétain spoke of the common soldier of the Great War: 'We who have known him know that he is simply a man, with his virtues and his vices, a man of the people, to whom he remained attached . . . to the circle of his family, to his workshop, his office, his village, to the farm where he grew up.' Doing his duty, 'he went up the line without enthusiasm but without weakness'.

This war democratized suffering. In most combatant countries, roughly 50 per cent of the male population between the ages of eighteen and forty-nine were in uniform. Nothing like this had ever happened before. France and Germany mobilized the highest proportion: about 80 per cent of men of military age were conscripted. Austria-Hungary mobilized 75 per cent of its adult male population; Britain, Serbia and Turkey called up between 50 and 60 per cent. In Russia, about 16 million men or 40 per cent of the male population between fifteen and forty-nine served during the war. In the United States, in the brief space of eighteen months about 4 million men, or roughly 16 per cent of the same age group, were in uniform.

Total casualties and losses as a proportion of those who served passed a threshold beyond previous experience: the total of roughly 9 million dead soldiers (according to varying estimates) constitutes one in eight of the men who served. Adding statistics on other casualties, roughly 50 per cent of the men who served were captured, wounded or killed.

Overall, the Western Front was the most murderous theatre of operations. But a higher proportion of those who fought on the Eastern Front died. There, disease and enemy action killed combatants with equal force. This [the Eastern Front] was a nineteenth-century war waged with twentieth-century weapons. Of the Serbs who served in the war, 37 per cent were killed; roughly one in four Romanians, Turks and Bulgarians also perished. On the Western Front, where the war was won and lost, combat was perhaps only half as lethal: German and French losses were about one in six of those who served; British losses one in eight.

Another feature of total war may be more surprising. Initially, casualties among social élites were higher than among the rest of the population. The reason is casualties of officers who led from the front were significantly higher than those in the ranks—about 10 per cent of men in the ranks were killed; between 12 and 20 per cent of all officers perished. And who were the officers? Men from the upper and upper middle class, since social selection of the officer corps mirrored the inequalities in pre-war life. Consequently in the early stages of the war, the higher up the social scale a man was, the greater were his chances of serving as an officer and of becoming a casualty of war. But by 1917 these strata of society had been sufficiently reduced to require the armies to draw junior officers from wider social groups, still mostly middle-class but now from commercial or shopkeeping families. These groups in their turn suffered disproportionately higher casualties in the last two years of the war.

Among the poor and the underprivileged, the story is different. Pre-war deprivation saved the lives of millions of working-class men, whose stunted stature and diseases made it impossible for them to pass even the rudimentary standards of medical fitness for military service. In Britain, roughly 35 per cent of men examined for military service were either unfit for combat or unfit to wear a uniform at all. They were the lucky ones. Inequality was their salvation.

Broken Faces, Missing Limbs

During and after the war the wounded were there—on street corners, in public squares, in churches. No village or town in Europe was without them. The French textile worker Mémé Santerre described her village in the north of the country:

The agricultural laborers came back as amputees, blind, gassed, or as 'scar throats', as some were called because of their disfigured, crudely healed faces. We began to see more and more returning. What a crowd! What a rude shock at the railway station, where the wives went to meet their husbands, to find them like that—crippled, sick, despairing that they would be of no use anymore. At first, we had the impression that all those returning had been injured. It wasn't

until later that those who had escaped without a scratch returned. But, like their comrades, they were serious, sad, un-
smiling; they spoke little. They had lived in hell for four
years and wouldn't forget it.

The wounded came in many forms: psychologically damaged men, men who suffered from illness contracted during
the war, men literally torn apart. Among them were thousands of ordinary men afflicted with extraordinary wounds.
These were the *gueules cassées*, men with broken faces. Estimates vary, but at least 12 per cent of all men wounded suffered from facial injuries, and perhaps one third of these
were permanently disfigured. Since in Britain, France and
Germany alone roughly 7 million men were wounded, about
280,000 disfigured men in these three countries returned
home after the 1914–18 war. Not all were severely disfigured, but those who were could no longer look in the mir-
ror: they had literally lost their identities. For these men, the
road back to some semblance of ordinary life was tortuous.

Henriette Rémi was a French nurse who knew first-hand
of their fate. In the spring of 1918 she visited a friend, an officer who had in his care a man with no face: 'He has only
one leg; his right arm is covered by bandages. His mouth is
completely distorted by an ugly scar which descends below
his chin. All that is left of his nose are two enormous nostrils,
two black holes which trap our gaze, and make us wonder for
what this man has suffered? . . . All that is left of his face are
his eyes, covered by a veil; his eyes seem to see. . . .'

The wounded man talked of home, where his mother and
sister lived: ' "I cannot see them, it is true, but they will see
me. Yes, they will see me! And they will care for me. They
will help me pass the time. You know, time passes terribly
slowly in hospital. My sister is a teacher, she will read to me.
My mother's eyes are weak; she can hardly read; she sewed
too much when we were kids; she had to provide for us; my
father died when we were little." '

The authorities at the hospital did not encourage family
visits, which were potentially traumatic. But the time had
come when this veteran would return to his family. He asked

Rémi if they would recognize him. 'Certainly,' was her hesitant answer, hoping that if their eyes did not find the man, their hearts would. Then the sister came:

> A young woman, fresh, pretty, approaches quickly; she searches in the crowd for her brother. All at once, her face pales, an expression of terror forms; her eyes grow in fright, she raises her arms as if pushing away a vision of horror, and murmurs, 'My God . . . it's he.' A little further away, a woman in black, a bit bent, advances timidly, searching with an expectant smile. And in an instant, those poor tired eyes grow terrified, those tired hands raised in fear, and from this mother's heart comes the cry: 'My God . . . it's he.' . . .

Other disfigured men and their companions succeeded in forming a new, collective identity. The Union of Disfigured Men . . . was just one of a host of veterans' associations in post-war France, but it remained separate from the larger organizations—the disfigured had special problems of sociability which only their own association could address.

The idea was hatched by two disfigured men who had met at the Val-de-Grâce military hospital in Paris, and who invited all those whom they had known there to band together. Their first meeting was held on 21 June 1921, four years after other, inclusive groups of veterans began to create their own associations. Their leader, Colonel Picot, then aged fifty-nine, was a towering figure in the veterans' movement as a whole, but he always affirmed the special character of this association. Its members met at a banquet twice a year, and drew on each other's strength to face their terrible problems. In 1927 the association turned a country house with parkland at Moussy-le-Vieux, 25 miles from Paris, into a place where disfigured men could rest away from a still uncomfortable public. As Colonel Picot put it, it would be 'a place worthy of them, a château like those acquired by the men who got rich when we lost our faces'. Some men came for short stays; others for good. Their families were welcome too. All were invited to join in farming activities; even those who thought they were unemployable found work.

The presence of these victims was commonplace in the

post-war generation. In Paris on Bastille Day, 14 July 1919, the crippled, the blind and the disfigured led the victory parade, creating an ambiance [environment, or atmosphere] which converted celebration into sombre meditation. An entire industry grew to service the needs of men without limbs. In Britain, the money collected on 11 November each year in exchange for an artificial poppy went to the families of ex-soldiers in need. Some 80 per cent of the unemployed in the mid-1920s were ex-veterans; they were all in need. How much greater, then, the plight of those whose injuries would not go away.

Appendix of Documents

Document 1: Assassination at Sarajevo: June 28, 1914

Rising tensions between Austria-Hungary and Serbia finally exploded with the assassination of Austro-Hungarian archduke Franz Ferdinand at Sarajevo in Bosnia. The following account by Borijove Jevtic, a member of the Bosnian Serb secret nationalist society Narodna Odbrana, *was given to the* New York World *ten years later.*

A tiny clipping from a newspaper, mailed without comment from a secret band of terrorists in Zagreb, capital of Croatia, to their comrades in Belgrade, was the torch which set the world afire with war in 1914. That bit of paper wrecked old, proud empires. It gave birth to new, free nations.

I was one of the members of the terrorist band in Belgrade which received it.

The little clipping declared that the Austrian Archduke Francis Ferdinand would visit Sarajevo, the capital of Bosnia, June 28, to direct army maneuvers in the neighboring mountains.

It reached our meeting place, the café called Zeatna Moruna, one night the latter part of April, 1914. To understand how great a sensation that little piece of paper caused among us when it was passed from hand to hand almost in silence, and how greatly it inflamed our hearts, it is necessary to explain just why the *Narodna Odbrana* [Bosnian Serb secret society] existed, the kind of men that were in it, and the significance of that date, June 28, on which the Archduke dared to enter Sarajevo. . . .

How dared Francis Ferdinand, not only the representative of the oppressor but in his own person an arrogant tyrant, enter Sarajevo on that day? Such an entry was a studied insult.

June 28 is a date engraved deep in the heart of every Serb, so that the day has a name of its own. It is called the *vidovnan*. It is the day on which the old Serbian kingdom was conquered by the Turks at the battle of Amselfelde in 1389. It is also the day on which in the second Balkan War the Serbian armies took glorious revenge on the Turk for his old victory and for the years of enslavement. . . .

As we read that clipping in Belgrade we knew what we would do to Francis Ferdinand. We would kill him to show Austria there yet lived within its borders defiance of its rule. We would kill him to bring once more to the boiling point the fighting spirit of the revolutionaries and pave the way for revolt.

Our decision was taken almost immediately. Death to the tyrant! . . .

When Francis Ferdinand and his retinue drove from the station they were allowed to pass the first two conspirators. The motor cars were driving too fast to make an attempt feasible and in the crowd were many Serbians; throwing a grenade would have killed many innocent people.

When the car passed Gabrinovic, the compositor, he threw his grenade. It hit the side of the car, but Francis Ferdinand with presence of mind threw himself back and was uninjured. Several officers riding in his attendance were injured.

The cars sped to the Town Hall and the rest of the conspirators did not interfere with them. After the reception in the Town Hall General Potiorek, the Austrian Commander, pleaded with Francis Ferdinand to leave the city, as it was seething with rebellion. The Archduke was persuaded to drive the shortest way out of the city and to go quickly.

The road to the maneuvers was shaped like the letter V, making a sharp turn at the bridge over the River Nilgacka. Francis Ferdinand's car could go fast enough until it reached this spot but here it was forced to slow down for the turn. Here Princip had taken his stand.

As the car came abreast he stepped forward from the curb, drew his automatic pistol from his coat and fired two shots. The first struck the wife of the Archduke, the Archduchess Sofia, in the abdomen. She was an expectant mother. She died instantly.

The second bullet struck the Archduke close to the heart.

He uttered only one word, "Sofia"—a call to his stricken wife. Then his head fell back and he collapsed. He died almost instantly.

The officers seized Princip. They beat him over the head with the flat of their swords. They knocked him down, they kicked him, scraped the skin from his neck with the edges of their swords, tortured him, all but killed him.

The next day they put chains on Princip's feet, which he wore till his death.

Louis L. Snyder, ed., *Historic Documents of World War I.* New York: Van Nostrand Reinhold, 1958, pp. 52–56.

Document 2: The "Blank Check": Germany Backs Austria-Hungary: July 6, 1914

As the Austro-Hungarian government prepared to punish Serbia for the Sarajevo assassination in early July 1914, it received crucial support from Germany. The telegram below is considered the "blank check" that widened and intensified the crisis. Austria-Hungary was preparing to humiliate Serbia with its demands for redress, and Russia aligned with Serbia.

Telegram from the Imperial Chancellor, von Bethmann-Hollweg, to the German Ambassador at Vienna. Tschirschky, July 6, 1914

Berlin, July 6, 1914

Confidential. For Your Excellency's personal information and guidance
The Austro-Hungarian Ambassador yesterday delivered to the Emperor [Germany's Wilhelm II] a confidential personal letter from the Emperor Francis Joseph, which depicts the present situation from the Austro-Hungarian point of view, and describes the measures which Vienna has in view. A copy is now being forwarded to Your Excellency [Tschirschky].

I replied to Count Szögyeny [Austrian ambassador to Germany] today on behalf of His Majesty that His Majesty sends his thanks to the Emperor Francis Joseph for his letter and would soon answer it personally. In the meantime His Majesty desires to say that he is not blind to the danger which threatens Austria-Hungary and thus the Triple Alliance as a result of the Russian and Serbian Pan-Slavic agitation. . . .

Finally, as far as concerns Serbia, His Majesty, of course, cannot interfere in the dispute now going on between Austria-Hungary and that country, as it is a matter not within his competence. The Emperor Francis Joseph may, however, rest assured that His Majesty will faithfully stand by Austria-Hungary, as is required by the obligations of his alliance and of his ancient friendship.

BETHMANN-HOLLWEG

Louis L. Snyder, ed., *Historic Documents of World War I.* New York: Van Nostrand Reinhold, 1958, pp. 57–58.

Document 3: British Indecision on the Brink of War

By 1914, Great Britain had joined in the so-called Triple Entente with France and Russia to counter German ambitions in Europe. This did not, however, firmly commit the British to come to France's aid in case of war. The following note to the French government from Britain's foreign secretary, Sir Edward Grey, suggests the ambiguity of official British support for intervention, even on the eve of war.

Sir Edward Grey to Sir F. Bertie

Foreign Office, July 31, 1914

Sir,

M. Cambon [French ambassador to Britain] referred today to a telegram that had been shown to Sir Arthur Nicolson [British official] this morning from the French Ambassador in Berlin saying that it was the uncertainty with regard to whether we would intervene which was the encouraging element in Berlin, and that, if we would only declare definitely on the side of Russia and France, it would decide the German attitude in favor of peace.

I said that it was quite wrong to suppose that we had left Germany under the impression that we would not intervene. I had refused overtures to promise that we should remain neutral. I had not only definitely declined to say that we would remain neutral; I had even gone so far this morning as to say to the German Ambassador that, if France and Germany became involved in war, we should be drawn into it. That, of course, was not the same thing as taking an engagement to France, and I told M. Cambon of it only to show that we had not left Germany under the impression that we would stand aside.

M. Cambon then asked for my reply to what he had said yesterday.

I said that we had come to the conclusion, in the Cabinet today, that we could not give any pledge at the present time. The commercial and financial situation was exceedingly serious; there was danger of a complete collapse that would involve us and everyone else in ruin; and it was possible that our standing aside might be the only means of preventing a complete collapse of European credit, in which we should be involved. This might be a paramount consideration in deciding our attitude.

I went on to say to M. Cambon that though we should have to put our policy before Parliament, we could not pledge Parliament in advance. Up to the present moment, we did not feel, and public opinion did not feel, that any treaties or obligations of this country were involved. Further developments might alter this situation and cause the Government and Parliament to take the view that intervention was justified. The preservation of the neutrality of Belgium might be, I would not say a decisive, but an important factor, in determining our attitude. Whether we proposed to Parliament to intervene or not to intervene in a war, Parliament would wish to know how we stood with regard to the neutrality of Belgium, and it might be that I should ask both France and Germany whether each was prepared to undertake an engagement that she would not be the first to violate the neutrality of Belgium.

M. Cambon expressed great disappointment at my reply. He repeated his question of whether we would help France if Germany made an attack on her.

I said that I could only adhere to the answer that, so far as things had gone at present, we could not take any engagement. The latest news was that Russia had ordered a complete mobilization of her fleet and army. This, it seemed to me, would precipitate a crisis, and would make it appear that German mobilisation was being forced by Russia.

M. Cambon urged that Germany had from the beginning rejected proposals that might have made for peace. It could not be to England's interest that France should be crushed by Germany. We should then be in a very diminished position with regard to Germany. In 1870, we had made a great mistake in allowing an enormous increase in German strength; and we should now be repeating the mistake. He asked me whether I could not submit his question to the Cabinet again.

I said that the Cabinet would certainly be summoned as soon as there was some new development, but at the present moment the only answer I could give was that we could not undertake any definite engagement.

I am, etc.

E. GREY

Louis L. Snyder, ed., *Historic Documents of World War I.* New York: Van Nostrand Reinhold, 1958, pp. 77–79.

Document 4: Enthusiasm for War: Summer 1914

The outbreak of war in early August 1914 evoked mixed responses throughout Europe, from profound anxiety to wild celebration. Austrian author Stefan Zweig in his memoir The World of Yesterday *recalls the enthusiasm that swept Vienna as Austria-Hungary went to war.*

The next morning I was in Austria. In every station placards had been put up announcing general mobilization. The trains were filled with fresh recruits, banners were flying, music sounded, and in Vienna I found the entire city in a tumult. The first shock at the news of war—the war that no one, people or government, had wanted—the war which had slipped, much against their will, out of the clumsy hands of the diplomats who had been bluffing and toying with it, had suddenly been transformed into enthusiasm. There were parades in the street, flags, ribbons, and music burst forth everywhere, young recruits were marching triumphantly, their faces lighting up at the cheering—they, the John Does and Richard Roes who usually go unnoticed and uncelebrated.

And to be truthful, I must acknowledge that there was a majestic, rapturous, and even seductive something in this first outbreak of the people from which one could escape only with difficulty. And in spite of all my hatred and aversion for war, I should not like to have missed the memory of those first days. As never before, thousands and hundreds of thousands felt what they should have felt in peace time, that they belonged together. A city of two million, a country of nearly fifty million, in that hour felt that they were participating in world history, in a moment which would never recur, and that each one was called upon to cast his infinitesimal [infinitely small] self into the glowing mass, there to be purified of all selfishness. All differences of class, rank, and language were swamped at that moment by the rushing feeling of fraternity. Strangers spoke to one another in the streets, people who had avoided each other for years shook hands, everywhere one saw excited faces. Each individual experienced an exaltation of his ego, he was no longer the isolated person of former times, he had been incorporated into the mass, he was part of the people, and his person, his hitherto unnoticed person, had been given meaning. . . .

[W]hat did the great mass know of war in 1914, after nearly half a century of peace? They did not know war, they had hardly given it a thought. It had become legendary, and distance had made it seem romantic and heroic. They still saw it in the perspective of their school readers and of paintings in museums; brilliant cavalry attacks in glittering uniforms, the fatal shot always straight through the heart, the entire campaign a resounding march of victory—"We'll be home at Christmas," the recruits shouted laughingly to their mothers in August, 1914. Who in the villages and the cities of Austria remembered "real" war? A few ancients at best who, in 1866, had fought against Prussia, which was now their ally [as Germany]. But what a quick, bloodless, far-off war that had been, a campaign that had ended in three weeks with few victims and before it had well started! A rapid excursion into the romantic, a wild, manly adventure—that is how the war of 1914 was painted in the imagination of the simple man, and the young people were honestly afraid that they might miss this most wonderful and exciting experience of their lives; that is why they hurried and thronged to the colours, and that is why they shouted and sang in the trains that carried them to the slaughter; wildly and feverishly the red wave of blood coursed through the veins of the entire nation.

Stefan Zweig, *The World of Yesterday*. London: Cassell, 1953, pp. 222–24, 226–27.

Document 5: Hating the Enemy: Ernst Lissauer's Hymn of Hate

German Jewish writer Ernst Lissauer was rejected for service by the German military, but sought to prove his patriotism in the following anti-British poetic diatribe. The poem displays the rampant nationalism that made World War I possible by 1914. Lissauer's poem was a sensation in Germany. In the poem, "Weichsel" is the German name for the Vistula River on the eastern front and the "Vosges gate" is likely a position on the western front.

French and Russians, they matter not,
A blow for a blow and a shot for a shot;
We love them not, we hate them not,
We hold the Weichsel and Vosges gate.
We have but one and only hate,
We love as one, we hate as one,
We have one foe and one alone.

He is known to you all, he is known to you all.
He crouches behind the dark gray flood,
Full of envy, of rage, of craft, of gall,
Cut off by waves that are thicker than blood.
Come let us stand at the judgment-place,
An oath to swear to, face to face,
An oath of bronze no wind can shake,
An oath for our sons and their sons to take.

Come, hear the word, repeat the word,
Throughout the Fatherland make it heard.
We will never forego our hate,
We have all but a single hate,

We love as one, we hate as one,
We have one foe and one alone—
ENGLAND!

Marilyn Shevin-Coetzee and Frans Coetzee, eds., *World War I and European Society: A Sourcebook*. Lexington, MA: D.C. Heath, 1995, pp. 30–32.

Document 6: A Soldier's Idealism Early in the War: Franz Blumenfeld

Following the Great War, a German university professor gathered private letters of students who served with the German army between 1914 and 1918. Three months after writing this letter to his mother, Franz Blumenfeld was killed in France.

In the train, September 24th, 1914

My dear, good, precious Mother, I certainly believe and hope that I shall come back from the war, but just in case I do not I am going to write you a farewell letter. I want you to know that if I am killed, I give my life gladly and willingly. My life has been so beautiful that I could not wish that anything in it had been different. And its having been so beautiful was thanks above all to you, my dear, good, best of Mothers. . . .

I want to write to you about something else, which, judging from bits in your letters, you haven't quite understood: why I should have volunteered for the war? Of course it was not from any enthusiasm for war in general, nor because I thought it would be a fine thing to kill a great many people or otherwise distinguish myself. On the contrary, I think that war is a very, very evil thing, and I believe that even in this case it might have been averted by a more skilful diplomacy. But, now that it has been declared, I think it is a matter of course that one should feel oneself so much a member of the nation that one must unite one's fate as closely as possible with that of the whole. And even if I were convinced that I could serve my Fatherland and its people better in peace than in war, I should think it just as perverse and impossible to let any such calculations weigh with me at the present moment as it would be for a man going to the assistance of somebody who was drowning, to stop to consider who the drowning man was and whether his own life were not perhaps the more valuable of the two. For what counts is always the readiness to make a sacrifice, not the object for which the sacrifice is made.

This war seems to me, from all that I have heard, to be something so horrible, inhuman, mad, obsolete, and in every way depraving, that I have firmly resolved, if I do come back, to do everything in my power to prevent such a thing from ever happening again in the future.

Marilyn Shevin-Coetzee and Frans Coetzee, eds., *World War I and European Society: A Sourcebook*. Lexington, MA: D.C. Heath, 1995, pp. 39–40.

Document 7: Slaughter on the Somme, 1916: British "Blokes and Chaps"

The summer of 1916 saw the wholesale slaughter of British, as well as German, troops in the epic battle of the Somme. The following accounts of volunteer enlisted men with different British regiments depict the carnage and futility of the great offensive. The brutalization of war is apparent in the first excerpt by W.H. Shaw. In the second account, Sergeant J.E. Yates reveals how commonplace horrible wounds and comradely courage were amid the hell of battle. In the third excerpt, Private W. Hay reflects on the stupidity of frontal infantry attack in the face of artillery and machine-gun fire. He also notes how ordinary soldiers increasingly questioned the decisions of their commanders who ordered the attacks.

Our artillery had been bombing that line for six days and nights, trying to smash the German barbed-wire entanglements, but they hadn't made any impact on those barbed-wire entanglements. The result was we never got anywhere near the Germans. Never got anywhere near them. Our lads was mown down. They were just simply slaughtered. It was just one continuous go forward, come back, go forward, come back, losing men all the time and there we were, wondering when it was going to end. You couldn't do anything. You were either tied down by the shelling or the machine-guns and yet we kept at it, kept on going all along the line, making no impact on the Germans at all. We didn't get anywhere, we never moved from the line, hardly. The machine-guns were levelled and they were mowing the top of the trenches. You daren't put your finger up. The men were just falling back in the trenches.

Now there was a saying in the Royal Welch Fusiliers [Shaw's unit], 'Follow the flash.' Now, I don't know whether you've ever seen a Royal Welch Fusiliers officer, but there's a flash on the back of his collar. The officers were urging us on, saying, 'Come on, lads, follow the flash!' But you just couldn't. It was hopeless. And those young officers going ahead, that flash flying in the breeze, they were picked off like flies. We tried to go over and it was just impossible. We were mown down, and that went on and if some of the Battalions did manage to break through, it was very rare and it was only on a small scale. If they did, the Germans would counter-attack and that's what was going on. You'd attack, fall back, the Germans would counter-attack, they'd fall back, and that's how it was, cat and mouse all the time.

When they were counter-attacking, well, they were mown down, just the same as what we were, and yet they were urged on by their officers just the same as our officers were urging us on. They were coming over just like cattle, whole Battalions of them. You just felt, 'You've given it to us, now we're going to give it to you,' and you were taking delight in mowing them down. Our machine-gunners had a whale of a time with those Lewis machine-guns. You just couldn't miss them.

* * * * *

Almost imperceptibly the first day merged into the second, when we held grimly to a battered trench and watched each other grow old under the day-long storm of shelling. Big shells landed in the crowded trench. For hours, sweating, praying, swearing, we worked on the heaps of chalk and mangled bodies. Men did astonishing things at which one did not wonder till after. Here is an instance of fortitude.

A man had his right arm and leg torn off clean. His mind was quite clear as I laid him on the fire-step. His left hand wandered over his chest to the pulp where his right shoulder had been. 'My God,' he said, 'I've lost my arm.' The hand crept down to the stump of the right thigh. 'Is that off too?' I nodded. It was impossible to move him at the time. For five hours he lay there fully conscious and smoking cigarettes. When at last we tried to carry him out the stretcher stuck in the first traverse. We put him on a groundsheet and struggled on. But our strength was gone: we could not hold his weight. 'Drag me,' he suggested then, and we dragged him along the floor of the trench to the medical dugout.

At dawn next morning we were back in a green wood. I found myself leaning on a rifle, and staring stupidly at the filthy exhausted men who slept round me. It did not occur to me to lie down until someone pushed me into a bed of ferns. There were flowers among the ferns, and my last thought was a dull wonder that there could still be flowers in the world.

* * * * *

You were between the devil and the deep blue sea. If you go forward, you'll likely be shot, if you go back you'll be court-martialled and shot, so what the hell do you do? What can you do? You just go forward because that's the only bloke you can take your knife in, that's the bloke you're facing.

We were sent in to High Wood in broad daylight in the face of heavy machine-gun fire and shell fire, and everywhere there was dead bodies all over the place where previous battalions and regiments had taken part in their previous attacks. We went in there and C Company got a terrible bashing there. It was criminal to send men in broad daylight, into machine-gun fire, without any cover of any sort whatsoever. There was no need for it; they could have hung on and made an attack on the flanks somewhere or other, but we had to carry out our orders.

But there was one particular place just before we got to High Wood which was a crossroads, and it was really hell there, they shelled it like anything, you couldn't get past it, it was almost impossible. There were men everywhere, heaps of men, not one or two men, but heaps of men everywhere, all dead. Then afterwards, when our battle was all over, after our attack on High Wood, there was other battalions went up and they got the same! They went on and on. They just seemed to be pushing men in to be killed and no reason. There didn't seem to be any reason. They couldn't possibly take the position, not on a frontal attack. Not at High Wood.

Most of the chaps, actually, they were afraid to go in because they knew it was death. Before we went in, we knew what would happen, some of the blokes that had survived from previous attacks knew what they'd been through. It was hell, it was impossible, utterly impossible. The only possible way to take High Wood was if the Germans ran short of ammunition, they might be able to take it then. They couldn't take it against machine-guns, just ridiculous. It was absolute slaughter. We always blamed the people up above. We had a saying in the Army, 'The higher, the fewer'. They meant the higher the rank, the fewer the brains.

Lyn MacDonald, ed., *1914–1918: Voices and Images of the Great War*. London: Michael Joseph, 1988, pp. 155–57, 160–61.

Document 8: Total War: A German Volunteer's View

By late 1916 the war was becoming mechanized slaughter, dispelling the romantic notions that prevailed among armies of both sides in August 1914. The following account of German soldier Reinhold Spengler of the 1st Bavarian Infantry Regiment suggests the growing disillusionment.

The brutality and inhumanity of war stood in great contrast to what I had heard and read about as a youth. I really wanted to go off to the Front at the beginning of the war because in school we were taught to be super patriots. This was drilled into us— in order to be men we should go off to war and, if necessary, bravely die for Kaiser and Fatherland.

When I had joined the army in the spring of 1916 I still carried presumptions that the war would be fought like the 1870 War between Germany and France. Man-to-man combat, for instance. But in the trenches friend and foe alike suffered from the effects of invisible machinery. It was not enough to conquer the enemy. He had to be totally destroyed. The fighting troops of the front lines saw themselves mired hopelessly in this hellish wasteland. Whoever lived through it thanked his good luck. The rest died as 'heroes'. It seemed quite unlikely to me in late 1916 that I should live through it. When you met someone you knew who belonged to a different outfit, he was greeted with the words, 'Well, are you still alive?' It was said humorously but meant in deadly earnest. For a young man who had a long and worthwhile future awaiting him, it was not easy to expect death almost daily. However, after a while I got used to the idea of dying young. Strangely, it had a sort of soothing effect and prevented me from worrying too much. Because of this I gradually lost the terrible fear of being wounded or killed.

Lyn MacDonald, ed., *1914–1918: Voices and Images of the Great War.* London: Michael Joseph, 1988, pp. 181–82.

Document 9: Poison Gas and Poetry: Wilfred Owen

Wilfred Owen was one of a number of British soldier-poets, including Siegfried Sassoon and Robert Graves, who contributed through their ordeal to the literary legacy of the Great War. The following is Owen's most famous poem. It evokes the horror of poison gas warfare on the western front, and ends with a bitterly ironic comment on patriotism. The closing Latin passage, "Dulce et decorum est / Pro patria mori," translates as "It is sweet and proper to die for one's country." Wilfred Owen died one week before the end of the war.

Dulce Et Decorum Est

Bent double, like old beggars under sacks,
Knocked-kneed, coughing like hags, we cursed through sludge,
Till on the haunting flares we turned our backs
And towards our distant rest began to trudge.
Men marched asleep. Many had lost their boots
But limped on, blood-shod. All went lame; all blind;
Drunk with fatigue; deaf even to the hoots
Of tired, outstripped Five-Nines that dropped behind.

Gas! Gas! Quick, boys!—An ecstasy of fumbling,
Fitting the clumsy helmets just in time;
But someone still was yelling out and stumbling
And flound'ring like a man in fire or lime . . .
Dim, through the misty panes and thick green light,
As under a green sea, I saw him drowning.
In all my dreams, before my helpless sight,
He plunges at me, guttering, choking, drowning.

If in some smothering dreams you too could pace
Behind the wagon that we flung him in,
And watch the white eyes writhing in his face,
His hanging face, like a devil's sick of sin;
If you could hear, at every jolt, the blood
Come gargling from the froth-corrupted lungs,
Obscene as cancer, bitter as the cud
Of vile, incurable sores on innocent tongues,—
My friend, you would not tell with such high zest
To children ardent for some desperate glory,
The old Lie: Dulce et decorum est
Pro patria mori.

Jere Klemens King, ed., *The First World War.* New York: Walker, 1972, pp. 223–24.

Document 10: The November Revolution in Russia: Trotsky Arouses the People

N.N. Sukhanov was a Russian revolutionary of the Menshevik faction that lost out to the Bolsheviks. His classic memoir of the events of 1917 includes the following sketch of the brilliant Leon Trotsky whipping up support for the second stage of the revolution three days before the Bolsheviks captured power. Trotsky emphasized the key, popular Bolshevik demands—bread, land, and peace—to end the "suffering in the trenches."

The mood of the people, more than 3,000, who filled the hall was definitely tense; they were all silently waiting for something. The audience was of course primarily workers and soldiers, but more than a few typically lower-middle-class men's and women's figures were visible.

Trotsky's ovation seemed to be cut short prematurely, out of curiosity and impatience: what was he going to say? Trotsky at once began to heat up the atmosphere, with his skill and brilliance. I remember that at length and with extraordinary power he drew a picture of the suffering of the trenches. Thoughts flashed through my mind of the inevitable incongruity of the parts in this oratorical whole. But Trotsky knew what he was doing. The whole point lay in the mood. The political conclusions had long been familiar. They could be condensed, as long as there were enough highlights.

Trotsky did this—with enough highlights. The Soviet regime was not only called upon to put an end to the suffering of the trenches. It would give land and heal the internal disorder. Once again the recipes against hunger were repeated: a soldier, a sailor, and a working girl, who would requisition bread from those who had it and distribute it gratis to the cities and front. But Trotsky went even further on this decisive "Day of the Petersburg Soviet."

"The Soviet Government will give everything the country contains to the poor and the men in the trenches. You, bourgeois [upper middle class], have got two fur caps!—give one of them to the soldier, who's freezing in the trenches. Have you got warm boots? Stay at home. The worker needs your boots. . . ."

These were very good and just ideas. They could not but excite the enthusiasm of a crowd who had been reared on the Tsarist whip. In any case, I certify as a direct witness that this was what was said on this last day.

All round me was a mood bordering on ecstasy. It seemed as though the crowd, spontaneously and of its own accord, would break into some religious hymn. Trotsky formulated a brief and general resolution, or pronounced some general formula like "we will defend the worker-peasant cause to the last drop of our blood."

Who was—for? The crowd of thousands, as one man, raised their hands. I saw the raised hands and burning eyes of men, women, youths, soldiers, peasants, and typically lower-middle-class faces. Were they in spiritual transport? Did they see, through the raised curtain, a corner of the "righteous land" of their longing? Or were they penetrated by a consciousness of the *political occasion*, under the influence of the political agitation of a *Socialist?* Ask no questions! Accept it as it was. . . .

Trotsky went on speaking. The innumerable crowd went on holding their hands up. Trotsky rapped out the words: "Let this vote of yours be your vow—with all your strength and at any sacrifice to support the Soviet that has taken on itself the glorious burden of bringing to a conclusion the victory of the revolution and of giving land, bread, and peace!"

The vast crowd was holding up its hands. It agreed. It vowed. Once again, accept this as it was. With an unusual feeling of oppression I looked on at this really magnificent scene.

Trotsky finished. Someone else went out on to the stage. But there was no point in waiting and looking any more.

Throughout Petersburg more or less the same thing was going on. Everywhere there were final reviews and final vows. Thousands, tens of thousands and hundreds of thousands of people. . . . This, actually, was already an insurrection. Things [revolution] had started.

Marvin Perry, Matthew Berg, and James Krukones, eds., *Sources of Twentieth-Century Europe.* Boston and New York: Houghton Mifflin, 2000, pp. 111–12.

Document 11: The United States Intervenes: Wilson's War Message, 1917

Germany's decision at the end of 1916 to unleash unrestricted submarine warfare led the United States to declare war on Germany on April 6, 1917. President Woodrow Wilson in his address of January 22, 1917, had spoken of U.S. global objectives as "peace without victory" among the belligerents. The following war message of April 2, 1917, however, shows Wilson shifting to a new strategy of peace through victory. Germany's aggressive U-boat campaign was seen as endangering American principles, interests, and lives.

Gentlemen of the Congress: I have called the Congress into extraordinary session because there are serious, very serious choices of policy to be made, and made immediately, which it was neither right nor constitutionally permissible that I should assume the responsibility of making.

On the third of February last I officially laid before you the extraordinary announcement of the Imperial German Government that on and after the first day of February it was its purpose to put aside all restraints of law or of humanity and use its submarines to sink every vessel that sought to approach either the ports of Great Britain and Ireland or the western coasts of Europe or any of the ports controlled by the enemies of Germany within the Mediterranean. That had seemed to be the object of the German submarine warfare earlier in the war, but since April of last year the Imperial Government had somewhat restrained the commanders of its undersea craft. . . . The new policy has swept every restriction aside. Vessels of every kind, whatever their flag, their character, their cargo, their destination, their errand, have been ruthlessly sent to the bottom without warning and without thought of help or mercy for those on board, the vessels of friendly neutrals along with those of belligerents. Even hospital ships and ships carrying relief to the sorely bereaved and stricken people of Belgium . . . have been sunk with the same reckless lack of compassion or of principle. . . .

The present German submarine warfare against commerce is a warfare against mankind.

It is a war against all nations. American ships have been sunk, American lives taken, in ways which it has stirred us very deeply to learn of, but the ships and people of other neutral and friendly nations have been sunk and overwhelmed in the waters in the same way. There has been no discrimination. The challenge is to all mankind. Each nation must decide for itself how it will meet it. The choice we make for ourselves must be made with a moderation of counsel and a temperateness of judgment befitting our character and our motives as a nation. We must put excited feeling away. Our motive will not be revenge or the victorious assertion of the physical might of the nation, but only the vindication of right, of human right, of which we are only a single champion.

When I addressed the Congress on the twenty-sixth of February last I thought that it would suffice to assert our neutral rights with arms, our right to use the seas against unlawful interference, our right to keep our people safe against unlawful violence. But armed neutrality, it now appears, is impracticable. . . .

With a profound sense of the solemn and even tragical character of the step I am taking and of the grave responsibilities which it involves, but in unhesitating obedience to what I deem my constitutional duty, I advise that the Congress declare the recent course of the Imperial German Government to be in fact nothing less than war against the Government and people of the United States; that it formally accept the status of belligerent which has thus been thrust upon it; and that it take immediate steps not only to put the country in a more thorough state of defense, but also to exert all its power and employ all its resources to bring the Government of the German Empire to terms and end the war. . . .

While we do these things, these deeply momentous things, let us be very clear, and make very clear to all the world, what our motives and our objects are. . . . Our object . . . is to vindicate the principles of peace and justice in the life of the world as against selfish and autocratic power, and to set up among the really free and self-governed peoples of the world such a concert of purpose and of action as will henceforth ensure the observance of those principles. Neutrality is no longer feasible or desirable where the peace of the world is involved and the freedom of its peoples, and the menace to that peace and freedom lies in the existence of autocratic governments, backed by organized force which is controlled wholly by their will, not by the will of their people. We have seen the last of neutrality in such circumstances. We are at the beginning of an age in which it will be insisted that the same standards of conduct and of responsibility for wrong done shall be observed among nations and their governments that are observed among the individual citizens of civilized States.

We have no quarrel with the German people. We have no feeling towards them but one of sympathy and friendship. It was not upon their impulse that their government acted in entering this war. It was not with their previous knowledge or approval. It was a war determined upon as wars used to be determined upon in the old, unhappy days when peoples were nowhere consulted by their rulers and wars were provoked and waged in the interest of dynasties or of little groups of ambitious men who were accustomed to use their fellow-men as pawns and tools. . . .

The world must be made safe for democracy. Its peace must be planted upon the tested foundations of political liberty. We have no selfish ends to serve. We desire no conquest, no dominion. We seek no indemnities for ourselves, no material compensation for the sacrifices we shall freely make. We are but one of the champions of the rights of mankind. We shall be satisfied when those rights have been made as secure as the faith and the freedom of nations can make them. . . .

It is a distressing and oppressive duty, Gentlemen of the Congress, which I have performed in thus addressing you. There are, it may be, many months of fiery trial and sacrifice ahead of us. It is a fearful thing to lead this great peaceful people into war, into the most terrible and disastrous of all wars, civilization itself seeming to be in the balance. But the right is more precious than peace, and we shall fight for the things which we have always carried nearest our hearts—for democracy, for the right of those who submit to authority to have a voice in their own governments, for the rights and liberties of small nations, for a universal dominion of right by such a concert of free peoples as shall bring peace and safety to all nations and make the world itself at last free. To such a task we can dedicate our lives and our fortunes, everything that we are and everything that we have, with the pride of those who know that the day has come when America is privileged to spend her blood and her might for the principles that gave her birth and happiness and the peace which she has treasured. God helping her, she can do no other.

Leon Fink, ed., *Major Problems in the Gilded Age and the Progressive Era: Documents and Essays.* Lexington, MA: D.C. Heath, 1993, pp. 527–30.

Document 12: A Liberal American Blueprint for Peace: Wilson's Fourteen Points

With the new Bolshevik government in Russia demanding immediate peace and rising calls for defining more liberal peace aims on the home fronts of both the Allies and the Central Powers, Woodrow Wilson skillfully seized the initiative in his Fourteen Points address to Congress on January 8, 1918. The Fourteen Points are credited with persuading Germany to sue for peace later that year but found only partial realization in the Paris peace treaties ending the war.

The program of the world's peace . . . and the only possible program, as we see it, is this:

I. Open covenants of peace, openly arrived at . . . diplomacy shall proceed always frankly and in the public view.

II. Absolute freedom of navigation upon the seas, outside territorial waters, alike in peace and in war, except as the seas may be closed in whole or in part by international action for the enforcement of international covenants.

III. The removal, so far as possible, of all economic barriers and the establishment of an equality of trade conditions among all the nations consenting to the peace and associating themselves for its maintenance.

IV. Adequate guarantees given and taken that national armaments will be reduced to the lowest point consistent with domestic safety.

V. A free, open-minded, and absolutely impartial adjustment of all colonial claims, based upon a strict observance of the principle that in determining all such questions of sovereignty the interests of the populations concerned must have equal weight with the equitable claims of the government whose title is to be determined.

VI. The evacuation of all Russian territory and such a settlement of all questions affecting Russia as will secure the best and freest coöperation of the other nations of the world in obtaining for her an unhampered and unembarrassed opportunity for the independent determination of her own political development and national policy. . . .

VII. Belgium, the whole world will agree, must be evacuated and restored, without any attempt to limit the sovereignty which she enjoys in common with all other free nations. . . .

VIII. All French territory should be freed and the invaded portions restored, and the wrong done to France by Prussia in 1871 in the matter of Alsace-Lorraine, which has unsettled the peace of the world for nearly fifty years should be righted. . . .

IX. A readjustment of the frontiers of Italy should be effected along clearly recognizable lines of nationality.

X. The peoples of Austria-Hungary . . . should be accorded the freest opportunity of autonomous development.

XI. Roumania, Serbia, and Montenegro should be evacuated; occupied territories restored; Serbia accorded free and secure access to the sea. . . .

XII. The Turkish portions of the present Ottoman Empire should be assured a secure sovereignty, but the other nationalities which are now under Turkish rule should be assured an undoubted security of life and an absolutely unmolested opportunity of autonomous development, and the Dardanelles should be permanently opened as a free passage to the ships and commerce of all nations under international guarantees.

XIII. An independent Polish State should be erected which should include the territories inhabited by indisputably Polish populations, which should be assured a free and secure access to the sea, and whose political and economic independence and territorial integrity should be guaranteed by international covenant.

XIV. A general association of nations must be formed under specific convenants for the purpose of affording mutual guarantees of political independence and territorial integrity to great and small States alike.

Quoted in Louis L. Snyder, ed., *Historic Documents of World War I.* New York: Van Nostrand Reinhold, 1958, pp. 164–66.

Document 13: Total War and State Interference: The German Home Front

The following report by a German government official in 1915 suggests how total war on land and sea generated pressures for expanded economic controls on the German home front. The British maritime blockade of Germany intensified nationalism within Germany, as well as government control of limited resources and supplies, a phenomena sometimes called "war socialism." Similar pressures were at work in other belligerent nations.

The present world war is being waged with weapons which were unknown to any earlier age. Economic weapons have been added to military means of annihilation. In the forefront stands a scheme from which our opponents hoped great things even before the war, and which is now, after a succession of fearful defeats, doubly important to them. It is the famous starvation scheme. Our flourishing economic life has brought us into the closest connection with every country, and it is apparently only this connection which has enabled us to feed the ever-increasing population within our narrow borders; now our enemies desire to seal us hermetically [completely] from the outside world and to tie the veins of our economic life. Our army and fleet having shown themselves a match for half the world, our nation is to be conquered by hunger.

Germany and Austria are for the most part surrounded by hostile countries, the only neutral frontiers being those of Holland, Denmark, Switzerland, Italy, and Roumania. By means of a so-called command of the sea and by influencing our neutral neighbours it is hoped to cut off Germany and Austria from the rest of the world and so force them to their knees. Our enemies suppose that Germany and Austria cannot exist for any length of time without their enormous foreign trade. . . . While much is hoped from tying up the export trade, greater results are expected from hindering the importation of all that we need for manufacture and daily life—wool, cotton, petroleum, copper, and the like, but, above all, food for man and beast. It is believed that we should find it difficult to hold out for any length of time without our exports—and quite impossible without our imports. This plan of campaign was originated by England, who, in her ruthless desire for power, has never hesitated to countenance the use of any weapon, and in her colonial wars has quite forgotten how to fight decently. The concentration camps of the Boer War [South African war, 1899–1902] afford the latest proof that the English gentleman is not ashamed to make war against women and children; now England desires to use this well-tried weapon on a large scale, and would like to make the whole of Germany one vast concentration camp. France, corrupted by her English alliance, has taken up the starvation idea with rapture, though it is little worthy of so chivalrous [gallant, honorable] a nation. . . .

Among the great acquisitions for which we have to thank the war, perhaps the greatest is that it has put new life into our national consciousness. Two dangers threatened us: love of everything foreign (or internationalism), and personal egotism (or individualism). In the most diverse paths of life, in art, literature, fashion, German characteristics seemed either to be forgotten in the general admiration of the foreigner, or to have lost all coherence in the strife of self-assertion. The war has changed all this. With our whole hearts we feel ourselves to be Germans. The cults of the foreigner and egotism have fallen from us as if they were unfitted to us. Each sees his highest aim in serving the Fatherland to the best of his ability, and it now seems absolutely natural that world connections as well as private interests should be placed in the background of our economic life, and that we should think only of the economic weal of the German people. Should circumstances compel Germany and Austria to become one isolated State, each one of us will adapt his thought and deeds to the necessity without further ado.

In an isolated State, economic thought experiences a complete transformation. So long as our national economic life was bound up with that of the rest of the world, the idea of production stood in the foreground; if we produced valuable goods no matter of how one-sided a nature, no one doubted the possibility of exchanging them abroad for all that we needed in our daily life. . . .

So long as our economic life was bound up with that of the rest of the world, great personal freedom in our economic demeanour was possible. Even those who had given up the principle of boundless *laissez faire* still feared any far-reaching restrictions of economic freedom; but in the difficult position which has arisen through the sudden isolation of German economic life that fear must disappear. Our economic life is subject to State regulation to an extent hitherto unheard of. The . . . [German government] has extensive powers to prohibit the export or fix the highest prices of objects of daily necessity, and they can also demand any restrictions of economic freedom which the situation may require. Patriotic feeling has, however, accepted this far-reaching State regulation as absolutely justified. Nowadays everyone is a Socialist, so to speak.

Quoted in Marilyn Shevin-Coetzee and Frans Coetzee, eds., *World War I and European Society: A Sourcebook.* Lexington, MA: D.C. Heath, 1995, pp. 237–39.

Document 14: The Propaganda War

The following British propaganda leaflet was aimed at German front-line soldiers near the end of the war. Economic and military pressure on Germany by 1918 was intense and this appeal might have furthered the weakening of German troop morale.

FOR WHAT ARE YOU FIGHTING, MICHEL?

They tell you that you are fighting for the Fatherland. Have you ever thought why you are fighting?

You are fighting to glorify Hindenburg, to enrich Krupp [armaments manufacturer]. You are struggling for the Kaiser, the Junkers [aristocrats], and the militarists. . . .

They promise you victory and peace. You poor fools! It was promised your comrades for more than three years. They have indeed found peace, deep in the grave, but victory did not come! . . .

It is for the Fatherland. . . . But what is your Fatherland? Is it the Crown Prince [Kaiser's son, an army commander] who offered up 600,000 men at Verdun? Is it Hindenburg, who with Ludendorff is many kilometers behind the front lines making more plans to give the English more cannon fodder? Is it Krupp for whom each year of war means millions of marks? Is it the Prussian

Junkers who still cry over your dead bodies for more annexations? No, none of these is the Fatherland. You are the Fatherland. . . . The whole power of the Western world stands behind England and France and America! An army of ten million is being prepared; soon it will come into the battle. Have you thought of that, Michel?

Quoted in Louis L. Snyder, ed., *Historic Documents of World War I*. New York: Van Nostrand Reinhold, 1958, p. 135.

Document 15: Warning America Against Spies and Subversives

The Wilson administration's Committee on Public Information (CPI) mobilized American sentiment for total war with propaganda like the following CPI public advertisement. In effect, the federal government asked the public to engage in counterespionage. The ad suggests that criticizing government policy in wartime might sabotage victory over the "Hun."

German agents are everywhere, eager to gather scraps of news about our men, our ships, our munitions. It is still possible to get such information through to Germany, where thousands of these fragments—often individually harmless—are patiently pieced together into a whole which spells death to American soldiers and danger to American homes.

But while the enemy is most industrious in trying to collect information, and his systems elaborate, he is *not* superhuman—indeed he is often very stupid, and would fail to get what he wants were it not deliberately handed to him by the carelessness of loyal Americans.

Do not discuss in public, or with strangers, any news of troop and transport movements, or bits of gossip as to our military preparations, which come into your possession.

Do not permit your friends in service to tell you—or write you—"inside" facts about where they are, what they are doing and seeing.

Do not become a tool of the Hun [derogatory: German] by passing on the malicious, disheartening rumors which he so eagerly sows. Remember he asks no better service than to have you spread his lies of disasters to our soldiers and sailors, gross scandals in the Red Cross, cruelties, neglect and wholesale executions in our camps, drunkenness and vice in the [American] Expeditionary Force, and other tales certain to disturb American patriots and to bring anxiety and grief to American parents.

And do not wait until you catch someone putting a bomb under a factory. Report the man who spreads pessimistic stories, divulges—or seeks—confidential military information, cries for peace, or belittles our efforts to win the war.

Send the names of such persons, even if they are in uniform, to the Department of Justice, Washington. Give all the details you can, with names of witnesses if possible—show the Hun that we can beat him at his own game of collecting scattered information and putting it to work. The fact that you made the report will not become public.

You are in contact with the enemy *today*, just as truly as if you faced him across No Man's Land. In your hands are two powerful weapons with which to meet him—discretion and vigilance. *Use them.*

Quoted in *This Fabulous Century: 1910–1920*, vol. 2. New York: Time-Life Books, 1969, p. 234.

Document 16: The Treaty of Versailles: June 28, 1919

The Treaty of Versailles was a long, complicated document. The following are its key provisions. Germans and some Allied spokesmen thought the treaty terms vindictive and contrary to Wilson's liberal peace proposals that shaped the armistice of November 11, 1918.

PART III *Political Clauses for Europe*

ARTICLE 31. Germany, recognizing that the Treaties of April 19, 1839, which established the status of Belgium before the war, no longer conform to the requirements of the situation, consents to the abrogation of the said treaties and undertakes immediately to recognize and to observe whatever conventions may be entered into by the Principal Allied and Associated Powers, or by any of them, in concert with the Governments of Belgium and of the Netherlands, to replace the said Treaties of 1839. If her formal adhesion should be required to such conventions or to any of their stipulations, Germany undertakes immediately to give it. . . .

ARTICLE 42. Germany is forbidden to maintain or construct any fortifications either on the left bank of the Rhine or on the right bank to the west of a line drawn 50 kilometres [30 miles] to the East of the Rhine. . . .

ARTICLE 45. As compensation for the destruction of the coal mines in the north of France and as part payment towards the total reparation due from Germany for the damage resulting from the war, Germany cedes to France in full and absolute possession, with exclusive rights of exploitation, unencumbered and free from all debts and charges of any kind, the coal mines situated in the Saar Basin [after the Franco-Prussian War of 1870]. . . .

ARTICLE 51. The territories [Alsace and Lorraine] which were ceded to Germany . . . are restored to French sovereignty as from the date of the Armistice of November 11, 1918. . . .

ARTICLE 80. Germany acknowledges and will respect strictly the independence of Austria. . . .

ARTICLE 81. Germany, in conformity with the action already taken by the Allied and Associated Powers, recognizes the complete independence of the Czecho-Slovak State. . . .

ARTICLE 87. Germany, in conformity with the action already taken by the Allied and Associated Powers, recognizes the complete independence of Poland, and renounces in her favour all rights and title over the territory [of Poland].

The boundaries of Poland not laid down in the present Treaty will be subsequently determined by the Principal Allied and Associated Powers. . . .

PART IV *German Rights and Interests Outside Germany*

ARTICLE 119. Germany renounces in favour of the Principal Allied and Associated Powers all her rights and titles over her oversea possessions [colonies]. . . .

PART V *Military, Naval, and Air Claims*

ARTICLE 160. By a date which must not be later than March 31, 1920, the German Army must not comprise more than seven divisions of infantry and three divisions of cavalry.

After that date the total number of effectives in the Army of the States constituting Germany must not exceed one hundred thousand men, including officers and establishments of depots. The Army shall be devoted exclusively to the maintenance of order within the territory and to the control of the frontiers.

The total effective strength of officers . . . must not exceed four thousand.

. . . The Great German General Staff and all similar organisations shall be dissolved and may not be reconstituted in any form. . . .

ARTICLE 180. All fortified works, fortresses and field works situated in German territory to the west of a line drawn fifty kilometres to the east of the Rhine shall be disarmed and dismantled.

ARTICLE 181. After the expiration of a period of two months from the coming into force of the present Treaty the German naval forces in commission must not exceed:

6 battleships . . .
6 light cruisers,
12 destroyers,
12 torpedo boats,

or an equal number of ships constructed to replace them as provided in Article 190.

No submarines are to be included.

All other warships, except where there is provision to the contrary in the present Treaty, must be placed in reserve or devoted to commercial purposes. . . .

ARTICLE 198. The armed forces of Germany must not include any . . . air forces. . . .

PART VI *Reparation*

ARTICLE 231. The Allied and Associated Governments affirm and Germany accepts the responsibility of Germany and her allies for causing all the loss and damage to which the Allied and Associated Governments and their nationals have been subjected as a consequence of the war imposed upon them by the aggression of Germany and her allies. . . .

PART XIV *Guarantees*

ARTICLE 428. As a guarantee for the execution of the present Treaty by Germany, the German territory situated to the west of the Rhine, together with the bridgeheads, will be occupied by Allied and Associated troops for a period of fifteen years from the coming into force of the present Treaty. . . .

ARTICLE 431. If before the expiration of the period of fifteen years Germany complies with all the undertakings resulting from the present Treaty, the occupying forces will be withdrawn immediately.

Quoted in Louis L. Snyder, ed., *Historic Documents of World War I.* New York: Van Nostrand Reinhold, 1958, pp. 185–89.

Document 17: Failure at Versailles: John Maynard Keynes Attacks the Treaty

John Maynard Keynes (1883–1946) was a brilliant young economic adviser to the British delegation at the Paris Peace Conference of

1919. His Economic Consequences of the Peace *(1920) caused a sensation as a savage yet persuasive indictment of the economic blunders of the "Big Four" leadership. He especially attacked the German reparations settlement as a disastrous mistake.*

The Treaty includes no provisions for the economic rehabilitation of Europe,—nothing to make the defeated Central Empires into good neighbors, nothing to stabilize the new States of Europe, nothing to reclaim Russia; nor does it promote in any way a compact of economic solidarity amongst the Allies themselves; no arrangement was reached at Paris for restoring the disordered finances of France and Italy, or to adjust the systems of the Old World and the New.

The Council of Four paid no attention to these issues, being preoccupied with others,—Clemenceau to crush the economic life of his enemy, Lloyd George to do a deal and bring home something which would pass muster for a week, the President to do nothing that was not just and right. It is an extraordinary fact that the fundamental economic problems of a Europe starving and disintegrating before their eyes, was the one question in which it was impossible to arouse the interest of the Four. Reparation was their main excursion into the economic field, and they settled it as a problem of theology, of politics, of electoral chicane [trickery, deception] from every point of view except that of the economic future of the States whose destiny they were handling. . . .

The essential facts of the situation, as I see them, are expressed simply. Europe consists of the densest aggregation of population in the history of the world. This population is accustomed to a relatively high standard of life, in which, even now, some sections of it anticipate improvement rather than deterioration. In relation to other continents Europe is not self-sufficient; in particular it cannot feed itself. Internally the population is not evenly distributed, but much of it is crowded into a relatively small number of dense industrial centers. This population secured for itself a livelihood before the war, without much margin of surplus, by means of a delicate and immensely complicated organization, of which the foundations were supported by coal, iron, transport, and an unbroken supply of imported food and raw materials from other continents. By the destruction of this organization and the interruption of the stream of supplies, a part of this population is deprived of its means of livelihood. Emigration is not open to the redundant surplus. For it would take years to transport them overseas, even, which is not the case, if countries could be found which were ready to receive them. The danger confronting us, therefore, is the rapid depression of the standard of life of the European populations to a point which will mean actual starvation for some (a point already reached in Russia and approximately reached in Austria). Men will not always die quietly. For starvation, which brings to some lethargy and a helpless despair, drives other temperaments to the nervous instability of hysteria and to a mad despair. And these in their distress may overturn the remnants of organization, and submerge civilization itself in their attempts to satisfy desperately the overwhelming needs of the individual. This is the danger against which all our resources and courage and idealism must now cooperate. . . .

This is the fundamental problem in front of us [the economic reconstruction of Germany within an international economy], before which questions of territorial adjustment and the balance of European power are insignificant. Some of the catastrophes of past history, which have thrown back human progress for centuries, have been due to the reactions following on the sudden termination, whether in the course of nature or by the act of man, of temporarily favorable conditions which have permitted the growth of population beyond what could be provided for when the favorable conditions were at an end.

Quoted in Brian Tierney and Joan W. Scott, eds., *Western Societies: A Documentary History*, vol. 2. 2nd ed. Boston: McGraw-Hill, 2000, pp. 376–78.

Document 18: Disillusionment

Renowned French writer Paul Valéry (1871–1945) voiced the postwar mood of disillusionment and a wounded European spirit in the following selections. The first was written in 1919, and the second is an excerpt from a 1922 speech at the University of Zurich in Switzerland.

We modern civilizations have learned to recognize that we are mortal like the others.

We had heard tell of whole worlds vanished, of empires foundered with all their men and all their engines, sunk to the inexplorable depths of the centuries with their gods and laws, their academies and their pure and applied sciences, their grammars, dictionaries, classics, romantics, symbolists, their critics and the critics of their critics. We knew that all the apparent earth is made of ashes, and that ashes have a meaning. We perceived, through the misty bulk of history, the phantoms of huge vessels once laden with riches and learning. We could not count them. But these wrecks, after all, were no concern of ours.

Elam, Nineveh, Babylon [ancient civilizations noted in the Bible] were vague and splendid names; the total ruin of these worlds, for us, meant as little as did their existence. But *France, England, Russia* . . . these names, too, are splendid. . . . And now we see that the abyss of history is deep enough to bury all the world. We feel that a civilization is fragile as a life. The circumstances which will send the works of [John] Keats [English poet] and the works of [Charles] Baudelaire [French poet] to join those of Menander [ancient Greek poet] are not at all inconceivable; they are found in the daily papers.

* * * * *

The storm has died away, and still we are restless, uneasy, as if the storm were about to break. Almost all the affairs of men remain in a terrible uncertainty. We think of what has disappeared, we are almost destroyed by what has been destroyed; we do not know what will be born, and we fear the future, not without reason. We hope vaguely, we dread precisely; our fears are infinitely more precise than our hopes; we confess that the charm of life is behind us, abundance is behind us, but doubt and disorder are in us and with us. There is no thinking man, however shrewd or learned he may be, who can hope to dominate this anxiety, to escape from this impression of darkness, to measure the probable duration of this period when the vital relations of humanity are disturbed profoundly.

We are a very unfortunate generation, whose lot has been to see the moment of our passage through life coincide with the arrival of great and terrifying events, the echo of which will resound through all our lives.

One can say that all the fundamentals of the world have been affected by the war, or more exactly, by the circumstances of the war; something deeper has been worn away than the renewable parts of the machine. You know how greatly the general economic situation has been disturbed, and the polity of states, and the very life of the individual; you are familiar with the universal discomfort, hesitation, apprehension. *But among all these injured things is the Mind.* The Mind has indeed been cruelly wounded; its complaint is heard in the hearts of intellectual man; it passes a mournful judgment on itself. It doubts itself profoundly.

Marvin Perry, Joseph R. Peden, and Theodore H. Von Laue, eds., *Sources of the Western Tradition*, vol. 2, *From the Renaissance to the Present*. 3rd ed. Boston: Houghton Mifflin, 1995, pp. 297–98.

Document 19: Losses, 1914–1918

World War I devastated the generation that came of age during the war. Fifteen million people—8 million military and 7 million civilian—died during the war. The Spanish influenza epidemic at the end of the war was equally disastrous and promoted by wartime strains. The following table shows the terrible human price paid by big and small nations alike.

Country	Total men mobilized	Combat deaths	Percentage of forces killed
Austria-Hungary	7,800,000	1,200,000	15.4
Belgium	267,000	14,000	5.2
British Empire	8,900,000	947,000	10.6
Bulgaria	560,000	87,000	15.5
France	8,400,000	1,400,000	16.2
Germany	11,000,000	1,800,000	16.1
Greece	230,000	5,000	2.2
Italy	5,600,000	460,000	8.2
Montenegro	50,000	3,000	6.0
Portugal	100,000	7,000	7.2
Rumania	750,000	336,000	44.8
Russia	12,000,000	1,700,000	14.2
Serbia	707,000	125,000	17.7
Ottoman Empire	2,900,000	325,000	11.4
United States	4,740,000	115,000	2.4

Military casualties	Percentage of forces wounded	Civilian deaths	Total war dead	Percentage population killed
7,000,000	90.0	300,000	1,500,000	5.2
93,000	34.8	30,000	44,000	0.6
3,200,000	35.2	30,000	977,000	2.4
267,000	47.7	275,000	362,000	8.3
6,200,000	73.2	40,000	1,440,000	3.6
7,100,000	64.9	760,000	2,500,000	3.8
27,000	11.7	132,000	137,000	2.8
2,200,000	39.1	n.a.	n.a.	
20,000	40.0	n.a.	n.a.	
33,000	33.3	n.a.	n.a.	
536,000	71.4	275,000	611,000	8.1
9,200,000	76.3	2,000,000	3,700,000	2.4
331,000	46.8	650,000	775,000	17.6
975,000	34.2	2,200,000	2,500,000	10.1
204,000	6.7		115,000	0.1

Steven Hause and William Maltby, *Western Civilization: A History of European Society.* Belmont, CA: West/Wadsworth, 1999, p. 800.

Chronology

1914

June 28: Austro-Hungarian archduke Franz Ferdinand is assassinated at Sarajevo.

July 6: Germany gives a "blank check" to Austria-Hungary to attack Serbia.

July 28: Russia mobilizes.

August 1: Germany declares war on Russia.

August 3: Germany declares war on France.

August 4: Britain declares war on Germany.

August 26: The Germans defeat the Russians on the eastern front at Tannenberg.

September 5: The German invasion is halted at the First Battle of the Marne.

November 1: Turkey enters the war on the side of the Central Powers.

1915

April 22: Poison gas is used in the German attack at the Second Battle of Ypres in Belgium.

April 25: Allied landings at Gallipoli (Turkey) begin.

May 7: The British liner *Lusitania* is sunk by a German submarine, leading to a crisis in German-American relations.

May 23: Italy enters the war on the side of the Allies.

1916

February 12–December 18: The French blunt the German assault at Verdun; both sides suffer huge casualties.

June 1–November 13: A costly British offensive on the Somme River gains little ground.

June 5: The Arab revolt against the Turks starts, aided by Britain's T.E. Lawrence (Lawrence of Arabia).

December 7: David Lloyd George becomes British prime minister.

1917

January 31: Germany begins unrestricted submarine warfare.

March 12: The Russian czar abdicates.

April 2: President Woodrow Wilson asks U.S. Congress for a declaration of war against Germany.

April 6: Congress votes for war against Germany.

April 29: Mutinies begin in the French army.

October 24: The Italian army is routed at Caporetto by Austrian and German forces.

November 7: The Bolsheviks seize power in Russia.

1918

January 8: President Wilson announces his Fourteen Points for peace.

February 6: Women's suffrage is achieved in Britain.

March 3: The German-dictated Treaty of Brest-Litovsk confirms the Russian defeat in the east.

March 21: Germany's Ludendorff offensive begins on the western front.

May 28: The first American military action occurs at Catigny, France.

July 15: The Second Battle of the Marne stops the German drive; the final Allied counteroffensive begins on the western front.

October 9: Austria-Hungary leaves the war.

October 30: Turkey leaves the war.

November 9: Kaiser Wilhelm abdicates and Germany becomes a republic.

November 11: An armistice is signed at Compiègne, France, ending the war.

1919

January 18: The Paris Peace Conference begins.

June 28: The Treaty of Versailles is signed.

December 19: The U.S. Senate refuses to ratify the treaty.

For Further Research

Collections of Original Documents

Lyn MacDonald, ed., *1914–1918: Voices and Images of the Great War.* London: Michael Joseph, 1988.

Marilyn Shevin-Coetzee and Frans Coetzee, eds., *World War I and European Society: A Sourcebook.* Lexington, MA: Heath, 1995.

Louis L. Snyder, ed., *Historic Documents of World War I.* New York: Van Nostrand Reinhold, 1958.

Peter Vansittart, *Voices from the Great War.* New York: Franklin Watts, 1981.

General

Niall Ferguson, *The Pity of War.* New York: Basic Books, 1999.

Martin Gilbert, *The First World War: A Complete History.* New York: Holt, 1994.

John Keegan, *The First World War.* New York: Knopf, 1999.

Michael J. Lyons, *World War I: A Short History.* Englewood Cliffs, NJ: Prentice-Hall, 1994.

Keith Robbins, *The First World War.* New York: Oxford University Press, 1984.

James L. Stokesbury, *A Short History of World War I.* New York: William Morrow, 1981.

A.J.P. Taylor, ed., *History of World War I.* London: Octopus Books, 1974.

Jay Winter and Blaine Baggett, *The Great War and the Shaping of the Twentieth Century.* New York: Penguin, 1996.

J.M. Winter, *The Experience of World War I.* New York: Oxford University Press, 1989.

Origins of World War I

Orin J. Hale, *The Great Illusion, 1900–1914.* New York: Harper & Row, 1971.

Laurence Lafore, *The Long Fuse: An Interpretation of the Origins of World War I.* Philadelphia: Lippincott, 1965.

Robert K. Massie, *Dreadnought: Britain, Germany, and the Coming of the Great War.* New York: Ballantine, 1991.

Barbara Tuchman, *The Guns of August.* New York: Macmillan, 1962.

L.C.F. Turner, *The Origins of the First World War.* New York: Norton, 1971.

Military Aspects of the War

Corelli Barnett, *The Swordbearers: Supreme Command in the First World War.* New York: William Morrow, 1964.

E.M. Coffman, *The War to End All Wars: The American Military Experience in World War I.* New York: Oxford University Press, 1968.

John Ellis, *Eye-Deep in Hell: Trench Warfare in World War I.* London: Crown Helm, 1976.

William R. Griffiths, *The Great War.* Wayne, NJ: Avery, 1986.

Alistair Horne, *The Price of Glory: Verdun, 1916.* New York: Penguin, 1964.

Richard Hough, *The Great War at Sea, 1914–1918.* New York: Oxford University Press, 1983.

Lee Kennett, *The First Air War.* New York: Free Press, 1991.

Philip Knightley and Colin Simpson, *The Secret Lives of Lawrence of Arabia.* London: Nelson, 1969.

S.L.A. Marshall, *The American Heritage History of World War I.* New York: American Heritage, 1964.

Martin Middlebrook, *The First Day on the Somme.* London: Allen Lane, 1971.

———, *The Kaiser's Battle, 21 March 1918: The First Day of the German Spring Offensive.* London: Allen Lane, 1978.

Alan Moorehead, *Gallipoli.* New York: Harper's, 1956.

Colin Simpson, *The Lusitania.* Boston: Little, Brown, 1972.

Norman Stone, *The Eastern Front, 1914–1917.* New York: Simon & Schuster, 1986.

John Terraine, *To Win a War, 1918: The Year of Victory.* New York: Doubleday, 1981.

Denis Winter, *Death's Men: Soldiers of the Great War.* London: Allen Lane, 1978.

Leon Wolff, *In Flanders Field.* New York: Ballantine, 1960.

Diplomatic, Political, Economic, and Social Aspects of the War

Arthur Barbeau and Florette Henri, *The Unknown Soldiers: Black American Troops in World War I*. Philadelphia: Temple University Press, 1974.

Jean-Jacques Becker, *The Great War and the French People*. New York: St. Martin's, 1986.

Patrick Devlin, *Too Proud to Fight: Woodrow Wilson's Neutrality*. New York: Oxford University Press, 1974.

Robert H. Ferrell, *Woodrow Wilson and World War I, 1917–1921*. New York: Harper & Row, 1985.

Marc Ferro, *The Great War, 1914–1918*. London: Routledge & Kegan Paul, 1973.

Frank Freidel, *Over There: The Story of America's First Great Overseas Crusade*. New York: McGraw-Hill, 1990.

Maureen Weiner Greenwald, *Women, War, and Work: The Impact of World War I on Women Workers in the United States*. Westport, CT: Greenwood, 1980.

Ross Gregory, *The Origins of American Intervention in the First World War*. New York: Norton, 1971.

Gerd Hardach, *The First World War*. New York: Penguin, 1980.

Meirion Harries and Susie Harries, *The Last Days of Innocence: America at War, 1917–1918*. New York: Random House, 1997.

Cate Haste, *Keep the Home Fires Burning: Propaganda in the First World War*. London: Allen Lane, 1977.

Margaret Higonnet et al., *Behind the Lines: Gender and the Two World Wars*. New Haven, CT: Yale University Press, 1987.

David Kennedy, *Over Here: The First World War and American Society*. New York: Oxford University Press, 1980.

W. Bruce Lincoln, *Passage Through Armageddon: The Russians in War and Revolution, 1914–1918*. New York: Simon & Schuster, 1986.

Arthur Marwick, *The Deluge: British Society and the First World War*. Boston: Little, Brown, 1965.

———, *Women in War, 1914–1918*. London: Crown Helm, 1977.

Laurence Moyer, *Victory Must Be Ours: Germany in the Great War*. New York: Hippocrene, 1995.

Ronald Schaffer, *America in the Great War: The Rise of the War Welfare State.* New York: Oxford University Press, 1991.

The Peace Settlement and Legacy of World War I

Rene Albrecht-Carrie, *The Meaning of the First World War.* Englewood Cliffs, NJ: Prentice-Hall, 1965.

P.M.H. Bell, *The Origins of the Second World War in Europe.* London: Longman, 1997.

Paul Fussell, *The Great War and Modern Memory.* New York: Oxford University Press, 1975.

N. Gordon Levin, ed., *Woodrow Wilson and the Paris Peace Conference.* Lexington, MA: Heath, 1972.

Charles L. Mee, *The End of Order: Versailles 1919.* New York: Dutton, 1980.

Jack J. Roth, ed., *World War I: A Turning Point in Modern History.* New York: Knopf, 1967.

Alan Sharp, *The Versailles Settlement: Peacemaking in Paris, 1919.* New York: St. Martin's, 1991.

Jon Silkin, *Out of Battle: The Poetry of the Great War.* London: Oxford University Press, 1972.

Index

Africa
  war in, 16
agriculture
  in Britain, 171–72
  in Europe, women in, 187, 191
Aitken, William Maxwell, 97
Alexander II (Russian czar), 75–76
  collapse of Russian government
    under, 21–22
Alexandra, 75, 76–77, 81
Alexis, 76
Allenby (British general), 93
Allied Powers. *See* Triple Entente
All Quiet on the Western Front
  (Remarque), 30
American Political Tradition, The
  (Hofstadter), 126
Amiens, Battle of, 66
Andrew, Christopher, 64
antiwar movement, 13, 128
appeasement, 29
Armistice, 149, 157
arts
  influence of war on, 30–31
Asquith, Herbert, 56, 72, 97, 223
Atatürk. *See* Kemal, Mustapha
Austria-Hungary, 12
  annexation of Bosnia by, 13–14
  declaration of war by, 14
  nationalities problem in, 34–35, 48
  political centralization in, 164–65
  surrender of, 25, 148
  U.S. declares war on, 145

Baggett, Blaine, 16, 29–30, 235
Balfour Note, 218–19
Balkan Wars (1912–13), 35
  and nationalism, 13–14
Barbusse, Henri, 113
Bell, P.M.H., 209
Below, Fritz von, 93
Benedict XV (pope), 23, 146
Berchtold, Leopold von, 42, 54
Bernhardi, Friedrich von, 36
Bethmann-Hollweg, Theodor von,
  51, 62, 165
"Big Three" leaders

  see also Clemenceau, Georges;
    Lloyd George, David; Wilson,
    Woodrow
Bismarck, Otto von, 12, 48
  German international relations
    under, 36–37
Black Hand, 41
Blunden, Edmund, 94
Boer War (1899–1902), 37–38
Bolshevik revolution, 22–23,
  122–25, 232
  counterrevolution to, 148
Bosnia
  annexation by Austria-Hungary,
    13–14, 35
Braeman, John, 128
Braybon, Gail, 184
Brest-Litovsk, Treaty of, 24, 80, 125,
  147, 165
Briand, Aristide, 98
Brusilov, Aleksei, 121, 123
Brusilov offensive, 69–70
Bryce Report, 198
Buchan, John, 94
Bulgaria, 148
  entry into war by, 16, 71
  surrender of, 25
Bülow, Bernhard von, 61

Carden, Sackville, 100, 103
Carson, Sir Edward, 97
casualties
  at Gallipoli, 109
  total, of World War I, 227, 238–39
  at Verdun, 90
  the wounded, 240–42
censorship, 170
Central Powers. *See* Triple Alliance
Chaplin, Charlie, 20
chemical warfare. *See* gas warfare
Chemin des Dames campaign, 112
chlorine gas, 16, 116
Chotek, Sophie, 49, 53
Churchill, Winston, 62, 96, 108
  and Dardanelles campaign, 99,
    102–103
  and intervention in Russia, 148

on prewar military buildup, 47
Clemenceau, Georges, 25, 27,
  152–53, 166
  accession of, 174
  and Paris Peace Conference, 223
  settlement aims of, 203
Cleveland *Plain Dealer* (newspaper),
  199
Cobb, Frank, 130, 197
Committee on Public Information
  (CPI), 196
conscription
  military, 12, 19, 238
Contemporary Europe: A History
  (Hughes), 33
Coolidge, Calvin, 218
Cooper, James Milton, Jr., 144
Craig, Gordon A., 162
Creel, George, 197
Czechoslovakia, 28, 221
  creation of, 206

Daniels, Josephus, 126
Danterre, Mémé, 239
Dardanelles campaign. *See*
  Gallipoli/Dardanelles campaign
Delbrück, Hans, 61
Denikin, Anton, 124
d'Espérey, Franchet, 158, 159
Dix, Otto, 18, 166
Dreadnought (Massie), 47
Dreadnoughts, 13
Dreyfus Affair, 229
Dual Monarchy. *See* Austria-
  Hungary

eastern front, 67
  German offensive on, 77–79
*Economic Consequences of the Peace,
  The* (Keynes), 217, 224
Elisabeth (Hapsburg empress), 49
Ellis, John, 110
entente, 12
  see also Triple Entente
*Eye Deep in Hell: Trench Warfare in
  World War I* (Ellis), 110

Falkenhayn, Erich von, 67, 73, 78,
  168
  and Battle of Verdun, 68, 82–84
Farewell to Arms, A (Hemingway), 30
fascism
  postwar rise of, 29, 230, 231

Fayolle, Marie Emile, 93, 94
feminist movements, 187
Ferdinand, Franz, 49
  assassination of, 14, 38–39, 41,
  52–55
Ferguson, Niall, 56
Ferrell, Robert H., 222
Figes, Orlando, 122
First World War, The (Robbins), 150
Fischer, Fritz, 57, 58
Foch, Ferdinand, 29, 149, 153, 155
  and intervention in Russia, 148
  settlement aims of, 204
  on Versailles treaty, 210
Fort Douaumont, fall of, 85
Fourteen Points, 23, 25, 26, 146–49
France, 12
  acquisition of Morocco by, 35
  alliance with Russia, 37, 38
  effects of war on liberal democracy
  in, 229
  German concessions to, 203–204
  home front conditions in, 173–74
  mutiny in army of, 112–13
  political centralization in, 163, 166
  postwar policies toward women,
  193
  shell shortage in, 167
  war aims of, 20
  women in workforce of, 190–91
Franco-Prussian War, 216
Freud, Sigmund, 11

Gallipoli/Dardanelles campaign,
  99–109
  Allied failure at, 107–108
  amphibious landing in, 104–106
  human cost of, 109
  main attack, 106–107
  naval attack, 101–104
gas warfare, 16–17, 18, 115–16
  precautions against, 117
  see also individual types of gas
Generation of 1914, The (Wohl), 237
genocide
  Armenian, 17
George V (king of England), 54, 98,
  145
German War Practices, 198
Germany, 12
  alliance with Austria-Hungary,
  50–52
  declaration of war by, 14

economic controls in, 167–68
and escalation to war, 40
home front conditions in, 175–78, 179–83, 191–92
hyperinflation in, 219–20
limited prewar ambitions of, 57–59
loss of territory to, 214
manpower problem in, 175–76
nationalities problem in, 34
1915–1916 eastern offensive of, 77–79
political centralization in, 163–64, 165
prewar politics in, 38
rise of totalitarianism in, 231, 233–34
surrender of, 25, 157
terms of, 203–205
and Treaty of Brest-Litovsk, 24
war aims of, 20, 59–61
and "war guilt" clause, 26–27
war plans of, 15, 44
Weimar Republic of, 223, 230
Germany and the Next War (Bernhardi), 36
Gilbert, Martin, 119
Gough, Hubert, 152
Graves, Robert, 31
Grayson, Cary T., 224
Great Britain, 12
and Battle of the Somme, 17, 92–95
entry into war by, 14
as a mistake, 56–62
limits on liberty rights in, 169–70
losses of, to U-boats, 134–35
political centralization in, 164, 165–66
position on war debts and reparations, 218–19
prewar politics in, 38
and U.S., relationship between, 137–38, 145
war aims of, 21
Great Depression
effects on liberal democracy, 230
Great War, The (Griffiths), 99
Great War and the Shaping of the 20th Century (Winter and Baggett), 16
Greece
entry into war by, 16
Grey, Sir Edward, 45, 54, 56, 62
arguments of, against neutrality, 57

Griffiths, William R., 99

Haig, Douglas, 68, 70–71, 97, 153
and Battle of the Somme, 92–95
Hamilton, Ian, 104, 105
Hapsburg Empire. *See* Austria-Hungary
Harries, Meirion, 196
Harries, Susie, 196
Harrod, Roy, 225
Hemingway, Ernest, 30
Hervé, Gustave, 163
Hindenburg, Paul von, 21, 73, 77, 97
Hindenburg program, 175–76
Hitler, Adolf, 233
Ho Chi Minh, 26
Hoffman, Max, 123
Hofstadter, Richard, 126
home front
effects of total war on, 19–20, 162–70
in Britain, 172–73
in France, 173–74
in Germany, 175–78, 179–83, 191–92
Horne, Alistair, 69
Hötzendorf, Franz Conrad von, 42, 50, 54, 77, 78
House, Edward M., 127, 129, 146, 149, 224
Hughes, H. Stuart, 33
Hugo, Victor, 97

inflation, 211–12
in Germany, 219
influenza, 26
Italy, 12
defeat of Hapsburg forces by, 158
entry into war by, 16
rise of fascism in, 230, 231
war aims of, 21
and Paris Peace Conference, 28

Joffre, Joseph, 19, 64, 68, 98
and Battle of the Somme, 92, 93, 95
Joseph, Franz, 49, 54
death of, 22

Kaiser, the Beast of Berlin, The (film), 197–98
Keegan, John, 24–25

Kemal, Mustapha (Atatürk), 106, 159, 206
Kerensky, Aleksandr, 119
   Provisional Government of, 121–23
Keynes, John Maynard, 27
   on economic blunders in Versailles treaty, 217–18
   on personalities of the Big Three leaders, 224–25
King, Jere Clemens, 112
Kitchener, Lord Horatio, 64, 100, 108
Kollwitz, Kathe, 31

Lacaze, Marie Jean, 98
Lansing, Robert, 129
Law, Bonar, 97
Lawrence, T.E., 26
League of Nations, 23, 28, 203, 221
Le Figaro (newspaper), 54
Lenin, Vladimir, 22, 122, 125
   Declaration for Peace of, 124
Lettow-Vorbeck, Paul von, 160
liberal democracy
   effects of war on, 228–31
liberty rights
   wartime limitations on, 169–70
Lippmann, Walter, 146
literature
   influence of war on, 30–31
Lloyd George, David, 25, 72, 96–97, 108, 152, 165, 167, 174
   and Dardanelles campaign, 99
   and Paris Peace Conference, 223–24
   settlement aims of, 203
Ludendorff, Erich, 21, 24, 73, 97, 150
   influence on Nazi writers, 233
   1918 offensives of, 152–55
      Allied counteroffensives to, 155–57
Lusitania (ship), 133
   sinking of, 17
Lyautey, Louis, 98
Lyons, Michael J., 41

MacDonald, Ramsay, 164
Machiavelli, 221
machine guns, 18
   and amphibious warfare, 105–106
Mackensen, August von, 78

Mangin, Charles, 155
Marne, First Battle of, 15, 64
Marshall, S.L.A., 92
Marwick, Arthur, 171
Masefield, John, 94
Massie, Robert K., 47
Maximilian (emperor of Mexico), 49
Mayer, S.L., 20
Mein Kampf (Hitler), 233
Middle East
   Allied advances in, 159–60
   and Paris Peace Conference, 28
   and Versailles treaty, 206
Milan, Otto, 159
Mitford, Nancy, 209
Moltke, Helmuth von, 44, 52, 59, 64, 65, 166
Monro, Charles, 109
Montgomery, Bernard, 94
Moyer, Laurence, 179
Müller, Gustav, 61
mustard gas, 116

nationalism, 13
   and nationalities problem, in Central/Eastern Europe, 33–35
Nazism
   and German hyperinflation, 219–20
   rise of, as legacy of war, 29
New York Times (newspaper), 199
Nicholas (Russian grand duke)
   retreat of, 79–80
Nicholas II (Russian czar), 15
   command of Russian army by, 80–81
   overthrow of, 120–21
Nicolson, Harold, 25, 225
Nivelle, Robert-Georges, 89, 97, 112–13
Norris, George, 128

Operation Michael, 150
Ottoman Empire. See Turkey
Owen, Wilfred, 31, 116

Page, Walter Hines, 129
Paleologue, Georges, 44
Paris Peace Conference (1919), 25–27
   achievements and failures of, 206–208
   atmosphere of, 225

clashing personalities of, 222–25
conflicting Allied aims at, 202–203
and new independent states, 28
reasons for failure of, 225–27
Passchendaele offensive, 152, 236
Pershing, John J., 24, 151, 153
Pétain, Henri Philippe, 70, 152, 153, 238
  and Battle of Verdun, 86–87
  on Verdun, 88
phosgene gas, 116
Pity of War, The (Ferguson), 56
Plowman, Mark, 94
Poincaré, Raymond, 38, 44
Poland, 28, 34, 213, 221
  reconstitution as independent state, 206
Prager, Robert, 200
Princip, Gavrilo, 14, 15, 53–54
propaganda, 19–20, 170
  anti-German, in U.S., 197–98
Prost, Antoine, 238
Pursuit of Love, The (Mitford), 209
Putnam, Irving, 199

Rasputin, 76–77, 81, 119
Rathenau, Walther, 167–68
Rawlinson (British general), 93
Reizler, Kurt, 61
Remarque, Erich Maria, 30
Robbins, Keith, 150
Robeck, John de, 103–105
Romania
  entry into war by, 16, 71
Romanov dynasty, 75–76
Roosevelt, Theodore, 145
Roth, Jack J., 228
Rudolf (Hapsburg crown prince), 49
Russia, 12
  Bolshevik
    challenge to Allied war aims by, 146
    civil war in, 26
    counterrevolution against, 148
    treaty with Germany. *See* Brest-Litovsk, Treaty of
  czarist, collapse of, 21–22, 120–21
  and Dardanelles campaign, 100
  inefficient war machine of, 74–75
  losses on eastern front by, 67
  nationalities problem in, 34
  political centralization in, 164
  rise of totalitarianism in, 232–33
  social discontent in, 119–20
  support of Serbia by, 39–40, 55
  war aims of, 20
Russo-Japanese War (1904–1905), 75

Sanders, Limon von, 101
Sassoon, Siegfried, 31, 94
Sazonov, Sergei, 44
Scheffler, Karl, 182–83
Schlieffen Plan, 44, 65
  see also Germany, war plans of
Serbia
  anti-Austrian policy of, 34–35
  and Balkan wars, 14
  role in Ferdinand's assassination, 39
Seymour, Charles, 224
Sharpe, Alan, 29
Short History of World War I, A (Stokesbury), 73
Smuts, Jan Christian, 221, 225
Socialists
  and antiwar movement, 13
Somme, Battle of, 17, 19, 93–95, 114
  British losses in, 95
  political consequences of, 97–98
Speer, Albert, 180
Stevenson, David, 20
Stokesbury, James L., 73
Stone, Norman, 18
Stopford, Frederick, 109
strikes
  labor, 174
  women leading, 192
submarine warfare, 17
  Allied strategy against, 139–41
  convoy systems, success of, 141–43
  announcement of, U.S. response to, 127
  German plan for, 132–33
  effectiveness of, 134–35
  negative effects of, 136
  home front effects, in Britain, 172–73

Taft, William H., 145
tanks, 66
  and Battle of the Somme, 96
Tannenberg
  German victory at, 15

Thomas, Albert, 167
Thomson, David, 202
Tocqueville, Alexis de, 72
totalitarianism
  postwar rise of, 231–34
trade unions
  views on female labor, 186, 190
trench warfare, 18, 110–17
  annual casualties from, 110
  at Gallipoli, 108
Triple Alliance, 12, 38
  and blame for war, 41–43
  effects of Fourteen Points on,
    148–49
  see also Austria-Hungary;
    Germany; Italy
Triple Entente, 12
  and blame for war, 43–46
  defeat of Ludendorff offensives by,
    155–57
  Petrograd meeting of, 119
  see also France; Great Britain;
    Russia
Tschirschky, Baron von, 51
Tumulty, Joseph, 129
Turkey, 148
  and Armenian genocide, 17
  and Balkan Wars, 35
  defeat of, 159–60
  entry into war by, 16
  offensive in Caucasus, 100
  and Paris Peace Conference, 28
  surrender of, 25
  see also Gallipoli/Dardanelles
    campaign
Turnip Winter, 176, 179–81

U-boats. See submarine warfare
Union of Disfigured Men, 241–42
Union sacrée, 163, 229
United States
  and Allies, diverging aims of,
    144–45
  anti-German hysteria in, 196–200
  entry into war by, 21, 138
  and European balance of power,
    220
  and failure of Versailles treaty, 28
  and German U-boat campaign,
    133–34, 137
  and war debt–reparations linkage,
    218–19

Verdun
  Battle of, 19, 68–70, 114–15
  battle of the hills, 87–89
  beginning of, 84–85
  fall of Fort Douaumont, 85
  human cost of, 90
  Pétain on, 88
  historic significance of, 83
Versailles, Treaty of
  Allied second thoughts on, 216–17
  German disarmament provisions
    of, 214
  Keynes's criticism of, 217–18
  and nationalities problem, 207–208
  psychological effects on Germany
    of, 215
  significance of, 28–29
  terms of, 203–206
    debate over, 23
  "war guilt" clause, 26–27, 204,
    215–16
Viviani, René, 44

warfare, 17–19
  amphibious, 105–106
  mechanization of, 18
    and stalemate on western front,
      66
  see also gas warfare; submarine
    warfare
"war guilt" clause, 26–27, 204,
  215–16
Wavell, Archibald, 94
Weimar Republic, 223, 230
western front, 66–67
  stalemate on, 15–16
Why America Fights Germany (CPI),
  198
Wilhelm II, 12, 51, 86, 90
  German international relations
    under, 37
  plans for a united Europe by,
    61–62
  war aims of, 58–59
Williamson, Samuel R., Jr., 15
Wilson, Trevor, 132
Wilson, Woodrow, 23, 25, 27, 126
  on anti-Bolshevik campaign, 148
  decision of, for war, 129–31
  "peace without victory" plan of,
    127
  settlement aims of, 202–203
  support for peace aims of, 145–46

and "war psychosis," 226–27
Winter, Jay, 16, 26, 29–30, 235
Wohl, Robert, 237
women
  effects of war on status of, 184–86
  industrial mobilization of, 188–89
  job inequalities faced by, 189–91
  postwar experience of, 184–86
  in prewar workforce, 186–87
World Crisis, The (Churchill), 103
World War I
  causes of, 12–15
    Allies' contribution to, 43–45
    Central Powers' contribution to,
      41–43
    military buildup, 12–13, 47
    nationalism, 13, 15, 33–35
    rival alliances, 36–40
  effects of
    economic, 211–12
    on liberal democracy, 228–31
    on political ideologies, 235–36
    on women's status, 184–86
  escalation to, 38–40

European power vacuum after,
  220–21
on home front, 19–20, 162–70
  effects of blockades on, 171–78
human cost of, 227
legacy of, 29–31
new states created in wake of, 28
and political centralization, 163–66
political effects of, 212–13
as prelude to World War II,
  209–21
as total war, 162–63
World War I: A Short History
  (Lyons), 41
Wukovits, John F., 82

Ypres
  Second Battle of, 16, 115–16
  Third Battle of, 111
Yugoslavia, 28
  creation of, 205

Zimmerman, Alfred, 129
Zimmerman telegram, 138